THE
TRAFALGAR CHRONICLE

Dedicated to Naval History in the Nelson Era

New Series 1

~~~~~~~~~

Journal
of
THE 1805 CLUB

Edited by
PETER HORE

In association with The 1805 Club

Seaforth
PUBLISHING

Text copyright © individual contributors 2016

First published in Great Britain in 2016 by
Seaforth Publishing,
An imprint of Pen & Sword Books Ltd,
47 Church Street,
Barnsley S70 2AS

www.seaforthpublishing.com

British Library Cataloguing in Publication Data
A catalogue record for this book is available from the British Library

ISBN 978 1 4738 9572 0 (PAPERBACK)
ISBN 978 1 4738 9574 4 (EPUB)
ISBN 978 1 4738 9573 7 (KINDLE)

Designed and typeset in 10/12 Times New Roman by M.A.T.S, Leigh-on-Sea, Essex
Printed and bound in Malta by Gutenberg Press Ltd

CONTENTS

3

President's Foreword

I welcome this, the first of a new series of the *Trafalgar Chronicle*, the yearbook of The 1805 Club.

Over the last quarter of a century, the *Trafalgar Chronicle* has established itself as the leading depository of knowledge about the Georgian navy, while its subject matter has broadened to include not just new research and rare details of the life of Admiral Lord Nelson and the Battle of Trafalgar, but also about other men, great and small, about strategy, operations and tactics in the sailing navies of the Georgian era, and not just in the British navy, but in the navies of Britain's rivals and allies.

Last year The 1805 Club marked its silver jubilee with a twenty-fifth anniversary edition, in the year of the bicentenary of the Battle of Waterloo, which was devoted to the theme of the victory of sea power which made Waterloo possible. In 2016 the first volume of the new series takes a slightly different format, but continues the idea of being themed. The relationship between the Royal Navy and the United States Navy has been extremely important throughout their shared history, and I am delighted that this is celebrated in this edition which contains new information and the results of new research into North America and North Americans in the sailing era.

Another feature of the *Trafalgar Chronicle* has been the publication of rarely seen images of the age, and this practice is maintained here.

Over its life the *Trafalgar Chronicle* has taken on an international character and here too the contributors come from Britain and overseas. They include foremost experts in their fields of study, as well as antiquarians and amateurs who have addressed their interests with the thoroughness and energy which is unique to them, and I wish to thank them each and every one for their contribution.

ADMIRAL SIR JONATHON BAND GCB DL
Former First Sea Lord
President of The 1805 Club

5

Frontispiece from *Nelson's Letters from the Leeward Islands* by Geoffrey Wales, The Golden
Cockerel Press, 1953. (From the collection of Rear-Admiral Joseph F Callo, USN)

Editor's Foreword

On 23 June 1800, during the USA's Quasi-War with France, Commodore Thomas Truxton wrote from USS *Constellation* to George Cross commanding the US frigate *John Adams*:

> A good understanding with the British Navy officers is highly necessary as we are acting in one common cause against a perfidious enemy, and we should endeavour to cement our union by acts of kindness, civility and friendship to each other on all occasions for it is unquestionably our interest and their interest always so to do.

Then in 1859 Rear-Admiral Josiah Tatnall USN, who had fought against the British in the War of 1812, remarked during an incident in the Second Opium War, when he and his sailors voluntarily served British guns against the Chinese, that blood is thicker than water. *Blackwood's* magazine responded: 'Gallant Americans! You and your Admiral did more that day to bind England and the United States together than all your lawyers and pettifogging politicians have ever done to part us!'

For your editor, these two quotations sum up the special relationship which has existed down two centuries between the Royal Navy and the United States Navy, a relationship which, as Truxton reminds us, started as soon as the ink dried on the Treaty of Paris in 1783, in the era of the Georgian navy which has been the focus of the *Trafalgar Chronicle* over its twenty-five years.

I therefore have much pleasure in dedicating this edition to North America and North Americans in the era of the Georgian sailing navies. There are two articles about the Star-Spangled Banner – the first time that the flag was seen at sea, and the writing of the words to the US national anthem, another article which challenges accepted wisdom about impressment as the cause of the War of 1812, two about charting under sail, and, as much of what we know about the sailing navy has come down to us via the marine painters of the age, there is a superbly illustrated article about Thomas Buttersworth. Several other articles address the great men and small of the age, many of whom had mixed backgrounds in Britain and in the USA.

Again the editor is grateful to contributors from several countries who have written so ably for the *Trafalgar Chronicle*, contributors who include leading contemporary scholars, as well as some first-time writers. I am also grateful to all those who have kindly refereed articles, and to the new publishing and production team who include Julian Mannering, Stephanie Rudgard-Redsell and Michael Harrington, the quality of whose work is self-evident.

In 2017 the *Trafalgar Chronicle* will look at the Royal Marines and the US Marine Corps in the Georgian era: it is never too soon to sharpen your quills, and proposals for articles are welcome now. Please contact the editor at tc.editor@1805club.org.

PETER HORE

Nicholas Biddle: America's Revolutionary War Nelson

Chipp Reid

The explosion lit up the night, showering the sea and everything on it with debris. The crew of the 64-gun HMS *Yarmouth* stood dumbfounded at the scene. For nearly fifteen minutes, the nimble Yankee frigate *Randolph* had pummelled the much larger British warship, whose captain, Nicholas Vincent, appeared on the verge of surrendering the *Yarmouth* when his opponent suddenly exploded.[1] The rain of splinters, iron and copper caused even more casualties on the *Yarmouth*. Only four men survived on the American vessel.[2] Among the dead was the American commander, Captain Nicholas Biddle.

Portrait of Captain Nicholas Biddle by Orlando Lagman, after a painting attributed to James Peale. (US Naval History and Heritage Command)

If any Continental Navy officer could lay claim to being America's Horatio Nelson, it was Biddle. Arguably the most accomplished officer in the fledgling colonial fleet, Biddle's seamanship and courage were beyond question. Washington Irving, best known for 'Rip Van Winkle' and the 'Legend of Sleepy Hollow', wrote in a biography of Biddle sixty years after Biddle's and more than thirty after Nelson's death, that Nelson had warned his Royal Navy colleagues at the onset of the American Revolution that Biddle would be England's toughest opponent at sea.[3] Although Irving never gave the source of Nelson's warning, if anyone knew Biddle and the American's abilities, it was Nelson.

The two warriors met in 1773 when they served on Captain Constantine Phipps's (later Lord Mulgrave) expedition to find a passage through the Arctic. Biddle was eight years older than Nelson and already an accomplished mariner. His life to that point had been one in which he surmounted obstacle after obstacle as he worked toward his ultimate goal, which was to serve in the Royal Navy. Biddle was born in Philadelphia on 10 September 1750, the eighth child of William Biddle and Mary Scully.[4] Nicholas showed an early predilection to head to sea, like his older brother Charles, who had secured a rate on a merchant vessel thanks to his brother-in-law, William McFunn. Nicholas signed on as a cabin boy at fourteen on the snow *Ann and Almack*, in which McFunn had a one-third ownership interest and Charles was second mate.[5] He spent a year at sea, leaving Philadelphia on 11 October 1764[6] and returning on 2 September 1765.[7]

The voyage only whetted Nicholas's desire for adventure. He signed on for a second cruise and shipped out on 20 October 1765, bound for Jamaica. On 2 January 1766 the snow was in the eastern Caribbean, sailing just off the Northern Triangles, a particularly dangerous chain of reefs, when a gale sprang up, driving the *Ann and Almack* onto a reef. She stuck fast and the crew abandoned her. A wave carried away the ship's longboat, leaving just a small yawl in which to escape. McFunn put Nicholas in charge of the crew's only lifeboat and he calmly had it launched and expertly kept it away from the wrecked snow. 'He did everything he was ordered with as much coolness as he would have done alongside a wharf,' his brother said.[8]

The ten-man crew managed to reach an island eight miles away, where four of them would have to remain, as only six men could fit in the yawl. The crew drew straws to see who would remain behind and Nicholas was one of the four who had to stay.[9] The castaways spent thirteen days on the island, surviving on lizards they caught, a bit of ship's bread and salt pork, and a pool of brackish water.[10] Their misery ended 18 January 1766, when Charles Biddle arrived in a small sloop. The brothers remained with

10

McFunn, sailing the Caribbean, and did not return to America until July 1766. Nicholas continued sailing for McFunn, before becoming the first lieutenant on the ship *Rotterdam*, which made three trips to Europe.[11]

By 1770 Biddle had grown tired of merchant service and cast his eyes toward a career in the Royal Navy. He was twenty years old and his reputation as a mariner had spread throughout the colonies. A contemporary described him as having a 'temper [that] was uniformly cheerful, and his conversation sprightly and entertaining ... [he was] remarkably handsome, strong and active, with the most amiable mildness and modesty of manner. A sincere Christian, his religious impressions had a decided and powerful influence upon his conduct.'[12]

Biddle's family connections had grown just as steadily. His older brother, Edward, was a judge and politician, and he convinced Joseph Galloway, speaker of the Pennsylvania House of Representatives, to write to Benjamin Franklin, asking the famed colonial representative to petition for a warrant for Biddle. Franklin agreed. The two met in June 1771 in London. It left a lasting impression on Biddle, who told his brother James in a letter that Franklin, 'Made a long speech full of advice and encouragement'. Franklin's tone, more than anything, was what struck Biddle, as 'was the kind and free manner with which he delivered it.' At Sheerness, on 22 June 1771, Biddle joined the *Seaford* (20), commanded by Captain Walter Stirling.[13]

Biddle spent six months on the *Seaford* before transferring with Stirling, with his personal following of *Seaford*s, to the *Portland*. The 50-gun frigate was bound for the West Indies. War with Spain loomed over the faraway Falkland Islands, breathing excitement into Biddle's service. However, the war rumours soon proved false and Biddle settled into the monotonous routine of the peacetime navy.[14] The *Portland* spent a year in the West Indies, returning to England before going into ordinary on 13 October 1772. He spent that winter in London, waiting for a lieutenant's commission and orders to report for duty.[15] By March 1773, news of an expedition to find a passage through the Arctic swirled around London and it fired Biddle's imagination. He sought out his former captain, Walter Stirling, and asked him to secure Biddle a place on the expedition. Stirling demurred, telling Biddle that Phipps had already selected his officers and midshipmen.[16]

The old captain, however, failed to cool Biddle's enthusiasm. He decided to enter as a seaman on either the *Racehorse* or the *Carcass*, the two specially fitted bomb ketches then undergoing refit at Deptford and Sheerness. He went first to Sheerness, where he learned the *Racehorse* already had its full complement of ninety sailors. He then went to Deptford, where on 4 May he secured a berth in the *Carcass*.[17] A former sailor from the *Portland* was also among the crew and he recognised his former midshipman. Believing Biddle had been demoted, the sailor 'was greatly affected', and approached Biddle to ask what happened. Biddle explained why he had enlisted as a seaman, and the sailor 'was equally surprised and pleased when he learned the true cause of the young officer's disguise, and he kept his secret as he was requested to do.'[18] Although he gave his age as twenty-five, Biddle was just twenty-three when he volunteered on the *Carcass* and there, when Horatio Nelson joined the ship as a midshipman three days later, the two heroes met.[19]

Six weeks later Biddle's strong nautical background led Phipps to rate him as a coxswain.[20] Despite their age difference, Biddle and Nelson were kindred spirits. Both possessed an innate quality of leadership and a desire for adventure. Biddle likely fired Nelson's imagination with tales from his merchant marine service and the two became fast friends.[21] The expedition set out on 4 June 1773, and by 24 July was off Svalbard Island in the northern Greenland Sea. Ice abounded and within days it had trapped both vessels. Captain Skeffington Lutwidge, commander of the *Carcass*, sent Biddle and Nelson out in longboats to scout the few passages through the ice, while sailors tried to cut the ships loose.[22] As the ice continued to encase the vessels, the sailors took the opportunity to frolic on the ice. It was probably what gave Nelson the idea of disobeying Lutwidge's orders and striking out on his own trip of exploration. He needed an accomplice and found a ready one in Biddle.

The identity of Nelson's companion on his frolic is disputed, but according to a biography of Biddle published in 1949, one night while the *Racehorse* and *Carcass* remained trapped, the two coxswains sneaked past the mid-watch and set out across the ice for Svalbard Island.[23] A heavy fog covered their escape, although it lifted by 3am. Lutwidge soon realised he was missing two men and a sharp-eyed lookout spotted Biddle and Nelson trapesing over the ice in pursuit of a bear. Lutwidge called out for both to return to the *Carcass* immediately. Biddle hesitated, looking toward the ship, and called on Nelson to return with him. Nelson, however, refused and while Biddle made his way back, Nelson continued his hunt. His musket, however, misfired, leaving him at the mercy of the bear. Only a large chasm in the ice prevented the animal from getting at the future admiral and a shot from Lutwidge frightened it off. A chagrined Nelson returned to the *Carcass*, where both Biddle and Nelson received an earful from their captain.[24]

Biddle and Nelson served together for the remainder of the expedition. They returned to England in October 1773, and parted company, although neither would forget the other. Biddle spent the winter in London, waiting for assignment to a warship. In a letter to his sister Lydia, he expressed the lesson he learned from his adventure with Nelson on the ice, while espousing an outlook that embraced the boldness that defined his and Nelson's career. He told her, 'not to credit idle tales; for you must know I have been so frightened, so terrified at hearing of the surprising difficulties we encountered, the dreadful dangers we were in, that I am positive my hand shakes while I write, and what astonishes me most of all is that during the whole voyage, I did not apprehend danger.'[25] Biddle remained in London and submitted an application to take part in an expedition to the Antarctic, but events in the colonies scuttled his plans. By December 1773, the situation between England and her North American colonists had deteriorated to the point that bloodshed appeared inevitable. Biddle, unwilling to turn his hand against his own family, submitted his resignation to the Royal Navy and returned to Philadelphia.[26] Before he left England, his mentor, Captain Stirling, and 'many others', attempted to persuade Biddle to remain loyal to King George III. Whether Nelson was one of those who spoke with Biddle is unknown.[27]

On his return to Philadelphia in the spring of 1774, Biddle lost no time in offering his services to the state. When open warfare broke out in April 1775, Biddle found himself in charge of Pennsylvania's largest warship, a 65ft gunboat named the *Franklin*. The ship was part sail vessel, part row galley, and designed for use in the Delaware River. He commanded her for four months, when he accepted a commission into the fledgling Continental Navy and took command of the brig *Andrea Doria*, a converted merchantman Congress purchased in October 1775.[28] Biddle's new ship carried fourteen 4pdr cannon and a crew of 112 men.[29] She was part of a small flotilla Commodore Esek Hopkins assembled in the Delaware, which included the ships *Alfred* and *Columbus*, the brig *Cabot* and the sloops *Providence*, *Hornet* and *Fly*. Biddle, despite being just twenty-five years old, ranked third among the captains in the flotilla.[30] The *Andrea Doria* left Philadelphia on 4 January 1776, in company with the rest of Hopkins's squadron. Hopkins had orders to sweep the mouth of the Chesapeake Bay clear of an improvised flotilla Virginia Governor John Murray, Earl of Dunmore, had built to harass rebel shipping.[31] Hopkins, however, decided to change his flotilla's destination and instead sailed for Nassau in the Bahamas, which he believed held a large store of military supplies – supplies the fledgling Continental Army desperately needed.[32]

The flotilla arrived off Nassau in March and took the town on 4 March, although the Americans missed their chance to seize a massive haul of weapons. Biddle played only a small part in the raid, remaining on board the *Andrea Doria* while marines and sailors from the *Cabot*, *Columbus* and *Alfred* carried out the attack.[33] It proved fortuitous, as did his insistence that his crew receive vaccinations against smallpox, which had broken out in the American squadron. The sailors on the *Andrea Doria* were the only ones not infected and soon the sick from other ships crowded onboard the brig, which became a hospital ship to the flotilla, returning to New London, Connecticut, on 14 April 1776, where Biddle unloaded the war material captured at Nassau.[34]

Biddle returned to sea on 4 May and seventeen days later captured his first prize, a brigantine laden with rum, salt, and molasses bound for Liverpool. On 29 May he captured a pair of British ships transporting a group of 42nd Royal Highland Regiment officers and men to Halifax. Biddle sailed to Newport, Rhode Island, arriving 21 June 1776, and again set out on a cruise on 10 July, capturing four ships carrying refugees and supplies from Lord Dunmore, as well as a large schooner carrying rum and sugar bound for England. All told, he took fourteen prizes in his cruises, before relinquishing command on 17 September 1776 and transferring to the 32-gun frigate *Randolph*.[35] His tally was the top among any Continental Navy captain.[36]

Throughout his time in command of the *Andrea Doria*, Biddle forged a reputation as a bold mariner and a compassionate captain. He trained his crew daily in gunnery and ran his ship as though it was a Royal Navy vessel. When Congress authorised the construction of thirteen frigates, ranging in size from twenty-eight to thirty-six guns, Biddle was at the top of the list to command. At twenty-six he was the youngest of the thirteen captains and ranked fifth in seniority.[37] His reputation in the colonies and beyond was even greater. When his brother Charles fell into English hands during a voyage to the West Indies, his captor pointed to an article in the *Pennsylvania Gazette* extolling the virtues of the young captain and asked Charles whether he was related to 'Captain Biddle'. Charles told the Briton somewhat proudly that the captain was his brother and his captor immediately put Charles in irons.[38]

Bad luck plagued Biddle's initial time in command of the *Randolph*. The first purpose-built, keel-up warship launched for the Continental Navy, the ship, Biddle said, 'is the very best vessel for sailing that I ever knew.' That was, when she could sail. After her launch in October 1776, the British blockade and an early winter kept the frigate trapped in the Delaware until a thaw in late January 1777 allowed her to slip past the Delaware Capes into the Atlantic. She cleared the capes on 6 February 1777, and appeared ready for a cruise.[39] The sojourn in open water lasted barely a day. A gale sprang up and shattered the fore- and mainmasts, forcing Biddle to make for Charleston, South Carolina, under a jury rig. She arrived on 12 March and immediately drew crowds, despite her appearance.[40] A fever and desertions had reduced Biddle's crew to less than a hundred men and repairs to the *Randolph* proceeded slowly. The new masts did not arrive until 14 May, and the sailors and carpenters began the laborious process of stepping in the masts to restore the *Randolph* to duty. They finished on 10 June. Two days later, a freak bolt of lightning hit the new mainmast, shattering it 'from cap to deck'. Once more, sailors and carpenters went through the process of removing the broken mast and replacing it. They finished on 2 July, but just eight days later another storm and another bolt of lightning shattered the third mainmast.[41]

Biddle settled in to wait while his crew stepped in a fourth mast and this time the captain was taking no chances. Biddle became the first American naval officer to install a lightning rod on a US warship. The spindly antennae-like apparatus was a source of curiosity among the residents of Charleston, who turned out in droves to stare at Biddle's mainmast.[42] It was during this time of repair and waiting that Biddle met the woman who, like Lady Hamilton with Nelson, would change Biddle's life. She was Elizabeth Elliott Baker, an eighteen-year-old daughter of a wealthy Charleston plantation owner. The two fell madly in love and Biddle proposed on 4 July.[43] It was the turning point of the young captain's life. Although a popular and successful captain and a somewhat prosperous landowner, Biddle could not match his fiancée's wealth and he knew he would need a successful cruise to add to his own holdings.

In what was a confluence of events, Biddle got his chance to make his mark as both the Continental Congress and the governor of South Carolina decided on the same target. Since the war began, British warships operating from Jamaica had stifled trade, while protecting the lucrative convoys conveying sugar to the United Kingdom. British actions had severely damaged the local economy and South Carolina Governor John Rutledge was especially eager to reopen trade in the Caribbean. He approached Biddle with the idea of striking back at the Crown by targeting the Jamaica convoys.[44] The Marine Committee of Congress had the same idea and sent Biddle orders to head for Jamaica.[45] Biddle promised Rutledge he would send any prizes he took into Charleston, which would further boost the economy if the governor would approve enlistment bounties for new crewmen. Rutledge agreed and in September 1777 Biddle and the *Randolph* finally put to sea.[46] He was out just a week when he fell in with a five-vessel convoy heading north along the coast. The largest of them, the ship *True Briton*, opened fire on the *Randolph* the moment Biddle hoisted American colours. Biddle, however, continued to close and after taking several broadsides from the *True Briton*, he ranged up on the ship and demanded her surrender. Her captain hauled down the Union Jack. The other vessels in the convoy, unable to match the speed of the *Randolph*, also surrendered. Biddle had captured two ships and two brigs – a small sloop managed to escape – as well as more than six hundred puncheons of rum, tons of sugar and other material.[47] It was a rich haul and Biddle escorted his prizes back to Charleston, where the governor and the people greeted him as a hero.[48]

Before setting out again, Biddle wanted to have the *Randolph*'s bottom cleaned and coppered. At the same time, news reached Charleston that the British had captured Philadelphia and the Royal Navy was on its way to renew its southern blockade. By October 1777, the frigates *Carysford* (28) and *Lizard* (28), the sloop *Perseus* (20) and an 8-gun brig, the *Hinchinbrook*, were patrolling off Charleston. Within a month, the British had again choked off the seaway into the city, alarming Rutledge, who turned to Biddle and the *Randolph* for help. Rutledge asked Biddle to take command of a flotilla that included the South Carolina state ships *General Moultrie* (20), *Volunteer* (18), and *Notre Dame* (16), and drive off the British.[49] Biddle hesitated, pointing out the state ships were barely manned. Rutledge appealed to the state and Continental forces in the area for volunteers, but found none. General William Moultrie, the state's top commander, suggested it would be easier to recruit men if Biddle led a naval force and a cruise against the Jamaica convoy, which held the lure of rich prize money. Moultrie made a powerful argument and Rutledge agreed to equip the 20-gun *General Moultrie*, brigs *Notre Dame* and *Fair American* (16), and the 14-gun brig *Polly*, and place them under Biddle's command. The Continental Navy captain, sensing this was his moment, agreed.[50]

Weather and the blockade stranded Biddle and his flotilla in Charleston throughout the winter. It was not until 12 February that Biddle and the *Randolph* cleared the bar off Charleston and slipped into ocean waters. The British blockade had lapsed, allowing the five American ships to begin their cruise. At first, it was uneventful. The Americans did not see another ship until 6 March, when the *Polly* captured an English schooner.[51] The next day, Saturday, 7 March 1778, lookouts spotted several sail on the horizon. One of the shapes was larger than others and it headed for the American flotilla. Biddle knew that his old ship, the 50-gun *Portland*, was

The battle between the *Randolph* and the *Yarmouth*, 7 March 1778, as depicted by artist J O Davidson in 1891. (US Naval History and Heritage Command)

patrolling out of Antigua. What he did not know was the 64-gun *Yarmouth* was also on station.[52]

Biddle was itching for a fight and, with four other ships, he believed he could outgun any one opponent, unless it was a ship of the line. Only the 20-gun *General Moultrie*, however, carried artillery to match the *Randolph* – 9pdr cannon. The other four ships had 6- or 4pdrs, which would do little damage unless the gunners could get into a raking position. The *Randolph* had 12pdrs on her gun deck and 6pdrs on her foredeck. As the mystery ship approached the flotilla, Biddle came up on the wind and brought the *Randolph* to a halt. He tacked around to gain the windward side of the unknown vessel, as did the *General Moultrie* and *Notre Dame*. The *Fair American* and *Polly*, however, failed to complete to their tacks and fell off leeward.[53]

At 7pm the mystery ship was within hailing distance of the *Notre Dame* and it depended on her captain to identify the vessel. It was now clear to the Americans they were up against a sixty-four, her guns poking out of two decks. The captain of the unknown ship identified himself as Nicholas

Vincent of the *Yarmouth* as the British warship swept past the *General Moultrie* to approach the *Randolph*. Biddle let the *Yarmouth* come up. His gunners had loaded their 12pdrs with bar and chain shot, while on the foredeck they had grape and canister to sweep the enemy deck. Biddle

Nicholas Biddle sits in chair on the quarterdeck of the *Randolph* at the height of the battle with HMS *Yarmouth*, 7 March 1778, in this lithograph of a painting by George Gibbs, painted about 1910. (US Naval History and Heritage Command)

refused to answer repeated hails from Vincent, who hailed a last time, threatening to fire on Biddle unless he answered. Biddle's answer was concise. He ran up the Grand Union Flag and let loose a broadside that swept over the *Yarmouth*.[54]

On board the *Randolph*, the gunners went about their work with grim precision. The two ships were barely 30yds apart and blasted away at one another, but it was the Americans who made their shots count. The *Randolph*'s crew fired three broadsides for every one the *Yarmouth* fired and the British vessel was quickly a wreck. The American gunners shot off the British ship's bowsprit, shattered her mizzen and shredded most of her lower rigging, endangering her fore- and mainmasts. Above deck, fifty men selected from the crack 1st South Carolina Regiment, many armed with rifles, poured fired onto the deck of the *Yarmouth*. Vincent, his first and second lieutenants all went down with wounds, while a rifle shot killed the quartermaster at the *Yarmouth*'s helm. By then Biddle was also wounded. A splinter opened his left thigh, but instead of leaving the deck, he ordered a chair and continued to command his ship.

The *General Moultrie* and *Notre Dame* joined in the battle, firing three broadsides, although the wind forced both vessels to break off. The *Notre Dame* actually fired on the *Randolph* by accident. Both ships attempted to get into a raking position, the *Notre Dame* on the bow and the *General Moultrie* at the stern. It appeared to the captains of both American vessels that Vincent was ready to strike his colours, but just as they managed to get into position, a massive explosion rent the night sky. When the smoke and debris cleared, the *Randolph* was gone. Out of a crew of 302 sailors and marines, only four men survived. Nicholas Biddle was dead. American naval icon John Paul Jones reportedly wept on hearing the news of Biddle's death, while Horatio Nelson is also reported to have mourned the loss of his friend.[55]

Biddle's career was tragically short. In the few months he commanded ships of war, he displayed the same courage and audaciousness that would characterise the career of his former messmate, Horatio Nelson. In one of his last letters to his brother Charles, he embraced a philosophy that could have come from Nelson. Nicholas wrote:

I fear nothing but what I ought to fear. I am much more afraid of doing a foolish action than of losing my life. I am for character of conduct as well as courage and hope to never throw away the vessel and crew merely to convince the world that I have courage. No one has dared to impeach it yet. If any should I will not leave them a moment of doubt.[56]

The Earliest Known 'Stars and Stripes'[1]

Peter Hore

During the American War of Independence the American privateer *Hampden* was fitted out at Portsmouth, New Hampshire, in the spring of 1778 under Lieutenant Samuel Pickerin.[2] Owned by John Langdon,[3] at 400 tons, armed with twenty-two guns,[4] and with a crew of 150 men, she was one of the largest privateers intended to prey on English shipping.[5] A newspaper recruiting notice for marines to be commanded by 'Captain of marines George Waldron' on 9 June 1778 described her as:[6]

> Mounts twenty-two Guns, nine and six Pounders. The Accommodations on Board are elegant, and suited for Convenience of all concern'd. The said Hamden [*sic*], without any Complement, mental Reservation, or Equivocation, is suppos'd to be as fast a sailing Vessel as any yet that has been fix'd out in the Thirteen States, therefore can take or leave.

After two cruises which paid poor dividend during the American War of Independence, the American privateer *Hampden* sailed from Brest at the beginning of February 1779, leaving behind a lawsuit over one of her prizes and a dispute with John Paul Jones over the recruitment in France of American seamen.

This third cruise was uneventful until at 10am on 7 March, when *Hampden* was in mid-Atlantic, at 47° 13' N, 28° 30' W, in company with a schooner 'under one Smith, armed with twelve x 4-pounders', and Pickerin saw a sight which made up for his frustration of the previous months: a rich, homeward-bound, East Indiaman, a sight which would have gladdened the heart of any privateersman. The East Indiaman lay to the southwest, about six miles distant, and Pickerin promptly began chasing her. He signalled to Smith to follow him, until at 5pm the stranger raised a British blue ensign, which Pickerin answered with a British red ensign, and fired a gun. Pickerin's red ensign was a *ruse de guerre*, and he hoped that by pretending that *Hampden* was a British warship, the stranger would heave-to to enable him to board. What he did not know was the blue ensign was also a bluff. The chase took all day and at 9pm his prey disappeared in the gathering darkness, and Pickerin hoisted three lanterns at the stern as a signal for Smith to follow him.

During the night *Hampden* prepared for action, and dawn found the stranger about three miles ahead. A letter from an American officer, possibly her first mate, John Tanner, described what happened next:[7]

At 7 A.M. came under her lee quarter within hail, hoisted continental colours and gave her a broadside. She kept all her guns hous'd till just before we fired, altho' we could tell her ports thirteen of a side, a very great distance apart; she return'd the broadside without any damage, with twenty-four nine pounders and eight four pounders and had the advantage of a spar deck to cover her men. Being a beautiful large ship with two tier of cabin windows we knew her to be an East Indian and of much superior force, but supposing they were badly mann'd, were determined to fight her as long as we could.

Though the officers of *Hampden* never discovered the identity of their victim, the ship of 'much superior force' was the 800-ton Thames-built East Indiaman, *Bridgewater*, and she was indeed short-handed. Built at Dudman's yard in 1769, she was on her third voyage to the East, returning after two years from Bencoolen (now Bengkulu), a British possession (<1714–1824) on the southwest coast of Sumatra. Her master was Captain William Parker, 'a native of this City ... whose ancestors have been uniformly as highly respected for their virtues, as for the important offices which they repeatedly filled in Cork'.[8] Parker was about to display other qualities too. *Bridgewater* carried only twenty-six guns, four more than *Hampden*, but she was poorly manned with only eighty-four men, many of whom were sickly, and in such a poor state that Parker had been forced to refit for a month at anchor off St Helena.

According to the anonymous correspondent of the *New Hampshire Gazette*:

The engagement continued till half past Ten, close alongside, when finding our three masts and bowsprit very badly wounded, our starboard main shrouds totally gone, our rigging and sails cut to pieces, our double headed shott expended, and near twenty of our men killed and wounded, were obliged to our grief to leave her a mere wreck, her masts, yards, sails and rigging cut to pieces. Having ourselves only the foresail which we could set to get off with, the sheets being cut away, were obliged to use our tacks. During the action our brave and worthy commander, Capt. Pickerin, was killed. Mr. Peltier a Frenchman kill'd. Samuel Shortridge so badly wounded he died in two hours after. John Bunting, both legs shot away but liv'd nine days after. John Tanner, master's mate, left arm shot off. Micajah [*sic*] Blasdel, left hand shot off. Peter Derrick, his mouth shot to pieces, and twelve others wounded, but none dangerous. We gave them three different cheers during the action, and our men fought with the greatest Bravery and coolness possible. The Ship was about Eight Hundred Tons, and a Tier of Air Ports under her Gun Ports.[9]

Each ship overestimated the strength of the other. According to Parker, *Hampden* (misreported as *Campden*) was an American frigate of twenty-eight guns, and three hundred men, with a sloop in company. The frigate hoisted American colours, the fight started at eight o'clock in the morning and lasted three hours until the frigate sheered off with the loss of her captain and nineteen seamen killed, and twenty-five wounded, while the sloop or schooner 'it blowing fresh … could not get into action'.[10] It had taken a day for *Hampden* to catch *Bridgewater*, which tells us that *Bridgewater* was well sailed despite being short-handed, Parker held his fire (presumably because he could not man many of his guns) until *Hampden* had ranged up alongside, and the fight ended when *Bridgewater* put her helm over and raked *Hampden*, causing havoc in *Hampden* and killing Pickerin.

James Fenimore Cooper, in his history of the US Navy, accounted this engagement as one of the most closely contested actions of the war, 'both sides appearing to have fought with perseverance and gallantry'.[11] Winslow, in a history of New Hampshire privateering, went further and implied that the Indiaman was reduced to a hulk and 'sank within hours'.[12] However, despite her lighter guns and weakened complement, *Bridgewater* was not badly hurt in the action and reached England safely two weeks later on 23 March 1779. When the Court of Directors of the East India Company studied the log of the *Hampden* and examined Parker, and presumably had read their copy of the *New Hampshire Gazette*, they resolved at their meeting on 10 June 1779:[13]

That for such a masterly defence of his ship, and against such a very unequal force … and in consideration of the gallant defence made by the Officers and Seamen of the ship *Bridgewater*, against an American Ship of War of superior force, which after an engagement of some hours was obliged to sheer off, a gratuity of Two thousand pounds, be paid to the said Officers and Seamen, in such proportion as shall be settled by the Committee of Shipping. That Captain Parker do receive the Thanks of this Court for his gallant conduct, and that he be presented with a Piece of Plate of One hundred guineas value, with the Company's Arms engraved thereon.

Parker's heroic defence of his ship was widely reported.[14] However, we know so much about him because he chose to commemorate his victory over *Hampden* by spending some portion of his share of his reward on a painting, choosing Francis Holman (1729–1784) who was well-acquainted with the sea. Holman was born at Ramsgate in Kent and lived at Wapping on the Thames, his father was a master mariner and his younger brother, also a sea captain, ran the family shipping business. He began his artistic career painting portraits of ships for his father's friends, and learned to draw hulls, rigging and flags with scrupulous attention to detail and accuracy. Later he drew scenes on the Thames, and then patriotic themes, especially sea battles. Holman's painting of *Bridgewater*'s fight shows much of the detail which he must have learned at first-hand from William Parker, including the presence of a third ship, the brailed-up sails, the fresh wind, open sea, and the flags worn by the opposing vessels.[15]

The stars appear to be set either in a rectangular pattern: 4 up, 4 across = 12, plus one in the middle = 13, or 3–2–3–2–3.

An early eighteenth-century East Indiaman at anchor off the coast of China, wearing the Honourable East India Company's striped ensign. The thirteen stripes of the Honourable East India Company ensign derived from a seventeenth-century English naval ensign. From 1707 to 1801 the HEIC ensign bore a British Union flag in the upper canton: the flag was normally flown south of St Helena. (Private collection)

Noticeably, Holman chose to draw the beholder's eye to *Hampden's* ensign and used the painterly device of placing her flag in the centre of the painting. On the right, *Bridgewater* flies the British blue ensign, but *Hampden* is flying what the literature tells us was 'American colours' (Parker) or 'Continental colours' (*New Hampshire Gazette*). Until the USA's Flag Act of 1777, Continental colours (also known as the Grand Union flag, the Congress flag, the Cambridge flag, or the First Navy Ensign) was very similar to the flag of the Honourable East India Company: alternating thirteen red and white stripes with the British Union flag (without St Patrick's cross which was introduced in 1801) in the upper canton of the hoist. The US Flag Act kept '13 stripes alternate red and white', but replaced the British Union flag in the canton with '13 stars white in a blue field representing a new constellation'. Inspection under ultra-violet light confirms that there are thirteen stars in Holman's, though their distribution is not clear – perhaps Parker did not have a clear view during the battle which he could with certainty relay to Holman, who had, presumably, never seen an American flag (see close-up).[16] The date of Holman's painting is unknown, but assuming that William Parker commissioned it soon after he

Raising the Grand Union ensign onboard the Continental Ship *Alfred*, painted by
W Nowland Van Powell. *Alfred* was the merchant vessel *Black Prince*, named for Edward,
the Black Prince, and launched in 1774, purchased by the United States and commanded by
Captain Dudley Saltonstall. In 1776 the Great Union flag (as George Washington called it)
or the Grand Union flag or Continental Colors [*sic*] may have been derived from the HEIC
ensign and for the first year of its life, like the HEIC ensign, also carried a British Union flag
and thus was barely distinguishable from the HEIC ensign, except, perhaps, by its more
squarish shape. (US Naval History and Heritage Command)

was paid his share of the reward by the Court of Directors of the East India
Company, it dates from 1779 and is thus the second oldest representation,
and first known representation in maritime art, of the Stars and Stripes.[17]

Postscript.[18] On 19 April 1779, six weeks after the fight with *Bridgewater*,
Hampden limped into Portsmouth, New Hampshire. A week later, the
newspaper carried an advertisement for her sale. She was described as a
'remarkably fast sailing vessel, frigate built and measuring 400 tons, and
armed with six 9-pounders, fourteen 6-pounders and two 4-pounders'. All
her stores, including one ton of gunpowder, were to be sold.[19] However, at
the end of June, during the Penobscot Expedition,[20] John Langdon, to
whose 'mind there was nothing wrong with profiting from patriotic deeds',[21]
offered *Hampden* to the New Hampshire Committee of Safety if the
committee would insure her against loss: she struck when 'hard pressed' to
a fleet under Vice-Admiral Sir George Collier on 14 August 1779.[22]
Meanwhile, in May an armed brigantine arrived from France at

The First Flag ensign by Francis Hopkinson. From 1777 onwards The British Union flag was replaced by white stars on a field of blue. The earliest design by Francis Hopkinson featured six-pointed stars arranged in rows. Another design with the stars in a circle is known as the Betsy Ross.

Portsmouth, with good news for the survivors of her privateering career,[23] and on 29 June 1779 an advertisement appeared calling on anyone who had an interest in prizes captured by the *Hampden* to collect their money.[24]

New Hampshire privateer *Hampden*, see colour plate 1

Nelson in Troubled Waters[1]

Joseph F Callo

In March 1784 twenty-six-year-old Captain Horatio Nelson took command of HMS *Boreas*. Two months later he departed from Portsmouth for the West Indies. When he arrived on station, he was surprised and deeply troubled by the widespread failure of the British authorities in the area to enforce Britain's Navigation Acts. This series of maritime laws, which were designed to reserve trade among Britain and its colonies for British ships, was being blatantly circumvented. As the senior officer afloat in the West Indies theatre, Nelson took his responsibilities seriously, and he believed strongly that those responsibilities included enforcement of the Navigation Acts.

As is so often the case, Nelson's own words tell the story dramatically. In this case Nicolas and a relatively obscure book, *Nelson's Letters from the Leeward Islands* by Geoffrey Rawson, are prime sources.

Ouroboros portrait of Nelson from *The Life of Nelson* by Clarke and M'Arthur.
(Author's collection)

A hostile Caribbean environment

After only six months in the West Indies, Nelson wrote to his friend Captain William Locker: 'The longer I am on this Station the worse I like it. Our Commander ... is led by the advice of the Islanders to admit the Yankees to a Trade; at least to wink at it.'[2]

In that environment, American merchant ship captains vigorously renewed their pre-Revolutionary War trade among the British West Indian possessions, and as they did so, they used an array of subterfuges to skirt the Navigation Acts. One of the favourite devices of the American captains involved feigning a seagoing emergency. By declaring that their ship was in serious distress from storm or other damage, they were able to appeal to the unwritten but universal law of the sea: namely one must aid a ship in distress, whatever its official nationality. Once in port, the American captains would offload their cargo, and then reload new cargo in the same port, or another British West Indian port, for a northbound voyage to America. In America, the cycle would start over again.

Another subterfuge of the American captains involved temporarily converting their vessels to Spanish registry. Before calling at a British West Indian port, the American ship captains would stop at a Spanish island, and there, for a price, they would secure official papers identifying their vessel as Spanish. Then, flying the Spanish flag, the American ships could operate under trading rights in the British colonies granted by a 1763 British Order of the Treasury. Nelson described the practice on a number of occasions. In one letter to the Admiralty in August 1786, he concluded: 'I have but little doubt ... that in their holds they bring American produce.'[3]

In the same letter to the Admiralty, Nelson indicated in precise detail how he was not enforcing of the law for its own sake:[4]

> This traffic, I must take the liberty of observing, brings to the King of Spain a considerable revenue; it will increase the Ship-building of America, and raise the numbers of her Seamen, while, on the contrary, it will decrease the British Shipping and Seamen in these Islands. These Americans will take off our rum, and carry it to America, so that our vessels will shortly have no trade to those States. They will be again the Carriers between these Islands and America.

Captain Collingwood fuels the problem

In mid-December of 1785, Captain Cuthbert Collingwood – at the time captain of the 44-gun fifth-rate HMS *Mediator* – was patrolling off St

'Chart' of the West Indies theatre in which Nelson operated as senior officer afloat between 1784–87. (Author's collection)

John's, Antigua, when he encountered an American vessel making for the harbour. When questioned, the American master claimed that he had a major problem with his mainmast and he intended to enter St John's for repairs. Collingwood had the mast inspected by *Mediator*'s carpenter, who determined that the damage was not serious. Collingwood then ordered the American ship to anchor alongside *Mediator* in St John's Harbour, and he proceeded to have his own ship's carpenter carry out the repairs. At the first opportunity, the master of the American ship went ashore, where he complained to the governor of the Leeward Islands, Major-General Thomas Shirley. In classic bureaucratic fashion, Shirley immediately sought the advice of the local King's Counsel, who opined:[5]

> I have always apprehended that the coercion for obedience to the Laws of Trade, Navigation or the Revenue is peculiarly committed to the Board of Customs, and to the subordinate officers of the Customs ... Any military interference without requisition from these officers of the Customs in any port of the British Dominions is certainly very unusual and singular.

With the opinion of the King's Counsel in hand, Shirley then wrote to the British Secretary of State in London about the incident. In his letter to London, Shirley repeated his complaint about Collingwood's action and asked the Secretary of State for a plan to resolve the dispute. A few days after the incident, Shirley also wrote to Nelson's reporting senior in the West Indies, Admiral Richard Hughes. Shirley questioned what Collingwood had done and complained that his actions had in fact closed the port of St John's.

Nelson enters the fray

In essence, Governor Shirley and his government legal adviser were challenging not just the legality of Collingwood's specific action, but in broader terms, the navy's legal authority to take aggressive action against the direct trade between America and the British West Indian colonies. The battle lines were drawn between civilian and naval authority.

Nelson quickly entered the dispute, and began a testy exchange of correspondence, not only with Governor-General Shirley, but also with Admiral Hughes, who was his military commander in the West Indies. Nelson's challenges lacked even the slightest hint of conciliation or deference, and in January he laid down his marker on the question of the Royal Navy's authority in an astonishingly bold letter to Admiral Hughes:[6]

> I beg leave to hope that I may be properly understood when I venture to say that at a time when Great Britain is using every endeavour to suppress illicit Trade at Home, it is not wished that the ships upon this Station

should be singular, by being the only spectators of the illegal trade which I know is carried on at these islands. The Governors may be imposed upon by false declarations; we, who are on the spot, cannot ... Whilst I have the honour to command an English Man of War, I never shall allow myself to be subservient to the will of any Governor nor cooperate with him in doing illegal acts. Presidents of Council I feel myself superior to.

Several weeks later Nelson reinforced his position in a letter to Governor-General Shirley:[7]

I conceive it the duty of all Governors, officers of the Navy, in short all officers under the Crown to suppress illicit trade, and to take care that the Laws which the Wisdom of our Parliament has made be not evaded, either by Oaths, Protests or Otherwise ... The wisdom of our Legislature has directed the Act of Navigation to Admirals and Captains of the Navy well knowing that those whose profession is the sea must be the best judge of the accidents which may happen upon that element.

Nelson's mini-lecture to Shirley continued with references to civilian-military protocol, and ended with a thinly disguised threat: 'I have, since my being on this Station, transmitted Home such accounts relative to the Trade and Navigation of these Colonies as I have thought fit, and shall from time to time continue that practice whenever it is necessary.'[8]

The defiance in those statements was unmistakable, but its boldness was backed by the thoroughness with which Nelson marshalled his arguments and the accuracy of the verbal broadsides he fired at his opponents' vulnerabilities. It was a pattern that would be repeated in other times and different theatres.

Those and other equally aggressive letters were politically risky, particularly for a young captain, and they were early signs of Nelson's willingness to take major political risks to do what he considered 'the right thing.' It was a testing time for Nelson's predilection for defining his duty in his own terms.

The complicity of customs officers

Nelson was particularly harsh in his judgement of the local customs officials: as he observed, they were sworn to uphold British law, not to interpret it. Nelson went so far as to suggest that, for the customs officials, it was simply a matter of corruption. In January 1785 in another of his combative letters to Governor Shirley, he wrote: 'Since I have been appointed to the Station among these islands, I know that several

Americans have received Permits from the Custom House here to sell their Cargoes, and these Permits obtained upon very frivolous pretexts.'[9]

Again Nelson was making enemies to make a point. Despite his single-minded determination, however, it became clear over time that there were serious limits to Nelson's ability to do more than slow down the illegal trade. Nevertheless he continued to try mightily. The immediate result: he was ostracised by many of the islands' merchants and landowners, and eventually he faced a legal threat that could have thrown him into unmanageable debt and ended his naval career.

No anchor to windward

In theory, a hard-charging young naval captain should be able to pursue his duty without putting his career in danger, and the steadfast support of his immediate military senior would be crucial in that regard. Unfortunately, Nelson lacked that particular 'anchor to windward'. In fact, his reporting senior was a significant part of the problem he was addressing.

In October 1784, in a letter to Captain Locker, Nelson labelled Admiral Hughes as 'tolerable'. A month later, in another letter to Locker, he was much more cutting: 'The Admiral and all about him are great ninnies.' Later, in May 1785, in a letter to his brother William, Nelson expanded his criticism: '[O]ur Admiral does not support us. He is an *excellent fiddler.*' Then by March 1786 he was mocking in his tone in yet another letter to Captain Locker: 'Sir Richard Hughes ... is a fiddler; therefore, as his time is taken up tuning that instrument, you will consequently expect the Squadron is cursedly out of tune.'[10]

A second area of potential support that obviously was lacking involved the local customs officials. Particularly in his correspondence with the Admiralty, Nelson was bitter in his condemnation of their inaction in the face of what clearly was, by British law, illegal trade. In a 'Memorial to the King' in June 1785, Nelson was pointed:[11]

> [Y]our Majesty's proclamation prohibiting all Trade with America, to and from the West Indies, (except in British bottoms, owned and navigated by the people of your Majesty's Dominions and Territories,) was most shamefully evaded by colouring American vessels with British Registers, by which means ... nearly the whole Trade between America and your Majesty's said Colonies was carried on in American bottoms.

Finally, there was the lack of support from the local population in general, and this heightened the sense of isolation for Nelson while deployed on a foreign station. Normally, one's fellow countrymen in an overseas theatre of operations would be a most welcome and important source of support for a young Royal Navy captain, one who was struggling to correct corrupt practices in the system. However, because he was perceived to be a threat to the livelihoods of the local British colonists, the situation actually was reversed for Nelson. In general, the local West Indian population considered him a particularly dangerous threat and, with notable exceptions, the local plantation owners, merchants and officials displayed open animosity towards Nelson.

As it turned out, the local plantation owners and merchants eventually launched a legal suit against Nelson and threatened to have him arrested if he stepped ashore. For extended periods of time he was a virtual prisoner in his own ship. At one stage he pointed out in a narrative, probably sent to Prince William Henry: 'Seven weeks I was kept a close prisoner to my Ship; nor did I ever learn that the Admiral took any steps for my release.'[12]

A significant defender

A notable exception to the adversarial relationship Nelson had with Britain's West Indian populace was John Herbert, president of Nevis. As the influential owner of a major plantation on Nevis and the head of one of the island's most respected families, Herbert had much to lose by Nelson's active enforcement of the Navigation Acts. However, he obviously liked and respected Nelson, and to his credit, he even offered to post bond for him if he was arrested.

In addition, Herbert invited Nelson to his home at Montpelier, which was set high on a hillside, where there would almost always be a cooling ocean breeze. Considering the attitude towards Nelson among Herbert's peers and the lack of comfort in the close quarters of his ship, Montpelier was a welcome refuge. In time, the idyllic site high on the Nevis hillside would take on even greater significance, when Nelson met his wife-to-be, Frances Nisbet.

Emerging leadership qualities

The adversities that Nelson faced in the West Indies would have forced an accommodation to the then-political realities of the West Indies from many officers in his situation. However, with Nelson it produced tenacious resistance to the practices with which he disagreed. In the process, the cutting edge of his basic leadership qualities was tempered and sharpened.

Significantly, this process was taking place in a non-combat environment, and in sharp contrast with the usually compact violence of combat, it was drawn out over a long period of time. In those circumstances, fatigue, discouragement, self-doubt, and boredom could have worn down a less dedicated personality.

Defining duty under pressure

Nelson's distinctive sense of duty was severely tested in the West Indies. Under the intense pressure of the circumstances, that sense of duty became something that he continued to build and maintain within himself, rather than something that was imposed externally by orders or regulations. Not surprisingly, the subject was very much on his mind during his tour in the West Indies. The subject of duty even found its way into his correspondence with his future wife, Frances Nisbet. In May 1786 he wrote to her: 'Duty is the great business of a Sea-officer. All private considerations must give way to it, however painful it is.'[13] As it turned out, that statement about a naval officer's duty also was a subtle predictor of an issue that would contribute to the marital troubles to come for the couple.

One of the most thought-producing features of the statements by Nelson about the Navigation Acts and his duty was that they were so unequivocal. There were no lengthy musings about whether or not he might be right. There were no ongoing reservations about his actions, and clearly there were no doubts concerning his authority. Just how strongly he felt on this subject emerges from the words he wrote in a message to Admiral Hughes in January 1785. In that long letter to his commander, he distilled his thinking:[14]

> [A]t a time when Great Britain is using every endeavour to suppress illicit Trade at Home, it is not wished that the ships upon this Station should be singular, by being the only spectators of the illegal Trade which I know is carried on at these Islands. The Governor may be imposed upon by false declarations; we, who are on the spot, cannot.

The unvarnished language Nelson used in his arguments with Admiral Hughes and Governor Shirley stands in sharp contrast with their more tentative letters. Consistently, they seemed to be groping for arguments that would protect them if their actions were found to be wrong in the eyes of the Admiralty. Nelson, on the other hand, reflected only the unshakable conviction that his actions were consistent with the law and the greater interests of his country.

Nelson's letters to his reporting senior, Admiral Hughes, were particularly striking. They were extremely risky for a young officer, notwithstanding

Nelson's status as a commanding officer, and notwithstanding the strength of his arguments. The tone reflected in those letters infuriated many senior Royal Navy officers and government leaders of the time, as well as some of his naval contemporaries.

As it turned out, there is no doubt that Nelson's attitude had a negative effect on his standing at the Admiralty immediately after his tour in the West Indies. The five years he spent seeking his next assignment were ample proof that he had developed a reputation there as a troublemaker. It could also be argued that it was the shift in Britain's relationship with France, more than anything else, that resulted in Nelson's appointment to command of HMS *Agamemnon* in January 1793.

In the long run, Nelson's willingness to deal bluntly with his seniors and accept the consequences also made him a uniquely valuable naval leader, one who would fearlessly speak the truth to his seniors as he applied his characteristically blunt combat doctrine, which he articulated before the Battle of Copenhagen in 1801: 'The boldest measures are the safest.'[15]

Fig Tree Church on Nevis, where the marriage between Nelson and Fanny Nisbet is registered. (Author's collection)

HMS *Boreas*, see colour plate 2, Nevis stamps, see colour plate 3

The *Chesapeake–Leopard* Affair, 1807

Anthony Bruce

The Treaty of Paris in 1783 brought the War of American Independence to an end, but relations between the United States and Great Britain remained tense. The loss of America 'jolted the national pride, and the national system'[1] and formal diplomatic contact between the two governments was not established until 1791. Britain reacted to its defeat by adopting 'aggressive policies meant to exploit weaknesses in the American political and economic systems'.[2] It sought to restrict America's developing role in the Atlantic carrying trade and British West Indian ports were closed to American shipping. Import duties were imposed and British garrisons remained in seven forts located across the northern United States.[3]

Among the causes of continuing mistrust between the two countries were the rights of neutrals and impressment (recruitment by force or the threat of force), and both issues grew in significance in the second part of the Great War, the Napoleonic War 1803–15, when a British economic blockade against France was in force.[4] The USA gave British and French warships access to its ports, but complained that the Royal Navy frequently infringed its neutrality. French warships were attacked in American

USS Chesapeake fired on by HMS Leopard, 1807, by Fred S Cozens.
(US Naval History and Heritage Command)

territorial waters and press gangs were sent on board merchantmen at sea and in American ports. In 1806, for example, the British set fire to the French warship *L'Impétueux* (74) off the coast of Virginia, and President Thomas Jefferson ordered an investigation to determine whether the incident had occurred within US waters. Moreover, impressment was not always confined to British subjects or to American merchantmen, and the United States strongly objected when the practice was extended to American citizens and warships. From 1796 the United States issued American seamen with certificates of citizenship, but these did not always provide them with protection. Britain complained that deserters from its ships were widely employed on American warships (on better pay and conditions) and fake certificates were in use. In 1812 it was claimed that there were some twenty thousand British seamen serving on American ships, a loss that Britain could ill-afford as it battled to defeat the French.[5]

There had been several confrontations between the Royal Navy and American merchant ships since the War of Independence, including an incident on 25 April 1806 when the British fourth-rate warship *Leander* (52) opened fire on the American merchantman *Richard* and killed a member of the crew. In May 1807 *Driver* (18) was banned from American waters after an incident in Charleston when the captain threatened violence after facing difficulties in obtaining supplies. The ban may have been one of the factors that led to the first British attack on an American warship since 1783 when, on 22 June 1807, the fourth-rate warship *Leopard* (50) opened fire on the American frigate *Chesapeake* (38). It created far more anti-British feeling than previous incidents, which included the removal of five sailors from the American frigate *Baltimore* (20) in 1798, and was to have far-reaching consequences for relations between the two countries in the period leading to the War of 1812.[6]

In 1807 a British flotilla, based in Halifax, Nova Scotia, under the command of Vice-Admiral George Berkeley, commander-in-chief of the British North American station,[7] was patrolling the coast of Virginia. Acting under Berkeley's orders dated 1 June, the flotilla was charged with searching ships which were suspected of carrying deserters from the Royal Navy, as well as undertaking its main function of enforcing the British blockade against France. In pursuit of these orders, the *Leopard*, commanded by Captain Salusbury Humphreys, was dispatched from its anchorage near Cape Henry, which forms the southern boundary of the entrance to Chesapeake Bay, in the early morning of 22 June. Its mission was to intercept the 38-gun frigate *Chesapeake*, which was suspected of carrying British deserters, as she left for Europe. She was one of the original six frigates of the United States Navy (USN) whose construction was authorised by the Naval Act of 1794 and had seen routine service in the Quasi War against France and the Barbary War (and she would be taken by the British frigate *Shannon* (38) during the War of 1812). In 1807 *Chesapeake*, part of a squadron commanded by Commodore James Baron, an experienced and well-regarded officer who had joined the USN in 1798, left Chesapeake Bay with orders to relieve American warships on the Mediterranean station. *Chesapeake*'s captain, Master Commandant Charles Gordon, had no reason to expect any trouble from the British: the ship and her crew were unprepared for action, and she was not even stowed for sea. As she entered the open sea, she passed two British warships at anchor without incident.

By mid-afternoon of Monday, 22 June, Gordon observed a vessel closing on *Chesapeake* from astern. According to *Leopard*'s log, at 3pm, when she was some nine miles east-southeast of Cape Henry, she 'bore down on the United States frigate *Chesapeake* [and] at 3.32 hove to and sent Lieut. Meade on board with despatches'.[8] A note from Captain Humphreys enclosed a copy of Admiral Berkeley's orders of 1 June which referred to desertions from British warships to *Chesapeake* and instructed his captains to search the ship if it was encountered 'at Sea, and without the limits of the United States'. They were to secure the return of any deserters they found. Humphreys hoped the issue would be settled amicably but, in response, Commodore Barron said that he was not aware of any British deserters in *Chesapeake* from the six ships that were specifically mentioned in Berkeley's orders. He also pointed out that the United States did not permit any such search: 'I am instructed never to permit the crew of any ship that I command to be mustered by any other but her own officers'.[9] At first Barron suspected that the 'British arrangements were menace rather than anything serious', although *Leopard* had her lower-deck ports open and the tampions of her guns had been removed. At this point, neither Barron nor Gordon had ordered their men to their quarters, as was formally required under naval regulations when a foreign warship approached.[10]

Meade returned to *Leopard* with Barron's note refusing to permit a search of his ship. After reading the answer, Captain Humphreys 'repeatedly hailed [*Chesapeake*], saying he was under the necessity of enforcing his orders', but the only response he received from Commodore Barron was: 'I do not understand what you say.' By this point Barron, who was trying to buy some time, had concluded that British 'intentions appear serious', and he ordered Gordon to call the crew to general quarters. He

The Hon George Berkeley (1753–1818), Rear-Admiral of the Red Squadron.
(*Naval Chronicle*)

asked for this to be done as quietly as possible and when the ship's drummer began to call the crew to action, Gordon struck him with his sword, which inevitably added to the general sense of confusion on board. The men were asked not show themselves through the gun ports, in order to avoid the British charging *Chesapeake* with 'making the first hostile show', but the British were within pistol range and could see the ship's decks being cleared for action.

According to the British log, *Leopard* then ranged alongside *Chesapeake* and 'fired a gun across her forefoot & again hailed her without effect'. After a short delay, a second shot was fired before a broadside was discharged; two more broadsides then followed. As shot penetrated *Chesapeake*, Barron stood in an open gangway displaying great coolness under fire, but at first there was no other American response. The British log records that fire was

CAPT. SALUSBURY PRYCE HUMPHREYS. R.N.

Captain Sir Salusbury Pryce Humphreys (1778–1845) was given no further commands after the *Chesapeake–Leopard* affair and retired to his estates outside Manchester.
(*Naval Chronicle*)

eventually returned 'by a few guns', but it was much delayed, as *Chesapeake* was still 'unprepared and Ship much lumbered', according to her log.[11] There were no powder horns or matches readily available to fire the guns, the crew were not all at their action stations and the magazine was disorganised. Despite these shortcomings, Barron could not understand why *Chesapeake*'s guns remained silent, and later questioned the crew's loyalty and commitment and charged the lieutenants with inaction during the engagement.

With casualties mounting – and facing a more powerful enemy – Barron decided that anything more than token resistance would be too costly. He therefore implored Gordon: 'for God's sake to fire one gun for the honour of the flag, I mean to strike.' In the end, one of *Chesapeake*'s 18pdrs was fired using a burning coal from the galley stove. The US marines had loaded

Commodore James Barron USN (1768–1851) was found guilty of not preparing his ship in advance for possible action. (John S Phillips Collection)

their rifles but they did not participate in the action, as they were never given the order to fire. At about the same time as she finally opened fire, or possibly slightly earlier, at 4.45pm, *Chesapeake* surrendered. She had lost three men and sixteen, including Barron, had been wounded, and there was substantial damage to the ship's masts and rigging; twenty-two roundshot were embedded in the hull.

A boarding party from *Leopard* then arrived and mustered the crew. Four sailors, three of whom were American-born deserters from the British frigate *Melampus* (36), were removed. But this was only a small fraction of the total, as many other British seamen were known to be serving in *Chesapeake* (out of a crew of 329 and fifty-two marines). In a message to Captain Humphreys, Barron said that he considered 'the frigate your prize, and am ready to deliver her to an officer authorized to receive her'. Humphreys refused the offer of surrender, saying that he had fulfilled his instructions and expressed regret that lives had been lost.

Leopard then went to rejoin the rest of the British flotilla, while *Chesapeake* returned to Hampton Roads, arriving there at noon on 23 June, and reported the incident to the authorities. Commodore Barron had begun a post-mortem even before the vessel reached her anchorage. He asked his officers for their views on what had happened and it was quickly evident that they were anxious to avoid blame and sought to limit the damage to their reputations.[12] In response, one of his lieutenants went as far as saying the surrender was an act of cowardice that had disgraced the flag. Another pointed out that *Leopard* only had ten more guns than *Chesapeake*, and said that 'you had better Sir have suffered your ship to have been blown from under you than thus shamely dishonoured us'.[13] A court of enquiry found Barron guilty of negligence and a court martial followed. Early in 1808 he was tried and convicted by eleven officers during a trial which lasted for a month, and he was found guilty of not preparing his ship in advance for possible action. He was suspended from the navy for five years without pay. Although his subordinates had not performed well, Barron as the senior officer was held responsible for failing to respond to the British challenge, and the incident marked the end of his active naval career.

Many Americans held Barron solely responsible for a major national embarrassment, but there were divided views in the US Navy about his culpability. However, most officers blamed him for the lack of an effective response and he struggled to find further employment. Much later, one of Barron's most vocal critics, Commodore Stephen Decatur, who had served on his court martial, opposed his efforts to resume his naval career. In a period when duels between naval officers were commonplace, Barron, who never accepted the damning verdict of his peers, challenged Decatur to a fight. Fought with pistols in March 1820, the duel left both men wounded and Decatur later died of his injuries.

There was a strong reaction to the *Chesapeake* incident among the residents of Norfolk and anger spread quickly across the country.[14] A mob in Norfolk destroyed a large number of water casks belonging to *Melampus* and the British responded by moving some of their ships into Hampton Roads where they could blockade the port. In New York City, the police protected the home of the British consul from attack, and in Manhattan the residents removed the sails and rudder of a British merchant ship. President Jefferson commented: 'never since the Battle of Lexington [1775], have I seen the country in such a state of exasperation

Commodore Stephen Decatur USN (1779–1820), a hero of the Barbary Wars and the War of 1812, was killed in a duel with James Barron. (US Naval History and Heritage Command)

as at present. And even that did not produce such unanimity'.[15] In an initial response, which was 'cool and measured',[16] the president asked the British government for an explanation and ordered all Royal Navy vessels to leave American waters immediately. His actions were designed to avoid open conflict but, faced with strong public anger, he did not discount the possibility of war, and preparations were made during the summer of 1807. Despite the fact that the two countries appeared to be headed for war, the US Navy was simply not strong enough to face the Royal Navy in battle. However, funding for a fleet of gunboats to defend the American coastline, as well as for new forts and harbour defences, was approved by Congress before the *Chesapeake* incident.

Immediate priority was given to the defence of Norfolk, both on land and at sea. Decatur, who now commanded *Chesapeake*, was responsible for replying to any British attack on Norfolk by sea. His force now included a French frigate, 'which speaks volumes about [Jefferson's anti-British] foreign policy'.[17] Other targets for a British attack were thought to be New York, Charleston and New Orleans. Offensive American action was likely to be by land rather than at sea, and this might include the occupation of Nova Scotia in order to remove the threat from British ships based in Halifax. Fully committed to the war with France, Britain was unable to reinforce its small garrisons in Canada in order to counter this threat, but she took steps to renew her alliance with her Indian allies.

While preparations for war were being made, the United States sought a formal disavowal of the attack, the return of the four seamen taken from *Chesapeake*, and reparations paid to the families of the dead and injured. This was coupled with a renewed American demand for an end to impressment and the British boarding of American ships.[18] The initial British response was conciliatory: reparations would be offered if British officers were culpable, and the government in London disavowed Berkeley's action. He was removed from the command of the North American Station, although he was soon appointed to the Mediterranean. Like the Americans, the British did not have the naval and military resources to go to war on another front, but they had little incentive to resolve the dispute quickly. News of the American ban on British ships and the demand for the abolition of impressment inevitably led to the complete failure of negotiations: while Britain was at war with France it was inconceivable that she would resolve the impressment issue in America's favour. The execution of the only British-born deserter taken from *Chesapeake* in August 1807 did nothing to improve relations between the two countries.[19]

In the absence of a diplomatic solution, Jefferson, who remained unwilling to go to war with Britain, proposed a commercial embargo as an alternative. The Embargo Act of 1807 imposed a general embargo that made all exports from the United States illegal. This untried experiment, which he hoped would persuade Britain and France to recognise the USA's rights as a neutral, had a damaging impact on the American economy without having the desired effect on Britain. In fact, British shipowners generally welcomed the ban, as it removed growing competition from the American merchant fleet, while alternative markets in Spanish America opened up to the British when Napoleon invaded Spain in 1808. Domestic political support for the embargo quickly evaporated and it was repealed in 1809.

With Britain maintaining its right of impressment, further incidents between the two navies were inevitable. In 1810 the British sloop *Moselle* (18) opened fire on the American schooner *Vixen* (14) off Barbados, and other incidents followed as the British continued to seize American and British subjects from American ships. In May 1811 the American frigate *President* (44) opened fire on the British sloop *Little Belt* (20), and thirteen members of the crew were killed and nineteen wounded; *President* suffered a single casualty. *President*'s commander, Commodore John Rodgers, claimed that the British opened fire first, but this was disputed. The vastly unequal action was celebrated by 'most Americans as fair recompense for the *Chesapeake* affair. Besting the British ship had restored national pride'.[20] In 1811, under President James Madison, the United States and Britain finally reached an agreement to compensate the families and return the two surviving seamen, but they were not transferred until 12 July 1812. By this time the USA had already declared war on Britain.

Even if the attack on *Chesapeake* did not represent a direct cause of the War of 1812, conflict had only narrowly been avoided at the time and there is no doubt, as Alfred Mahan pointed out, that it marked 'conspicuously the turning-point' in Anglo-American relations.[21] It was 'an engagement impossible to overlook or forget'[22] and helped to set the stage for war five years later. Apart from the affront to American honour, there was no resolution of one of the principal issues raised by the *Chesapeake* incident – the demand for an end to impressment – and it was one of the main reasons why the USA eventually decided upon war. There were several other factors that led to the American declaration, including trade restrictions brought about by the British war with France, British support for the native American tribes fighting American settlers on the frontier, and American plans to expand in the northwest and annex British territory.[23] The 'Second War for Independence',[24] 1812–15, arguably ended in a British victory, with American trade being brought to a halt, the capital burned, and some northeastern states on the verge of secession. The Americans also failed to seize any Canadian territory or bring impressment to an end, although the practice was soon to fall into disuse as result of the rapid reduction in the Royal Navy's manpower requirements following the defeat of France in 1815.

USS *Chesapeake*, see colour plate 4

Impressment: Politics and People

Kathryn Milburn

The War of 1812 is little discussed and little loved in a modern world where the United States and the United Kingdom are often marked as the closest of allies. However, after the conclusion of the American Revolution, the return to positive relations between Britain and the United States was slow and not always peaceful. The War of 1812 has often been called America's Second War for Independence by those who sought to glorify a new nation standing up to tyranny, and sardonically called Madison's War by those who attempted to reframe the war as a needless conflict over a series of trumped-up charges. The British, engaged in a generation-long war against the evil empire of France, called it a 'stab in the back'.

The most important and common American complaint of the time was impressment: the forced conscription of American seamen into the Royal Navy. For many Americans, this was an outrage and an unacceptable attack on newly formed American sovereignty; there would be no tolerance of British tyranny by those who had fought to free themselves from the monarchy only thirty years prior. However, impressment was not a new phenomenon in the history of naval warfare. Long before the outbreak of the French Revolution and subsequent wars, British – and European – maritime history is riddled with the use of impressed sailors. The monarch's subjects were expected to participate in defending Crown and country, and impressment was a common way of gathering the sailors needed to man ships during a time of war. Reliable numbers of American men pressed into the Royal Navy are difficult to come by, and most of the war rhetoric surrounding impressment is marked by hyperbole. In 1812 the United States went to war with Great Britain without the support of the New England states, a surprising contradiction considering the northeast states were predominantly engaging in maritime activities. If the real grievance, that of impressment, were true, why did war to redress that grievance take so long to come to fruition? Why would the maritime states in New England so hotly contest the war if their sailors were really being snatched at such an alarming rate?

Background: impressment pre-1800

Long before the American Revolution, impressment was common practice in the British navy. The British government established the 'Impress Service' during the 1740s, a department of the Admiralty that regulated impressment in the British Isles.[1] Impressment was not a shadowy and semi-legal activity, but it is described by Sir Robert Walpole in 1740 as unpopular, and he refused to affirm that such a practice was actually legal.[2] However, Walpole also claimed that impressment was the state's sole safeguard for its defence until a voluntary, workable register could be created.[3] On 22 November 1770 Lord Chatham said: 'I am myself nearly convinced, and I believe every man who knows anything of the English Navy will acknowledge, that without impressing it is impossible to equip a respectable fleet.'[4] As such, the Impress Service reached into every major port in the United Kingdom; however, no comparable system was established in the North American colonies and the practice of impressing Americans developed informally.[5]

As British subjects, colonial American seamen had no choice but to become part of the Royal Navy's global manning system.[6] It was widely acknowledged that impressment was one of the key tools available to the Admiralty in procuring skilled sailors for naval service, especially in times of war. Since colonists enjoyed the benefits of being British citizens, they were expected to participate in its protection. In a 1743 case questioning the legality of impressment, Justice Michael Foster, a respected jurist in Bristol, argued that naval impressment took precedence over private rights in national security, and that although it was unfortunate that these obligations of personal service fell to one occupational class of men, they were not illegal.[7] Despite the controversy and the obvious loathing of impressment, it did help create the world's greatest navy and enabled British domination of the sea.

The main colonial complaint about impressment, however, was not that it existed, but that the colonies could not control it. In the 1740s Governor William Shirley of Massachusetts tried on repeated occasions to gain control of the activities of press gangs in his colony.[8] Instead of allowing press gangs to run wild in Massachusetts, he tried to activate an orderly process in the pressing of sailors into British service. Even Benjamin Franklin attempted to control impressment with his Albany Plan of Union in 1757; however, the eventual riots and politicisation of American seaports forced the press gangs from land.[9] Despite these attempts to moderate impressment, one of the major obstacles to controlling impressment was that it only existed during periods of war.[10] Although impressment was the most consistent cause of crowd violence directed against imperial officials before the American Revolution, by 1776 impressment of Americans at ports had become less important (as Britain was largely at peace with other nations) and impressment is rarely cited as a contributing aggravating factor of the American Revolution.[11]

After independence, the new American nation renewed their complaints about impressment, and in the spring of 1790 President Washington dispatched Gouverneur Morris, a trusted diplomat, to London to address the normalisation of British-American relations. Morris met with Prime Minister Pitt to protest that American sailors had been impressed by the Royal Navy in its mobilisation for war with Spain.[12] Morris expected that the United States and Britain would achieve full diplomatic and commercial relations, predicting Britain 'will give us a good price for our neutrality.'[13] Despite Prime Minister Pitt's promise to consider the requests of the United States, he never did submit a response to Morris's proposals.[14]

The renewed impressment of American seamen in the late 1790s and early 1800s spawned a national crisis in the United States over what it meant to be an American citizen in an Atlantic world dominated by European empires.[15] Knowing this, British seaman utilised the crisis to manipulate their way to safety. Sailors sometimes impersonated foreigners, especially after American Independence, when British seamen could plausibly claim they were citizens of the new republic and avoid service to Britain.[16] In a response to this malfeasance, the United States began issuing naturalisation certificates that would prove a sailor was American. However, by 1812 the British Admiralty estimated that ten thousand false certificates were circulating and the Royal Navy refused to recognise any American-issued certificates that did not come from a customs agent.[17]

The pressed

The press gang is often seen as the face of impressment – the concept of a rowdy gang of hooligans, armed with clubs, whose aim was to beat sailors into submission and force them to serve in the Navy, is fanciful, but not necessarily accurate. In the American colonies, the press gang was an infrequent visitor to port towns, and usually pressed sailors at sea instead of on land, where it was considered too dangerous to 'recruit'.[18] Overall, impressment was seen as a necessary evil, a detested institution that was wildly unpopular, but imperative to manning the Royal Navy.

The fact that impressment existed in such controversial territory meant that it had to follow strict rules to ensure that men were pressed legally. Press officers had to have properly dated warrants and had to be physically present before entering any vessel or port in search of men.[19] The success of impressment at sea can be accounted by the fact that boarding a merchant ship almost certainly guaranteed an officer the opportunity to find skilled men.[20] According to the Exemption from Impressment Act of 1739, every foreigner, being a mariner, seaman or landsman, serving in any merchant ship, trading vessel, or privateer belonging to the subjects of the Crown of Great Britain could not be legally pressed into the British Navy.[21] In theory, this meant that British press gangs were not allowed to press foreign sailors who were serving on British ships, but the fact that many Americans and Britons were indistinguishable led to questions of nationality and protections. However, in the British perspective, becoming the citizen of another nation did not release one from the obligations of service to the Crown. The British, therefore, retained the right to impress British subjects who had become naturalised American citizens.[22] In 1796 Congress attempted to define and protect American citizenship in the Act for the Relief and Protection of American Seamen. The law instructed customs collectors in American ports to issue US citizenship protections to seamen before they set sail on the high seas. Between 1796 and 1812 106,757 seamen registered at custom houses: however, these protections were not always observed by the press gang and they were easily counterfeited.[23]

Despite many claims that the British did not impress foreigners, and even the assertion that it was a prohibited practice, there was impressment of foreign sailors.[24] However, compared to the total number of men in the British Navy, impressment of foreign sailors was a rarity.[25] Dancy's research suggests that impressment of Americans made up a minimal part of the British navy, as he found only sixty-eight Americans pressed out of his study of almost eighteen thousand seamen.[26] Statistically, this means that Americans did have a right to complain that their men were being pressed into British service, but the able researcher must question if such a small number is statistically significant enough to start a war.

However, other researchers have claimed numbers of American pressed sailors as much larger. A L Burt notes that as the years passed, the number of kidnapped Americans serving in the Royal Navy mounted until it was several thousand.[27] Zimmerman's research suggests between 1799 and 1802 the total number of those impressed is 2,059, which is derived from the final report of David Lenox, the American agent in Britain.[28] However, Zimmerman goes on to suggest that as early as 1807 the British navy held fifteen thousand American seamen.[29] Donald Hickey claims that perhaps ten thousand Americans were impressed during the French Revolutionary and Napoleonic Wars.[30]

On 30 November 1807 a resolution was passed in the United States Senate, calling for the gathering of information on those pressed into the British Royal Navy. On 29 February 1808 a report was filed by the Secretary of State and future president, James Madison, with estimates recorded by General Lyman, an agent of the United States in London, who was responsible for submitting impressment grievances to the British government to obtain a release of the pressed sailors. According to the applications and remittances received, the Lyman report estimated that since the commencement of war in 1803, 4,228 men were pressed into British service and 936 were released.[31] In an 1811 speech before Parliament, Lord Castlereagh admitted that out of 145,000 seamen employed in the British service, the whole number claiming to be American subjects amounted to no more than 3,300.[32] Also worth noting is the fact that at the Battle of Trafalgar there were approximately 389 Americans in British ships.[33] Of the thirty Americans who in served in HMS *Victory*, an unusually high proportion, numbering ten of them, were pressed.[34] These numbers serve to illustrate the problem of discussing impressment as a true cause for war: with so many estimates and such a range of numbers, how can any researcher confidently suggest that impressment was, or more importantly, was not, a cause for war?

American reactions to impressment: myths and realities

In the United States, the concept of forced servitude in the name of national security was widely disliked. Despite efforts by Presidents Adams, Jefferson, and Madison, proposals for mass conscription were not passed in the United States – Congress consistently erred on the side of volunteering as opposed to compulsion in times of war.[35] The British response to the lack of skilled sailors was utilisation of the press gang. The legal aspect of press gangs was justified by Lord Mansfield as owing to the fact there was no alternative.[36] Many in the United States believed that impressment deprived the American merchants of much needed seamen, and undermined the honour of the young nation by showing that its flag could not protect those who served under it. Almost from the beginning of independence, at least since 1790, American statesmen protested against impressment, although at first they emphasised the kidnapping of American citizens.[37] For many Americans, impressment was much deeper than the British need for bodies on ships; it was a question of sovereignty. Only America's colonial past and the experience of the American people as subjects under the British Crown can explain the nation's deeply emotional response to impressment. Many foreign nations surrendered mariners to the British navy during the French

Revolutionary and Napoleonic Wars, but no other country went to war over the issue.[38]

Initially, the British claimed only to press deserters from the British navy and while there was peace in Europe, as there was between 1801 and 1803, Britain and America faced no great danger of going to war or squabbling over impressment. However, as time passed and war was renewed, the British once again needed to man their ships. Naturally, British seamen were attracted to American merchant service, which was booming. In a study of six British vessels, approximately 16 per cent deserted from 1806/1807.[39] During this time American exports were experiencing exponential growth and in 1807 peaked at $108 million.[40] The American merchant fleet offered stable wages, safety from war, and the implied added protection from impressment. However, for the British, a successful navy meant the difference between victory over Napoleon or being subjected to his tyranny. To check the vital loss of manpower, British warships searched American vessels and removed British fugitives from service.[41] To further man the Royal Navy, they also laid claim to all British subjects, including emigrants and other persons who would not have been subject to impressment in British ports.[42] In fact, the British Admiralty estimated in 1812 that some twenty thousand British subjects worked aboard American merchant ships, which was more than double the American government's estimate.[43] This is part of the reason the British targeted American ships for pressing: they were trying to reclaim their own sailors.

Worth noting, however, is the fact that in September 1804 President Jefferson wrote a letter to the Attorney General, Levi Lincoln, stating, 'the new administration in England is entirely cordial. There has never been a time when our flag was so little molested by them in the European Seas.'[44] Despite the positive outlook of the American executive, Anglo-American relations would continue to deteriorate in direct relation to the war in Europe. In the summer of 1807 the British frigate *Halifax* came into port at Norfolk for repairs, providing an opportunity for desertions, of which there were many: on 7 March a whole boat's crew of the *Halifax* made off with the jolly-boat and escaped to Norfolk.[45] One in particular, Jenkin Ratford, told his captain that he was now in the land of liberty and would do as he liked.[46] In the following months the British minister in Washington complained to the Secretary of the Navy, who would not grant redress. Many of the deserters, and some sailors from the *Halifax*, who proved to be American, joined the crew of the American frigate *Chesapeake*. In response, the British ship *Leopard* attempted to retake her sailors at sea; first through negotiation with Commodore Barron, commander of the

Chesapeake, and when that failed, the *Leopard* attacked, killing three and wounding eighteen, including Commodore Barron.[47] The *Leopard* reclaimed Jenkin Ratford, but also took three Americans and left the *Chesapeake* to hobble back to Norfolk. Afterward, the attack upon the *Chesapeake* monopolised America's attention – the indignity of an American warship molested at sea and American sailors taken away to serve Britain was an outrage, and viewed as a direct attack on American sovereignty. Despite ongoing negotiations, Britain had yet to fully make reparations for the *Chesapeake* and well into 1811 Augustus Foster, Minister Plenipotentiary to the United States, was still trying to seek a successful resolution.[48]

This event, and the press coverage that surrounded it, begs the question, why were insults to the nation more deeply felt in 1812, when impressments and even ship seizures were relatively few, than in 1807 with the attack upon the *Chesapeake*? Surely this brazen attack was a more obvious challenge to national sovereignty, but it failed to bring war. In the subsequent debates in Congress, many demands for war were heard, but Jefferson refused, instead opting for diplomatic and economic solutions.

Attempts to settle impressment
During Jefferson's tenure as the American president, he oversaw the negotiation to try and end the pressing of American sailors by the Royal Navy without utilising force. Jefferson dispatched Monroe and Pinkney to negotiate a peace between Britain and the United States. Their mission was threefold: Great Britain would have to repudiate impressment, restore the American trade with the enemy colonies, and give indemnity for captures made.[49] Jefferson was confident that 1806 would see the establishment of peace between Britain and the United States, but unfortunately his optimism was ill-founded. Monroe and Pinkney believed they had secured a British promise not to engage in impressment except in unusual situations, but this was not directly addressed in the Monroe–Pinkney Treaty – a feature that was so important to Jefferson, that he refused to sign the treaty or submit it to congress for ratification.[50] Contrarily, Madison, writing in 1810, claimed that the Monroe–Pinkney Treaty had been rejected largely because it had left untouched the Orders in Council and that even if impressment wasn't resolved entirely in favour of the Americans, Madison would accept that as a path for peace.[51]

During the congressional sessions of 1806, several bills were proposed in an attempt to curb British impressment, but it must be noted that these proposals were not just aimed at impressment, but also British interference in trade. Senator Wright of Maryland introduced a bill for the protection of American seamen which would have adjudged impressment as piracy. This bill was shelved because the majority of opinion was for a combined retaliation against both impressment and restrictions upon neutral trade.[52] Later, Andrew Gregg from Pennsylvania and Joseph Nicholson of Maryland would introduce bills that would fight the importation of British goods. During Gregg's introduction to his resolution, he spent quite as much time attacking the practice of impressment as attacking the new British regulations regarding American commerce.[53] This appears indicative that in the American perspective, impressment was at least equal in importance to the trade restrictions imposed by the British.

The year 1806 appeared to be the one in which Britain would appease American calls for reform. In July, Parliament passed the American Intercourse Bill which would allow for trade between the United States and the West Indies. In a further attempt to appease the Americans, Fox, the British Foreign Secretary, oversaw the modifications of the French blockade, effectively allowing neutrals to trade, provided that they did not carry contraband of war, and provided that they had not been laded at, nor were destined to, an enemy port.[54] Sadly, these efforts were not seen as active concessions by American politicians, but as further examples of British dictatorial practices at sea. However, the New England merchants benefited greatly from these policies and in 1807 American exports peaked at $108 million.[55] Clearly, the British were doing their part to address trade rights, but the rhetoric surrounding impressment was about to explode.

In 1807 Jefferson tried to take advantage of the national outcry produced by the attack on the *Chesapeake* by attempting to force Britain to give up her traditional policy of impressment. Jefferson persuaded Congress to pursue economic repercussions as a means of punishment. In December 1807 the American Embargo Act was passed, confining American vessels to American ports and permitting foreign vessels to leave only in ballast or with the cargo they already had on board.[56] The emphasis was now to change from seamen to ships and cargoes. Instead of taking centre stage, impressment was relegated to only one of many American grievances of the time. It was at this point that American discontent was now shaded with commercial frustrations and disgruntled views of the events on the continent affecting neutral nations.

Britain, under Spencer Perceval, Chancellor of the Exchequer, realised that if they could restrict American commerce according to British desires and yet still avoid war, it would be of considerable advantage. It is in this context that the conflict should have reached a breaking point. The Orders in Council issued from Britain in January 1807 essentially made plain that the United States would have no trade with Europe except through Britain.[57] In response, Napoleon issued the Milan Decree declaring that every neutral ship that allowed herself to be searched by the British, sailed to a British port, or paid a British duty, was a lawful prize for France.[58] Despite the fact that by this time the French navy had been largely destroyed by Britain, it was clear that the United States had been backed into a corner, but once again, the United States was disinclined to start a war.

At the end of 1808, American spirit was at a very low ebb – commerce ruined by the Embargo Act, the country split by factions debating how to proceed, and Britain and France apparently impervious to American threats and retaliation.[59] Both of the belligerent nations had rendered the American Embargo irrelevant and reason suggested that the United States would now have to declare war. Jefferson could have led the States to war in June 1807, just after the *Chesapeake* incident – it would have been a war fought over impressment and citizenship rights, but this did not happen, and in the spring of 1808 the embargo was repealed as a failure.[60] However, war was not declared in 1807, and the fact that it was put off for five more years implies that impressment could not be the leading cause of the War of 1812.

Further evidence exists that the often cited problem of impressment had been rendered largely irrelevant by the end of 1808. David Erskine had been named the British Minister to the United States in 1806 and he was tasked with negotiating a new peace with the states. Eager for an agreement, he toned down Britain's original requests, which would have been deemed unacceptable by most Americans, and instead offered to have Britain repeal the 1807 Orders in Council, the United States would remove all trade restrictions from Britain and apply the Non-Intercourse Act only to France.[61] The Americans eagerly accepted and the victory of the Erskine Agreement, or at least as it was viewed by the United States, spelled out the end of large and long hostilities. Hamilton wrote, 'there no longer exists a probability of war.'[62] As demonstrated by Hamilton's enthusiasm, impressment could not be such a large contributor to the cause of war if many felt war could be avoided by addressing economic complaints without even mentioning impressment.

Further evidence suggests that, even during the furore of 1811, the eleventh Congress put up for vote to make it obligatory for Britain to give up impressment as well as her Orders in Council if America were to give up Non-Intercourse, but this suffered a heavy defeat, obtaining only twenty-one votes in support.[63] However, the Non-Intercourse Bill was passed and it stipulated that in order for it to be repealed, Britain must repeal its Orders in Council that were so damaging to American trade. Once more, this demonstrates the lack of belief that impressment was the true evil, and instead, that British trade behaviour was the root of the cause for war.

A close study of the debates of the twelfth session of Congress sheds light on what many of the true causes of the war might be. Henry Clay contended that 'today we are asserting our right to the direct trade – the right to export our cotton, tobacco, and other domestic produce to the market.'[64] Similarly, Felix Grundy stated that the point of contention between the US and Britain 'is the right of exporting the productions of our own soil and industry to foreign markets.'[65] John Rhea noted, 'but it is asked, will you go to war for commerce? It is answered, England has been at war for commerce the greatest part of two hundred years; and shall not the United States protect their commerce?'[66] The commercial desire of the War Hawk party did not go unnoticed by the Federalist opposition; a famous quote from John Randolph is 'we have heard but one word – like the whip-poor-will, but one eternal monotonous tone – Canada! Canada! Canada!'[67] The conquest of Canada was often cheered by the warmongers in Congress as a viable option for revenge on Britain for all of the troubles the United States had suffered, but it also implies a different cause of the war: expansion.[68]

In 1811 Congress called for a list that would outline how many applications had been made to the Admiralty for release, so that a firm idea of the number of Americans held prisoner might be realised. The same name often appeared more than once, which demonstrates the fact that any such list could not be an accurate account of how many Americans were actually pressed onto British ships at the time.[69] Between 1809 and 1810 the American consul submitted 1,558 applications for dismissal, although studies of these applications included many duplicates.[70] Of the reported 1,558, only 144 of those men reported that they were taken off an American ship – the rest were employed on British merchant ships or were working in British ports.[71] According to a report issued by the state legislature of Massachusetts in 1813, only twelve Massachusites had been impressed into British service.[72] These lists further demonstrate that while impressment was accompanied by blustery rhetoric, it was not nearly as common as many have claimed.

Declarations of war

By the time 1812 approached, it was clear that British attitudes about impressment were unlikely to change without a show of force. This was demonstrated by the pro-American British magazine *Monthly Review* that claimed, even one month before Madison declared war: 'Our right to impress our seamen from on board the merchantmen of America, or of any country, admits of no question: but the difficulty is to exercise that right without infraction on the liberty of American citizens.'[73]

The British would continue to practise impressment, even if it meant harassing American ships and sailors and evoking the ire of the Americans – dominance of the sea equalled survival. It may be argued that continuing with the practice of impressing American seamen had made Britain mistress of the seas, but by 1812 the United States elected to tolerate such treatment no longer.

In Madison's address to Congress in November 1811, he enumerated a long list of grievances against Great Britain, but he did not expressly mention impressment among them, further indicating to the British that impressment had become a non-issue.[74] In recent years, impressment had scarcely been mentioned in diplomatic correspondence, implying that the United States preferred to focus on their economic woes. Britain had received no warning that America intended to make war on such a ground, and impressment, though bitterly resented, had up to this point been officially considered irrelevant.[75] Britain was particularly shocked in the summer of 1812 that the United States could have thrown her forces on the side of Napoleonic tyranny, for throughout the spring Augustus Foster resolutely stated that 'although the war bill might pass the House, it would never win approval from the Senate.'[76] Even in the height of the war frenzy, the British could not fathom that after all this time, the Americans would go to war.

In Madison's war message, delivered on 1 June 1812, he outlined five complaints that led to a declaration of war. The first listed, as chief among them was impressment. Madison said:

British cruisers have been in the continued practice of violating the American flag on the great highway of nations, and carrying off persons sailing under it, not in the exercise of a belligerent right founded on the law of nations against an enemy, but of a municipal prerogative over British subjects. British jurisdiction is thus extended to neutral vessels in a situation where no laws can operate but the law of nations and the law of the country to which the vessels belong ... The practice, hence, is so far from affecting British subjects alone that, under the pretext of searching for these, thousands of American citizens, under the safeguard of public law and of their national flag, have been torn from their country and from everything dear to them; have been dragged on board ships of war of a foreign nation and exposed, under the severity of their discipline, to be exiled to the most distant and deadly climes, to risk their lives in the battles of their oppressors, and to be the melancholy instruments of taking away those of their own brethren.[77]

The Federalist newspapers, on the other hand, urged that impressment had never been, and was not at this time, a just cause for war.[78] It should be noted that, despite Madison's many appeals to the ills of impressment, it was still not seen as the most important act for war. Even in the lead-up to his delivery of the war message, Madison was scrambling around for an inciting event for war, as evidenced by the Henry Affair.[79] At the same time Madison was making his war overtures, Britain was repealing the Orders in Council and the Blockade of 1806, two items that the Americans had deemed particularly injurious.[80] When addressing negotiations for peace, Monroe wrote that since this cause of war was removed, the United States was under no obligation to continue the war.[81] This was also debated in Congress; Congressman James Emott from New York argued in January 1813 that all ills besides impressment had already been addressed and solved, that all that remained was the issue of impressment, to which he stated that 'we are now fighting for the right of protecting British subjects in our own vessels.'[82]

Had the United States Congress been aware of the fact that Britain had already repealed the Orders in Council, it is unlikely that any war declarations would have been made and that cause of war, being removed, would have seen the other essential cause, the practice of impressment, subject to renewed negotiations.[83] However, having cited impressment as the primary cause for war, the United States could not suddenly backtrack, having received redress for almost all of her complaints. Madison had, perhaps foolishly, named impressment as the primary purpose for declaring war and now that peace was being instantly handed over to him, he had to be sure that the largest complaint he cited was also solved in its entirety before agreeing to peace.

Conclusion

What is really surprising is not that America declared war on Britain in 1812, but that she had not done so several years earlier. Tensions were much higher in 1806 and 1807, after the United States rejected the Monroe–Pinkney Treaty and the seizure of the *Chesapeake*. By 1809 it seemed as though the time of crisis incited by Britain was over. Yes, the Orders in

Council were still in place, as were the French Milan and Berlin decrees, but since the French essentially lacked a viable naval force, the US merchants did not have much to fear from them. Since the War of 1812 does not have a clear inciting event, it is difficult to measure how different factors affected the coming of war. Regardless of the actual number of Americans impressed into British service, the rhetoric surrounding impressment was too loud to be ignored and Madison's war message clearly cites impressment as the most important reason to go to war against Britain.

What is most interesting about the war declaration and subsequent debates is that support for the war came largely from the south and west, regions that had been little affected by impressment, but largely suffered the most from Britain's economic sanctions. South Carolina, home state of War Hawk John C Calhoun, made up 10.3 per cent of domestic exported goods in 1812, which mean they also felt the particular pinch of the embargoes.[84] So why did the region that suffered the most losses in manpower to British depredations, the New England States, mount one of the fiercest anti-war campaigns in American history?[85] Statistically, the numbers indicate that impressment was not nearly as common as claimed, but it did provide a powerful narrative about national identity and rights of neutral nations. There were plenty of economic and expansionist reasons to go to war against Britain and it is likely that these reasons were much more important to defending the concept of American nationalism than protecting British sailors claiming to be Americans.

The War of 1812 provided an opportunity for a young nation to assert herself among kings, but the reasons for war that were cited at the time cannot be accepted without further examination. Though impressment was often complained about by both Americans and Britons alike, it is unlikely that impressment was truly so great an ill as it was portrayed. At the very least, the vastly ranging estimates of the number of men pressed into the British Royal Navy should indicate to modern historians that despite being cited as the greatest challenge to peaceful relations between Britain and the United States, it was a trumped-up charge that was disputed at the time, and it should continue to be disputed today.

A Boy in Battle

Charles A Fremantle

Charles, my subject, was the second youngest of seven Fremantles who served in the navy, and army, during the Napoleonic Wars. He was born on 1 June 1800 and was therefore given a second name of Howe by his mother, the diarist Betsey Wynne, and his father Thomas,[1] Nelson's right-hand man.[2] The Fremantle careers were fostered by Lord Buckingham, the head of the Grenville family.

Charles went to sea at the age of ten with his father, newly promoted to rear-admiral and appointed to the fleet blockading Toulon in the Mediterranean. A letter to Betsey dated 25 September 1810 from his flagship *Fortunee* (36) on passage states that 'Charles is already climbing the rigging as if he had been at sea for years'.[3]

The blockade of the French fleet in Toulon was a strain on men and ships. His father's flagship was now *Ville de Paris* (110), where Charles would have heard many stories of sea battles. The French refused to confront Admiral Cotton's fleet, but their forces on land under Marshal Suchet were taking control of Catalonia and thereby threatening Menorca, where the magnificent harbour at Mahon was the base for the fleet.

The protection of the island was put in Fremantle's hands, which gave Charles a mixture of sea and shore service until he was sent home with a liver complaint in July 1811 in *Tigre* (74) under Captain Hallowell,[4] another of Nelson's 'Band of Brothers'. Betsey greeted him, full of tales of the sea and eager to go away again, at home in Swanbourne in October. He had a brief spell at Eton with his elder brother Tom, and then joined *Argo* (44) under Captain Frederick Warren, to meet up again at Palermo in June 1812 with his father, who had now been given command of the Eastern Mediterranean. Charles stayed in *Argo* in order to visit Constantinople.

On 12 December 1812 he was rated as a midshipman, one of twenty, in *Ramillies* (74), under the command of Sir Thomas Masterman Hardy.[5] The ship was tasked with the blockade of key ports in New England after war was declared on Great Britain on 18 June 1812. They also had to counter five hundred American US privateers and frigates which preyed on British merchant ships throughout the Atlantic. The convoy system provided protection for British merchant ships, and *Ramillies* collected a convoy off

Betsey Wynne (age about 17), later Lady Elizabeth Fremantle, authoress of the Wynne Diaries, artist unknown. (Lord Cottesloe)

Madeira bound for the West Indies, before commencing the blockade of New London in February 1813.

Charles's father was in the Mediterranean at the capture of Trieste on 23 October, when he heard that his son had been taken prisoner, and wrote to reassure Betsey: 'I was quite astonished to hear of poor Charles being made a prisoner. I think it will not do him much harm, and I have no doubt Hardy will soon get him exchanged.' Sir Thomas Hardy also wrote to Betsey via his wife Lady Hardy to emphasise that he had not willingly put Charles into danger! Once Charles was freed he told him to write too:[6]

My Dear Mother, I suppose you will be surprised to hear that I have been for this last month a prisoner but it was all my own fault as I asked the Captain to let me go in a sloop with Mr Claxton fitted out for a tender to take prizes but we were not in her long before we were taken by a privateer which came out on purpose and carried us into New London where I was very comfortable as the British Consul let us have his house and was very kind to us and it was about a month ago that they let us come back to the ship. I don't like the Yankees at all as they took my Spy Glass which Lord Buckingham had given me and some of my bedding and behaved very ill to us while we were on board Fluke. I liked Mr Stewart very much likewise his wife who are very good kind of people. We are regularly exchanged yet only on parole but expect to be every day. Sir Thomas told me to write last week and asked me to say if I had, and so I am making haste and I believe there is soon a vessel going. The Ship has taken about a dozen, and I am getting as rich as Croesus.

We are I believe going to Halifax in about a month but Sir Thomas don't want to go for fear of losing the prizes as I expect as soon as I am exchanged to go away on a prize and then I will have a vessel of my own as all the midshipmen are gone.

I heard the other day that Lord Buckingham was dead which I hope is not true, if he is not, you must tell him I am very sorry I lost the Spy Glass but I tried very Hard to save it but the Blackguard American would have it because it was a good one.

I suppose by this time that my father is come home. I will write to him the next opportunity. I have only received one old letter from you since I have been out. I have wrote [sic] several.

Give my love to every body & believe yours ever affectionate, C H Fremantle.

Charles's 'seadaddy' was Lieutenant Christopher Claxton, who described the boy and his actions in a series of letters to Betsey, letters intended to reassure her, but which presumably she dreaded to receive and to open (Betsey noted in her diary 'found letters of Charles. He behaved so gallantly at the battle near Baltimore ... thank God he escaped unhurt'):[7]

I write Madam neither under constraint or diffidence although it is the first time I ever had the honour of addressing you for I write to tell you of the good conduct of your son who deserves to be beloved by everybody – It must be a pleasing satisfaction to you to hear of his behaviour and as (from having been a constant witness of all his actions) I have it in my power I will not withhold so great a satisfaction.

He particularly requested to go with me in a tender to the *Ramillies* and much against Sir Thomas' inclination (conceiving it a place of danger) he went – we had several little trying businesses in all of which he behaved as a youth much beyond his years – but his conduct at the time of our capture outcapt [sic] everything that could be expected from him. We were taken by a much superior force of 40 men to ten –

assistance was in vain. It was in the dark, consequently it was some time before I could ascertain the strength of our opponents, to have surrendered before would have been cowardice – during this interval we were exposed at 5 yards distance to a galling fire from a great gun and musketry – so warm it was that I was obliged to order all my men down below and three were hit – I used all my endeavours to force Charles also down but he remained firm on deck with a match in one hand and a pistol in the other, declaring that he would not leave the deck til I did myself – how he escaped I do not know, everything was shot to pieces, but we miraculously escaped. They boarded us, we were drove below and there was absolutely a consultation whether to give us quarter or no. This was awful indeed but your son never forgot himself.

I have since been a witness in boats on many occasions in action, in all of which he behaved like a hero. Sir Thomas is very proud of him, and that alone is an honour to him.

Hardy and his supporting ships continued their blockade of New England, but stayed on quite friendly terms with the locals who had been against the war in the first place, and were seeing their trade disappearing with a huge loss of revenue to the United States government.[8] In another letter to his mother, Charles records the price being paid by Hardy's ships for provisions bought in New England, far cheaper than his mother is paying![9]

There was excitement on 10 July 1813 when the blockading flotilla captured or destroyed the US privateers *Wampoa*, *Holkar* and *Vesta*, and bottled up the celebrated Commodore Decatur for the rest of the war.[10] Charles was hopeful that the 'cowardly' Yankees would come out and fight. They sailed to Halifax in September 1813 with four hundred American prisoners, and a captured transport. Charles writes about it in French to his mother, worried that he will lose Claxton, his friend and tutor, to duty in command of the prize. The ship re-equipped, refitted and rested before returning to the New London blockade in early December 1813, where the powerful US frigate *United States* (56)[11]and the captured *Macedonian* (38) had taken refuge. He writes to his mother on 2 January 1814, describing a visit with his friend Claxton under a flag of truce to tour the US ships and meet Decatur, whom he describes as polite and civil:[12]

My dearest Mother, As I do not have one single opportunity of writing to you I must not let this one pass without letting you know that I am well – though once again off this despicable place New London laying within 5 miles of the American frigates United States & Macedonian, it is very

Young Charles, by Christopher Fremantle. (Sir John Waters Kirwan)

tedious and unpleasant as we are always obliged to be on the 'qui vive' as they determined to get out. The United States is an immense ship compared to our frigates. Mr Claxton went in with a flag of truce & as he generally does me the honour to take me wherever he goes himself, I also went with him & saw the Renowned Commodore Decatur – he was very polite and civil as were also his officers – we went all over the United States. The Macedonian is much smaller in comparison & the (US) has 24 on the main deck & 12 more on the quarter deck and 500 men – it is not at all surprising she should dwarf the other with only 18 X 32" & 300 men. We expect shortly to be relieved by the Victorious (74) Captain Talbot when we shall proceed to Bermuda. I wrote you in my last that I wanted some clothes. I have now double need of them as the Americans have caught all our washing 40 dozen from this ship. You must therefore send me out double supply of shirts, at least 2 dozen & let them be made longer than the others as I have been growing very fast. They had better be too large than too small and cannot have much folding frills to them but something a little more manly. As for my trousers & stockings I am not an atom fatter than I was when I left you. You had better send them to Sir Thomas as they will be much safer. We have more prize money (before ordered here). I should think I have made about 80 pounds 'fort bien'. I should be very glad if I had my skates here as there is plenty of ice & I would enjoy having it. We do not find it so very particularly cold as we thought it would be. I suppose Emma cannot drive her little carriage now as it would be buried in the snow – I have not heard from her for these last six months – nor from you lately. I suppose the letters must have been lost or taken. Give my love to my Father & all & believe me. Your most affectionate son CH Fremantle

In June 1814 Hardy's flotilla embarked four hundred troops for a secret mission under General Sherbrooke[13] to capture as much of Maine as possible to become the colony of New Ireland.[14] The key ports were to be occupied, starting with the capture of Fort Sullivan, which commanded the entrance to the Passamaquoddy Bay. Sherbrooke had achieved fame with Wellington in India and in the Peninsula, where he was in command of a division at the bloody Battle of Talavera. This division included the first battalion of the Coldstream Guards in which served Charles's cousin John Fremantle, later an ADC to Wellington.[15]

Charles was given the command of a brass field gun, and was looking forward to 'spraying the Yankees with shot', but to his chagrin the fort, and all the islands in the bay, surrendered to Hardy on 19 July 1814 without a shot being fired. Possibly the fame of Hardy at Trafalgar and Sherbrooke in the Peninsula, and the pro-British sentiments of many in Maine, encouraged the lack of resistance. The captured territories remained British until the end of the war. Claxton wrote again to Betsey:[16]

My dear Madam, Charles of course informed you we were about to depart from Bermuda on a secret service with the 102nd Regiment on board. The denouement is the Capture of the Town and harbour of Eastport & of the Island of Moose in the Bay of Fundy – without loss as the Garrison surrendered at discretion – on our appearance. The business has been well conducted – The Enemy had not ten minutes notice – for in the space of that time, after their first seeing us, we were in the boats & they had not the slightest idea of our intentions. Charles had the honour of commanding a 6" Brass field piece, which no doubt he would have done justice to had the Enemy been possessed with pluck enough to have resisted. I remain my dear Madam, yours truly and sincerely C Claxton

In August, Hardy launched a three-day bombardment of Stonington in Connecticut. This was a town supplying torpedoes and powder to US forces, which were using them to attack the blockading ships. The torpedoes were mines to be taken by a submarine and attached to the hull of *Ramillies* below the waterline. Hardy introduced two-hourly cable sweeps of his hull as a countermeasure, but the mines were never attached.[17]

Attention now turned to the Chesapeake, where the population was more supportive of President Madison's war. Experienced troops were becoming available from Europe. Charles wrote to his mother regretting that the *Ramillies* had been unable to join the fleet under Admiral Cochrane which landed a combined force under General Ross and Rear-Admiral Cockburn:[18]

> I have but just time to write to you and tell you that Washington is destroyed, but I am sorry to say that we were just too late to join in the fun. They landed with 6,000 men and marched straight to Washington, but only 1,000 went into the town where they found 10,000 soldiers which they attacked and drove out of the Town. Mr Madison was seen driving about in a carriage with 4 white horses speaking to his troops, and had a large supper laid out in his house for as he thought his victorious Generals and Officers which our army partook of, they destroyed his house which cost £1,000,000, building and everything that was not private property, they destroyed a 60 gun Frigate, 2 Brigs, and Commodore Barney's Flotilla of gunboats which were 20. The damage that is done is supposed to be estimated at 50,000,000 dollars. I have not time to say any more as the vessel that is going to England has just shown herself and the boat is going away with the letters.

The combined British forces had defeated an American militia army three times their size at the Battle of Bladensburg, burned Washington and returned to their ships.[19] *Ramillies* joined the fleet while the commanders were debating whether to attack Baltimore, which was much larger and better defended than Washington. They were urged on by Cockburn, and this time Charles joined his friend Claxton in the Battle of North Point, described in a letter to Betsey from Claxton:[20]

> Your son Charles is well after having been in action with the Americans. My partiality for him may perhaps incline me to speak too favourably or at any rate may induce you to think I do. The Army (or a small body of 4,000 men so called) landed about 16 miles from Baltimore against which

Admiral Sir Charles Howe Fremantle GCB, artist unknown. (Lord Cottesloe)

place it was to act. As there were upwards of 30,000 Milititiamen it was deemed necessary to land all the marines of the fleet and as many seamen as could be mustered. I had the honour of commanding 100 men with musquets from the *Ramillies* who were regularly embodied with the Light Brigade of the Army consisting of the 4th Ship Marines, 44th and the seamen of the *Ramillies*, *Albion* (90), and *Diadem* (32) consisting of about 200 men. The whole about 2,500 – of which your son Charles commanded 20. We had the good fortune of being brought into action and of driving before us through a thick wood a large part of the American Army consisting it is supposed of 11 or 12 thousand men, of whom 7 hundred were killed or wounded, of the *Ramillies* 13 were wounded out of eighty seamen and 3 killed and 5 wounded of her marines. Each brigade had the same number of seamen attached to them, the whole under the command of Captain Crofton of the Navy, who was with us in the charge and who was pleased to take notice of your son's conduct and has made him a present as a memento of the victory.

Captain Crofton however thought the fatigue would be too much for him and so did I, and at my request he was sent back with the wounded, of which I was most happy as the enterprise we were about to undertake would have been most desperate. The Weather was intensely hot, but we marched 10 miles without stopping and went immediately into action – upwards of 200 men dropt with fatigue from the march. I feared much for Charles but he held out most nobly til the fight was over. The oldest soldiers never experienced such hot weather – it was impossible to resist his solicitations to accompany me – and nothing but a written order would make him go back. He tells me he amused himself on his way back by foraging to the right and left of the road with such men as were slightly wounded and ended by bringing back to the landing place 20 sheep and everything in proof, here he sent off his wounded, but remained himself until the whole army arrived. He was feeling ashamed to go on board without his party.

We advanced in dreadful weather to within 2 miles of Baltimore where we found the Americans 30,000 strongly posted on a height sustained and fortified by numerous cannon – which it was deemed impracticable to attack with 6,000 men, therefore we retreated at our leisure in good order for they were afraid to follow us – and we now hold them so cheap – Charles is writing you himself and I suppose will give you all the news. Our operations are now over, therefore you must not be under any alarm or uneasiness about him.[21]

This was followed by a reassuring letter from Hardy to Charles's father:[22]

I received your letter of the 3rd of June only a few days ago and I congratulate you most sincerely on your return to England. You will have seen by the Public Report all that we have been doing in this part of the world, and we have met with a very great loss in poor General Ross who was killed at Baltimore, he appeared to understand remarkably well what he was about and possessed the entire confidence of both Army and Navy. Colonel Brooke of the 44th now commands, but of course his rank is not sufficient to allow of his continuing it. I conclude our destination is New Orleans and if a sufficient force is sent out I see every prospect of success before us. Admiral Malcolm commands the Naval department, but Sir Alexander Cochrane is shortly to join us. Now my Dear Sir I have real satisfaction in being able to say with great truth that Charles is one of the finest young men in the Service, and I assure you he merits my full approbation in every respect. He is the most attentive boy I almost ever saw, and is very clever in his profession. He is quite perfect in Lunars and you must not forget to pay Percy Grace for a sextant which Charles got from him. Mr. Claxton has been very kind to him, and he is grateful for it. I am not a little annoyed at the neglect you have met with at the Admiralty, after your long service, but I am not without hope of hearing that you have got the Red Ribband [sic], which I think is the least they can do for you.[23]

Captain Crofton, who was being sent home with dispatches, left a letter for young Charles:[24]

My Dear Boy, As I am on the eve of my departure for England, I find it impossible to leave the Squadron without expressing to you how much I admired your gallantry and spirit in the Battle of the Twelfth Inst. I have spoken to Sir Alexander Cochrane and Admiral Cockburn of you and all the Ramillies who were with me on that day. Continue the same line of conduct and there will be little fear of your not being one day at the head of your profession.

If I have time I shall call on board before I sail.

I beg your acceptance of a pair pocket pistols as a testimony of the esteem and regard with which I am, my dear Charles, your affectionate friend, Edward Crofton.

Charles gave another version of the battle to his mother:[25]

I write to tell you that I am just returned from an Expedition against Baltimore with the Army and smallarmsmen of the ships. We landed about 16 miles from it and marched first without stopping about 10 miles in a hot sun and I can safely say 200 men fell down with fatigue. I do not know how I managed to keep up (it was hard work) then we had an entrenchment to attack of about 13,000 Americans and we only had 4,000 but we managed to drive them out in less than ten minutes, it was sharp work for all the time the balls were flying about like hail. We had altogether killed and wounded about 300, and the Yankees I can safely say had not less than 1,000, most of which died, all the rest went back to Baltimore. We had out of the smallarmsmen of our ship under Mr Claxton about 3 wounded, one of which I brought down to the ship and I was not able to join them again, but the next day they all returned finding the Yankees were too strongly encamped on a hill where they had 100 pieces of cannon and about 30,000 men. General Ross was killed who commanded the Army, he was very much liked and his death will be very much lamented. The troops are all embarked and it is not known where we will go to now. There is a report that we are going to attack Annapolis. I hope we may as it is a very pretty place and will annoy the Yankees very much. I forgot to tell you the Yankees had laid a plot for us on this hill, and if we had taken it, which we certainly would, they would have blown us all up and I believe that was the chief reason that we came back.

The fleet withdrew from the Chesapeake to attack New Orleans, hoping to secure the Mississippi, and thus surround the United States on all sides, and protect Britain's Indian allies from further encroachment. The attack was launched in December, but for once the American forces under Andrew Jackson included regulars, and were too strong. Lady Hardy wrote on 10 March 1815 to say that Charles had been employed in the boats, while her husband explored the shallow approaches to New Orleans. We do know that the boats had great difficulty making their way through muddy canals and creeks to land the British forces.

Meanwhile, in Europe, the Americans and British had signed the Treaty of Ghent in December which restored the status quo ante. By April 1815 Charles was with all his family in London where Captain Crofton joined them. According to his mother, who was presumably much relieved, he looked 'tanned and handsome'.[26] He was not yet fifteen years old.

For Charles, there was one more operation before the end of the Great War 1792–1815, under his father, who had been given the Channel Islands Command with his flag in the *Wye* (24) under Captain Green.[27] They landed French expatriates at Arromanches in Normandy on 7 July 1815, three weeks after the Battle of Waterloo, and a few days before Bonaparte surrendered to the British aboard HMS *Bellerophon*.[28]

Charles later joined his father's flagship *Rochfort* (74) in the Mediterranean, but it was not until 1819 that he acquired the six years' sea service required before he could be promoted lieutenant. After his father's early death in December 1819, Charles looked to Lord Buckingham, and his uncle William, the MP, for future advancement. In his later career he won the first RNLI gold medal for saving life; commanding *Challenger* (28), he proclaimed the colony of Western Australia in 1829 and the port was named after him; he surveyed the future colony of Hong Kong; circumnavigated the world; and visited Pitcairn Island.

In the long peace which followed the Great War, he was not promoted to rear-admiral until April 1854, when he reorganised the shipping required to maintain our forces in the Crimea. Promoted to full admiral in 1864, he became Commander-in-Chief of the Channel Squadron in July 1858 and Commander-in-Chief, Plymouth in 1863. He married a widow, Isabella Wedderburn, and, while they had no children, he retained close links to his brothers and sisters. His nephew Edmund, the third Admiral Fremantle, my great-grandfather, was his flag lieutenant in 1858.

The Rocket's Red Glare: Francis Scott Key and the Star-Spangled Banner

Charles Neimeyer

Throughout the long hot day of 13 September 1814, and into the morning hours of the next, specially trained Royal Marines and sailors fired Congreve rockets toward a star-shaped, stone and masonry structure the Americans called Fort McHenry. Originally built in the 1790s and intended to defend the inner harbour of the city of Baltimore from waterborne assaults, on this day the American fort became the primary focus of British naval commander-in-chief Vice-Admiral Sir Alexander Forrester Inglis Cochrane.

Adding to the cacophony of shrieking rockets, Cochrane's purpose-built bomb ships such as HMS *Terror*[1] and HMS *Aetna*[2] hurled 200lb naval shells

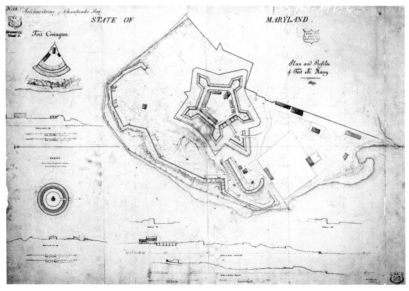

Plan of Fort McHenry, by William Tell Poussin, 1819. (Library of Congress)

towards the fort from over two miles away. Hence eyewitnesses to the bombardment of Fort McHenry literally saw 'the rocket's red glare' and 'bombs bursting in air' for a full twenty-five hours. Georgetown, Maryland, attorney and future author of the American national anthem, Francis Scott Key, was one of these eyewitnesses.

During the War of 1812 Vice-Admiral Alexander Cochrane was considered a veteran naval commander with significant experience in North American and Caribbean waters. He had fought against the French and Americans in the American War of Independence and had been wounded in action while serving under Admiral George Rodney. In the spring of 1814 Cochrane had been ordered by the Admiralty to replace Vice-Admiral Sir John Borlase Warren as station commander. The previous summer, Warren, and his highly capable second in command, Rear-Admiral George Cockburn, had raided the Chesapeake Bay region at will. While Cockburn urged a far more vigorous campaign against the Americans, Warren did not agree and was largely content with blockading the Chesapeake Bay and seizing enemy privateers and merchant vessels when the opportunity arose. However, while Warren failed to capture the vaunted 44-gun 'super-frigate' USS *Constellation* trapped at Norfolk, Virginia, and on 22 June 1813 an amphibious assault on the defences of Norfolk was severely repulsed at the battle of Craney Island, his forces dominated Chesapeake Bay, closed Baltimore, prevented dozens of privateers from sailing to prey on British shipping, and he accumulated prize money.

During the summer of 1814 Cochrane's concept for dealing with the Chesapeake region was far more expansive. One of his first actions was to declare liberation to slaves. As many as four thousand slaves took advantage of this brief window of opportunity to become free. Initially taken to Tangier Island off the Potomac, some four hundred former slaves volunteered to become colonial marines and served as a component of Cochrane's forces throughout the 1814 campaign season. Cochrane also wisely retained Rear-Admiral Cockburn as his second in command. Who knew the fighting capacity of the Americans and their defences in the region better than he?

Next, with the *Constellation* still firmly bottled up at Norfolk, Cochrane desired to eliminate the one remaining seagoing military threat that remained in the region in 1814 – the Chesapeake flotilla commanded by Acting Master Commandant Joshua Barney. During the previous summer, Barney had proposed building a 'poor man's navy' of approximately fifteen row galleys. Writing to Secretary of the Navy William Jones, Barney elegantly described the problem of defending the Chesapeake against the Royal Navy:

Sir George Cockburn, GCB, Rear-Admiral of the Red and one of His Majesty's
Lords of the Admiralty. (Library of Congress)

The question is, how to meet this force with a probability of success. *Our*
ships (two frigates) cannot act, our old-gunboats will not answer, they
are too heavy to Row, and too clumsy to sail, and are only fit to lay
moor'd, to protect a pass, or Assist a Fort. I am therefore of the opinion,
the only defense we have in our power, is a Kind of *Barge* or *Row-Galley*,
so constructed, as to draw a small draft of water, to carry *Oars*, light sails,
and *One heavy long gun*, these vessels may be built in a short time, (say
three weeks) [and] Men may be had, the City of Baltimore could furnish
Officers & men for *twenty Barges* [emphasis in the original].[3]

Jones bought off on Barney's idea. However, before much could come of
the concept, on a shakedown reconnaissance cruise down the bay toward
Tangier Island, Barney's flotilla ran into the 74-gun ship of the line HMS
Dragon (Captain Robert Barrie). It was not long before Barney and his
entire flotilla found themselves trapped up shallow St Leonard's Creek, a
tributary of the Patuxent River. However, Barney was able to break out of
St Leonard's Creek after a sharp engagement with three British blockading
vessels on 24 June 1814. Nevertheless, it was only a temporary respite, since
he and his flotilla were still bottled up the larger Patuxent River.

Cochrane's initial idea was to finish off the remaining credible military threat in the Patuxent River valley – Barney and his flotilla. After disposing of Barney, Cochrane believed he could then consider using his Royal Marines and promised army ground forces to attack either Washington, Annapolis, Maryland, or the large prize of Baltimore, then the third most economically important city in the United States.

In some ways, the war against the Americans in the Chesapeake region was personal to Cochrane. His older brother Charles had been killed in action at the battle of Yorktown in 1781. He also especially resented President James Madison, whom he believed started the war without adequate justification. However, it was the city of Baltimore that really angered him. At the beginning of the War of 1812, pro-British federalists in Baltimore were violently attacked by a Republican mob. Further, by 1814, Baltimore's maritime industry directed amazingly swift privateers who had long used the bay as a safe haven for raids against the West Indies and even British home waters. Cochrane strongly desired to do something about this heretofore untouched pro-war town.[4]

Although an advance squadron under Cockburn had been raiding the region for some weeks, Cochrane had been promised a substantial amount of ground forces with which to conduct a more aggressive campaign. However, as late as 17 July 1814 he remained mystified as to the amount of troops on the way, who commanded them, and exactly where the Crown wished for him to use his new reinforcements. In a rambling letter to the Admiralty, Cochrane suggested that once his reinforcements arrived, he might attack various locations all over the American coastline, to include Rhode Island, New Orleans, and possibly even the cities of Boston or New York. When Cochrane mentioned this indecisiveness on the part of the Crown to George Cockburn, it was Cockburn who responded with a 'secret' reply that the place to land his forces was Benedict, Maryland, on the Patuxent River. Cockburn was convinced that remaining in the Chesapeake was the right move for the British. Landing at Benedict would simultaneously threaten Washington, Annapolis, or even Baltimore. He further suggested that the fall of Washington would be 'a great blow to the Government of a country, as well on account of the resources as of the documents and records the invading army is sure to obtain.' Once Washington had been taken, Cockburn believed Annapolis and Baltimore would surely 'fall like dominos.'[5]

On 14 August 1814 Cochrane arrived at the mouth of the Potomac River in his massive 80-gun flagship HMS *Tonnant*, in order to rendezvous with George Cockburn's advance squadron. Two days later, the long-promised invasion force arrived with four combat regiments and an additional Royal Marine battalion – in all, about five thousand men. The troops had been aboard crowded transports for over seventy days and for health reasons alone, Cochrane was anxious to get them ashore as soon as possible. Three of the regiments, the 4th, the 44th, and the 55th Regiments of Foot had significant combat experience. The ground force commander was one of the Duke of Wellington's most able subordinates, Ireland-born Major-General Robert Ross.

Cochrane envisioned a three-pronged campaign that summer. A small squadron under Captain Sir Peter Parker in the 38-gun frigate HMS *Menelaus* would demonstrate off the Patapsco River near Baltimore and occupy the Americans in the upper bay, while a second reinforced squadron under Captain James Gordon in the 38-gun frigate HMS *Seahorse* would ascend the shoal-laden Potomac River, take out Fort Washington, which guarded the river approach to Washington and Alexandria, Virginia, and do what damage he could afterward. In between the two arms of this wide scale double envelopment, Ross would lead the main effort by landing his forces at Benedict, Maryland.

As planned, Ross and his troops began going ashore on 19 August 1814. Cockburn commanded the Royal Marines and bluejackets supporting the invasion task force. Barney's flotilla was known to be just a few miles upriver at the place called Nottingham, Maryland. Once fully ready, Ross would advance his troops up the west bank of the Patuxent, while Royal Marines and bluejackets covered his flank in ships' boats on the river. The idea was to force Barney to retreat until he literally ran out of river. At a place not too far distant from Prince George's County seat, Upper Marlboro, Maryland, this is exactly what happened. Barney reluctantly ordered his flotilla destroyed and he took his flotillamen overland to the Navy Yard at Washington to await further orders. As Cockburn's boats rounded a point in the river he noted that:

> upon nearing them [Barney's flotilla] we observed the sloop bearing the broad pendant [likely *Scorpion*] to be on fire, and she soon afterwards blew up. I now saw clearly that, they were all abandoned, and on fire, with trains to their magazines; out of the seventeen vessels which composed this formidable and much vaunted flotilla, sixteen were in quick succession blown to atoms.[6]

With the destruction of the Chesapeake flotilla, Ross and Cockburn were at a decision point. Moving to occupy Upper Marlboro, Ross made his temporary headquarters at Academy Hill, the comfortable home of one the town's leading citizens, the sixty-five-year-old Dr William Beanes. Much of the rest of the town's citizens had fled prior to Ross's arrival. Ross remained at Academy Hill until the afternoon of 23 August 1814, when he and Cockburn made the decision to march on Washington, a mere sixteen miles away. According to observers, Dr Beanes had been very accommodating to the British officers.

By the late afternoon of 23 August 1814, Ross and his army were on their way to Bladensburg, Maryland, where an American army of mostly militia under Brigadier-General William Winder stood. Ross's 85th Regiment of Foot, which was in reality a light brigade, having been reinforced by light infantry companies from the other regiments, was in the van of Ross's column and approached the town just after noon on 24 August. It was here that Colonel William Thornton, commanding officer of the 85th Regiment, found the American army arrayed in what appeared to be two very loose battle lines on the ground rising opposite the town and on the other side of a small bridge that spanned the eastern branch of the Potomac River. Winder's regular army troops and Barney's flotillamen and US Marines from the Washington DC barracks had been placed in a third line about a mile from the militia – too far away to provide any support or any assistance in opposing the river crossing the 85th Regiment was sure to make. Acting as a volunteer aide to 1st Columbia brigade commander, Brigadier-General Walter Smith, was Georgetown attorney Francis Scott Key. During the fighting, Key had the temerity to suggest to General Smith as to where he should place his artillery. Smith wisely ignored Key's amateurish advice.[7] However, in the end it did not matter. With the notable exception of Barney's naval brigade, Ross's crack troops easily routed Winder's militia. It was not long before the British army entered the District of Columbia itself and began their relentless destruction of all public buildings they could find, including the White House. As for Francis Scott Key, the battle of Bladensburg was notable in one other respect. It was here he saw first-hand what the face of defeat looked like.

Ross and his army remained in Washington for less than twenty-six hours. They marched out of the city late on 25 August, intent on returning to their shipping at Benedict, Maryland, via the road that led from Upper Marlboro. However, during their retrograde movement, a number of British stragglers were seen looting some of the unoccupied homes and farms near the vicinity of Upper Marlboro. A group of citizens, led by former governor Robert Bowie, appealed to Dr William Beanes to place these marauders under arrest. Beanes and some other citizens soon rounded up a number of prisoners and sent them to a local jail at nearby Queen Anne's Town. However, before the prisoners could be safely marched away, a British army deserter named Tom Holden, who had allegedly been caught raiding the good doctor's garden, was able to give his captors the slip. Unknown to everyone in Upper Marlboro at the time, Ross had sent his trusted aide George de Lacy Evans on a reconnaissance mission on captured horses back toward Upper Marlboro, to ascertain whether Winder's forces were mounting any kind of pursuit. Instead of finding American militia, Evans ran into Holden who claimed that Dr Beanes and other residents of Upper Marlboro had 'risen in arms', arresting 'innocent soldiers' like himself and had even killed some of the stragglers. When informed of this turn of events, General Ross was enraged over what he perceived was a violation of honour by Dr Beanes and he ordered the immediate arrest of anyone involved in the incident.[8]

As for Dr Beanes, his role in arresting British stragglers at Upper Marlboro had tremendous consequences for him. Beanes was arrested by George Evans's patrol in the middle of the night at Academy Hill. They also took two other prisoners, Dr William Hill and Philip Weems, and all three men were transported to the fleet landing at Benedict, Maryland. Made aware that there were other British prisoners in the vicinity, Evans threatened to fire the town if they were not immediately released. Earlier, a local citizen named John Hodges had taken five British prisoners to the Queen Anne's Town jail. Alarmed over this turn of events, frightened Upper Marlboro citizens appealed to Hodges to release the prisoners. In order to save Upper Marlboro, Hodges travelled back to Queen Anne's Town and convinced officials there to release the prisoners. For his troubles one year later, John Hodges was tried for treason by the United States federal government for 'delivering up prisoners to the enemy'. John Hodges 'is the only known [US citizen] to be tried for treason during the War of 1812.'[9]

Thanks to the efforts of Hodges in promptly freeing the men arrested by Dr Beanes, Hill and Weems were eventually released once they reached Benedict, Maryland. Beanes, however, was going to remain a prisoner. Many friends of Dr Beanes, including Prince George's County neighbour Richard Williams West, the brother-in-law of Francis Scott Key, remonstrated on the doctor's behalf, but to no avail. General Ross was known to be especially 'unforgiving in matters of honour', and he was adamant that Beanes had violated a tacit agreement not to take up arms against the British when he first met them under a flag of truce on the outskirts of Upper Marlboro.[10] Beanes, therefore, was going with

Cochrane's fleet as the British prepared to make their next move in the region – a direct attack on Baltimore itself.

As the British fleet pulled out of the Patuxent River, Richard West was already on his way to see his brother-in-law, attorney Francis Scott Key. Key was known as a man of great tact and propriety, and just the person West believed might convince Robert Ross to free William Beanes. On 1 September, 'Key secured permission to go on the Beanes mission from President James Madison and from General John Mason in charge of matters related to military prisoners.' Key would be accompanied by twenty-five-year-old Colonel John Skinner, a lawyer from Annapolis, and a man who had some experience with prisoner exchanges. In an interesting sidebar, General Mason took the initiative to contact the senior surviving wounded British officer still recovering in Washington (following his wounding at Bladensburg), Colonel William Thornton, the commanding officer of the 85th Regiment. Mason stated that Key would be happy to take any letters from the British wounded to their fleet once he met up with them.[11]

Francis Scott Key departed his Georgetown home for Baltimore, Maryland, on 2 September 1814, and reached the city and met up with Colonel Skinner two days later. The following day, both men departed in the American packet *President* under a flag of truce, in search of Cochrane's fleet, which they knew was headed up the bay toward Baltimore. On 7 September they located Cochrane's flagship, the British 80-gun *Tonnant* (Captain Charles Kerr), near the mouth of the Potomac River. Going on board, Key and Skinner were invited to dinner with all three senior British commanders, Cochrane, Cockburn, and Ross. Numerous accounts mention that Dr Beanes had not been treated particularly well, and Key later wrote that the British officers seemed 'filled with a spirit of malignity against every thing American'. Nevertheless, Key turned over the letters he carried from Colonel Thornton, and these seemed to be enough to change the British attitude toward their erstwhile prisoner of war, William Beanes.[12] However, the Americans had arrived at a very inopportune time. It was evident to one and all that Cochrane's fleet was preparing for a major operation, as his ships moved north toward the mouth of the Patapsco River.

According to a letter written by Skinner long after the war, while Key was still at dinner with Cochrane and Cockburn, Ross invited him to a private sidebar discussion. Ross told Skinner he was not persuaded by Key's legal arguments for the release of Beanes, but once he had seen the content of the letters sent by Colonel Thornton, which indicated the kind treatment he and his fellow wounded soldiers received from the Americans, he changed his mind and would release Beanes from captivity. However, Key was soon informed 'that neither he, nor anyone else would be permitted to leave the fleet for some days.' They had overheard too much. Since the *Tonnant* was crowded with staff officers planning the attack on Baltimore, on 8 September all three men were transferred to the 28-gun frigate *Surprize*.[13]

The Americans stayed aboard *Surprize* for the next three days as the fleet edged its way toward Baltimore harbour. The relatively shallow Patapsco River would not easily admit Cochrane's larger ships of the line, so these vessels remained twelve miles away at the mouth of the river. The frigates, sloops, and bomb ships could get closer. Early on the morning of 12 September, Ross and his troops were disembarking on the peninsula east of the city called North Point. Key was genuinely taken aback when he overheard British officers talking openly of their plans for the 'plunder and desolation' of Baltimore, but he diplomatically added, 'perhaps however, I saw them in unfavourable circumstances.'[14] Just as Ross made his landing on North Point, Cochrane transferred his flag to the *Surprize* so that he could better manage the overall operation. This necessitated the three Americans being returned under Royal Marine guard to the deck of their packet boat, *President*. At first, Cochrane likely kept the American vessel close to the *Surprize*, owing to a belief that Key and company might be useful in negotiating a surrender of the city. It is impossible to tell exactly where the *President* was located at all times during the operation but a sketch by an American militia officer showed a small vessel flying the American flag 'positioned [at one time] on the left edge of the bombardment squadron.'[15]

As Ross's forces advanced up the North Point peninsula, they ran into a forward reconnaissance force under Maryland militia Brigadier-General John Stricker. Stricker had been sent to a point halfway down the neck by the overall American commander at Baltimore, Major-General Samuel Smith, to ascertain the enemy strength. Stricker, however, did more than that. Sending a party of riflemen (who were actually armed with muskets) toward the British advance guard, a couple of militiamen shot an exposed Robert Ross from his horse and the general was soon dead. His death cast a pall over the entire operation. Nevertheless, Ross's senior-ranking colonel, Arthur Brooke of the 44th Regiment, took command, and later that afternoon fought a sharp engagement with the rest of Stricker's militia, known as the Battle of North Point. Although the Americans were ultimately driven from the field, it was not their main effort. Stricker performed exactly as ordered by Smith. Moreover, as Brooke would soon find out, Smith had turned the eastern side of the town into a veritable Gibraltar, with dozens of artillery emplacements and thousands of dug-in infantry in prepared trenches and rifle pits. Brooke soon recognised that driving the Americans from this position was well beyond his capabilities. He needed the Royal Navy to break into the harbour.

Meanwhile, Cochrane edged his battle line of bomb ships, *Terror*, *Devastation*, *Aetna*, *Meteor* and *Volcano* closer to the harbour. The *Volcano* fired special shells called carcasses. These bombs were filled with 'pitch, powder, sulfur, and saltpeter', and were designed to set things on fire. For good measure, the *Erebus* was specially outfitted as a Congreve rocket ship and could fire volleys of these highly inaccurate but terrifying weapons. All these vessels were designed to flatten forts and set cities on fire. There was nothing in the arsenal at Fort McHenry that could even come close to hitting back at them.[16] By the early morning of 13 September, Cochrane ordered his bomb ships and his rocket boat to begin shelling Fort McHenry. With the premature death of Ross, Cochrane was already concerned that the land operation was not going as expected. Nevertheless, with a little luck, the tremendous pounding of his bomb ships just might convince the Americans to surrender.

All through the day and into the evening hours, the relentless bombardment continued. Key later wrote he could clearly see the American flag flying from the flagstaff at the fort. Since it was bad weather on 13 September, the fort's commander, Major George Armistead, flew a smaller, storm flag that measured 17ft by 25ft. Most likely, during the bombardment the American packet boat was forced to move back to a position further behind the bombardment line, but Key was still able to see the flag with a glass at least until it got dark. British Midshipman Robert Barrett stated that 'all this night the bombardment continued with unabated vigor; the hissing of the rockets and the fiery shells glittered in the air the rain fell in torrents – the thunder broke in mighty peals after each successive flash of lightning that for a moment illuminated the surrounding darkness.'[17]

Towards dawn on 14 September, the fire upon the fort noticeably slackened. As the first rays of the sun broke through the clouds, Key trained his glass on the American flagpole in the fort. He could see a larger flag hanging there. This one actually measured 30ft by 42ft, but without a breeze Key could only wonder if the fort had somehow fallen during the night. At that exact moment, a slight wind caught the folds of the flag. Key later wrote, 'through the clouds of war, the stars of that banner still shone.' Absolutely thrilled by the sight, on the spot Key penned a poem he first called 'The Defence of Fort McHenry'. In his mind he wrote the words to correspond to an English drinking song he was fond of called 'To Anacreon in Heaven'.[18]

During the late afternoon of 16 September the British had fully back-loaded their forces from North Point. Cochrane informed the Americans in their packet boat that they were free to go. Carefully weaving its way past the sunken obstructions the Americans had placed in the inner harbour, the *President* edged up to Hughes Wharf near Fell's Point toward evening. Key took lodging that night at the Indian Queen Tavern and made some minor changes to his inspired poem. Little did he know that his poem would eventually become the national anthem known as 'The Star-Spangled Banner'. Buried in the fourth verse of Key's poem are the words 'in God is our trust.' This phrase was said to have also helped later inspire the American national motto, 'In God We Trust', adopted during the Civil War with a slight modification by Treasury Secretary Salmon P Chase. Thus Key's spontaneous poem can be said to have been the inspiration for both the American national anthem and the national motto (and is found on most US currency today).

Handbills of the song/poem soon appeared all over the city of Baltimore. A local newspaper, the *Baltimore Patriot*, published it on 20 September 1814. Other newspapers around the country soon picked up the story. Carr's music store in Baltimore printed it 'for the first time in sheet music form in November.' The store used the title 'Star-Spangled Banner' from words in the first verse. The new title, to use a modern phrase, went viral, and from this point on this was the name of Key's famous song written on the spot on 14 September 1814 from the deck of the American packet boat *President*.[19]

Battle of Baltimore, see colour plate 5
Bombardment of Fort McHenry, see colour plate 6

Frédéric Rolette: Un Canadien héros de la guerre de 1812

Samuel Venière and Caroline Girard

HMS *General Hunter* and HMS *Queen Charlotte* fire salvos at the fort and the fortified city of Detroit: *Bombardment of Fort Detroit, 1812*, by Peter Rindlisbacher.
(© Naval Museum of Québec)

Reconstructing the past

History is like broken glass – it starts out as a cohesive whole, but time weakens its structure, shattering it into a thousand tiny fragments that disperse and lose their significance. The archivist must painstakingly collect the shards and piece them back together, while the historian is responsible for imbuing this reassembled window to the past with meaning and clarity. It is precisely those tasks that the authors have undertaken in this article.

Frédéric Rolette is one of those men whose story is little known, forgotten in the annals of history, where the same names are tirelessly repeated. Aside from a Quebec township named after him, there is no

82

monument or commemorative plaque to remind Quebeckers of his actions during the War of 1812, a conflict that saw Great Britain, represented by Upper and Lower Canada,[1] take up arms against the United States, a fledgling nation at the time. Even today, most people know very little about the war itself. By retracing Frédéric Rolette's journey using first-hand documents, recently acquired by the Naval Museum of Québec through the Chatillon family, who are Frédéric Rolette's descendants, we will give readers a close look at the life and exploits of this forgotten *Canadien*[2] and a better understanding of the 1812 conflict and the stakes and major events that defined it.

Blurred beginnings: from history to legend

We know very little about Frédéric Rolette's early years – only that he was born on 25 September 1785 in Quebec City. He lived on Du Marché Street, near the actual Old Port neighbourhood. Royal Navy ships would regularly come to the city, and Rolette may have developed an early fascination with them, as he began working on an English ship at a very young age. The city archives show that his father was living alone in the family home in 1798, so Frédéric was no older than thirteen when he joined the navy.[3] While that may seem very young, it is important to bear in mind that, starting in 1794, boys were able to go to sea at very young ages. But why would Rolette leave home so early? His father was a merchant, and in those days merchants were often sailors. Rolette's aunt had married Samuel Holland, who had worked with James Cook on the drawings of the St Lawrence Basin in preparation for James Wolfe's arrival in 1759. It is possible that Rolette was captivated by his uncle's stories. Whatever his reasons for being interested in the sea, he set sail and we lose track of him until 1805, when he returned to Quebec. His time at sea does not appear to be documented.

The dearth of historical documentation for nearly a decade of Rolette's life led to much speculation on the part of nineteenth-century Canadian authors, both Francophones and Anglophones. This was in the early days of Canadian Confederation, and the new country was trying to lay the foundation for its own historical identity and create its own national history. On 5 February 1868, an article in *La Minerve* told Rolette's story with appropriate historical rigour, citing primary sources while presenting him as a hero.[4] The *Revue Canadienne* of March 1870 continued in the same vein and vaunted Rolette's merits.

However, new information appeared in 1884, with the publication of Benjamin Sulte's *Histoire des Canadiens-français, 1608–1880*. Sulte, a historian fascinated with Canadian history, claimed that Frédéric Rolette had participated in the Battle of the Nile in 1798 and had suffered five injuries, and that he had also fought in the Battle of Trafalgar, in which the illustrious Horatio Nelson perished on 21 October 1805.[5] That surprising piece of information is not cited in any earlier publication, which raises the question: what was Benjamin Sulte's source? There is still no historical documentation supporting it.

Be that as it may, the news was too good to pass up, and it was repeated in most of the subsequent publications on Rolette. Everything from the *Bulletin des recherches historiques*[6] of the late nineteenth century to modern-day biographies, all place Frédéric Rolette at the heart of the two famous battles, elevating his heroic status in the process.[7] But did he really fight in those battles?

It is not impossible, but it is unlikely. Because there is no known documentation of Rolette's life from the period in question, it is impossible for us to check those facts, but the chronology of events provides a few clues. As there was no recruiting centre at that time in Lower Canada, all a person had to do to join the navy was board a ship. Rolette enrolled in either 1797 or 1798; before that, he would have been too young. The only English ships visiting Quebec City during the two years in question were frigates – HMS *Hind*, HMS *Eurydice* and HMS *Nemesis* – escorting convoys between Portsmouth or London and Quebec City. The big ships of the line that were part of the Royal Navy's Mediterranean fleet were based in Lisbon.

One of the more unusual aspects of the Battle of the Nile was that only ships of the line (except Hardy's little *Mutine*) were involved in it. The frigates that were passing through Quebec City therefore would not have taken part in the battle, and it is highly unlikely that Rolette was transferred to one of the ships that did. Benjamin Sulte wrote that our hero suffered five injuries,[8] but Rolette was only twelve years old at the time, which makes the story hard to believe. The Battle of Trafalgar took place on 21 October 1805, but an eyewitness quoted in the memoirs of Verchères de Boucherville (who himself knew Frédéric Rolette well) confirmed that Rolette was working in the business of a certain Mr Reynolds, in Amherstburg, in the summer of 1806 (a number of authors say that he returned in 1807, but they do not back up that claim with any evidence). It is highly unlikely that, after being away for several years, Rolette would go directly from serving in the Royal Navy to his position in Amherstburg without taking a few weeks off to see his parents, who were still alive. It is more likely that he returned to Quebec in 1805, which would remove Trafalgar from the equation.

What we do know is that Frédéric Rolette was commissioned as a lieutenant in the Provincial Marine, the government's maritime service on

Capture of the Cuyahoga (1992), Peter Rindlisbacher. Lieutenant Frédéric Rolette can be seen on the right, standing up in his boat and brandishing his pistol. This is the only known painting of him in existence. (Private collection)

the Great Lakes in British North America, when the War of 1812 broke out, and he would not have been able to obtain that rank if he had not previously been a lieutenant in the Royal Navy.[9] Our *Canadien* would therefore have had to significantly distinguish himself to achieve that rank. This again raises the question of whether Rolette fought in the Battle of the Nile and at Trafalgar – especially since we know that at least five men from Quebec were present at Trafalgar – but the fact that there is no specific evidence pointing to his involvement leads us to believe that he did not. There may be as yet undiscovered documents that will invalidate this hypothesis, and we know that some boys went to sea at ages younger than eleven. In any case, we believe that Rolette's involvement in those famous battles is not necessary to cement his war hero status. The official documents and missives from 1812 that mention him are already full of praise, as we will see.

The man with the gaze of a lion

Is 'hero' the right word to describe this career warrior? Readers will soon be able to make that judgement for themselves. Frédéric Rolette's descendants, the Chatillon family, recently bequeathed to the Naval Museum of Québec documents dating from their ancestor's time that are useful in reconstructing events. These original documents – correspondence, letters of congratulations, surgeon's reports – grant us privileged access to Rolette's life and enable us to debunk certain myths.

In June 1812 war was declared between Great Britain and the United States. Word did not travel quickly in those days, and it took a while before the units in the most remote locations received the news. Very early in the war, Lieutenant Frédéric Rolette distinguished himself by performing a dazzling and daring feat:[10]

> His Majesty's Ship Queen *Charlotte*
> Amherstburg, Dec 24th 1812
>
> I do hereby certify that Lieut Rolette of his Majesty's Prov. Marine in the Lakes and Frontiers of Canada, was Commander of his majesty' Brig Genereal Hunter by appointment from His Excellency Sir George Prevost commanding his majesty's Forces in North America, on the morning of the 3 July 1812 when a part of his Crew [left the dock and] captures the Cuyahoga Packet an American [schooner] with part of the baggage of General Hull's army on board, and that it was his zeal for the service which induced him to [leave] the General Hunter to perform the above mentioned service in which he served before he received any [appointment] from any other naval force in this Harbour – and it is decidedly my opinion that he is entitled to every emolument which may arise from said capture to him, as commander of the said Brig Gene. Hunter. [...]
>
> George B Hall, Master & Comd
> PM Lieut off. Lakes Erie & Huron

It was not common at the time to decorate warriors for their bravery, but Rolette's zeal was often mentioned in letters addressed to the commander. The capture of the *Cuyahoga Packet* is known as the first belligerent act of the war. And what a capture it was! The American schooner was transporting a troop of some forty soldiers and officers in addition to the crew. Rolette captured the vessel by leading the assault from a longboat with a crew of five or six men. Seizing upon the opportunity to surprise the crew, who still had not received the news that war had been declared, Rolette approached the boat, forced the crew and troops to surrender at gunpoint, and then found General William Hull's war documents, which provided the

British with a trove of information on the American forces and their deployment.[11] Three of the people who survived the assault later told Rolette's son of: [trans] 'their admiration for his father's conduct, and they all agreed that they did not understand how they had been mesmerised by him. "He was so wild-eyed," they said, "that we looked at him trembling, like frightened soldiers receiving strict orders from their captain"'.[12] There are a number of references to Frédéric Rolette's fierce gaze in the documents.

That deed was but the beginning, as the lieutenant remained very active throughout the rest of the conflict. In August 1812 Major-General Isaac Brock, who had just arrived at Fort Amherstburg (Malden), decided to attack and take Detroit, against the advice of his officers. The British forces, supported by Tecumseh's Shawnees and protected by fire from HMS *General Hunter* and HMS *Queen Charlotte*, moved towards the town. At ten o'clock in the morning on 16 August, the colony was seized and the British took control of all of Michigan.[13] To Rolette, Brock said: 'I have watched you during the action. You have the gaze of a lion and I will remember you.'[14] Is this history or legend? We are not sure, but first-person accounts from members of Rolette's entourage paint a clear picture of the warrior's temperament, and the way that he responded to later events only confirmed those impressions.

Battle scars and steadfast persistence

On 22 January 1813 Rolette was fighting in the Battle of Frenchtown, near Rivière aux Raisins, as an artillery officer under Major-General Henry Procter, when he was shot in the back of the head by friendly fire and seriously injured. It appears as though he once again distinguished himself through his actions, as he was commended by his superiors yet again:[15]

Sandwich 28 January 1813

Sir,

General Procter having particularly noticed your excellent conduct in the action at Frenchtown on the 22nd has desired me to return you his most sincere thanks and to assure you that he will lose no opportunity of rewarding you as far as lies in his power according to your merits.
I have the honor to be, Sir

Your most [obedient humble] servant
Felix Throughton [Provincial Art]

Despite the seriousness of Rolette's injury, he survived. Major-General Procter wrote:[16]

> I do hereby Certify that Lieutenant Frederick Rolette of the Provincial Navy served as an Artillery officer on the 22nd day of January 1813 at the Defeat and Capture of Brigadier General Winchester and the [four] under his command at French Town on La Riviere aux Raisins and that while performing his duty entirely to my satisfaction, as on every other occasion, he was Dangerously wounded.

Certification letter from Major-General Henry Procter to Lieutenant Frédéric Rolette, November 1816. (Chatillon family collection © Naval Museum of Québec)

It is advisable to beware of secondary sources glorifying the extraordinary feats of Frédéric Rolette. For example, nineteenth-century Canadian biographers recounted that, after our *Canadien* was injured at Frenchtown, he stubbornly refused to stop fighting, saying, [trans] 'I was chosen to direct the fire of this gun, and it would be a disgrace for me to leave now'.[17] The phrase has a nice ring to it and definitely stirs the imagination, but the assessment of the Royal Artillery surgeon who examined Rolette's injuries is somewhat more grounded in reality: 'The wound alluded to was inflicted by a musket ball on the back part of his head while he was in the act of hoping to point a gun; and that he fell senseless and remained in that state for some hours in consequence of the blow.'[18]

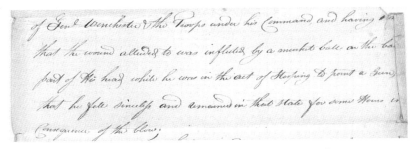

(Chatillon family collection © Naval Museum of Québec)

The shock knocked Rolette unconscious, which is not surprising, as friendly weapons are fired at much closer range than enemy ones. The injury took him out of service until the end of the year. It is already extraordinary that Rolette survived, and we do not feel that it is necessary to embellish his accomplishments, which were, in any case, warmly lauded and acknowledged by his superiors. Even more surprisingly, the injury, which was yet another in a long series, did not prevent him from continuing to fight: as soon as he was back on his feet, he participated in the Battle of Lake Erie on 10 September 1813, during which he once again impressed everyone with his zeal and level-headedness.

He was the first lieutenant (second in command) of the British schooner *Lady Prevost* at the Battle of Lake Erie. The battle, also known as the Battle of Put-In-Bay, saw the British flotilla of six vessels, commanded by Commodore Robert Barclay, fight the nine-vessel-strong American forces commanded by Commodore Oliver Hazard Perry.[19] The British ships were equipped with an assortment of guns that were poorly suited to naval combat, as Barclay had not received the cannons he needed.[20] The fighting began and quickly turned to carnage. At the start of the battle, Captain Buchan of the *Lady Prevost* was grievously injured and command fell into Rolette's hands, who continued the fight: 'until being severely wounded in the right side and seriously burnt by an explosion of gunpowder, which killed and wounded a number of his men, he surrendered his ship to the

89

enemy only when it was an unmanageable and sinking wreck.'[21] Thus captured, he remained a prisoner of the Americans for some time before he was allowed to return to Quebec City.

Honouring a worthy warrior

After the war, as the sole compensation for his actions, Rolette was presented with an honorary sabre by his friends and the citizens of Quebec City in recognition of his brave deeds. Next to its scabbard of gilded copper, the steel blade with damascened finish, richly detailed with mythological figures, bears the following inscription:

> PRESENTED to Lieut. FREDERICK ROLETTE of the Provincial Navy a CANADIAN born Subject, who Distinguished himself on many Occasions during the late American War, particularly in the naval Action on LAKE ERIE of the 11th September 1813, under the brave, Captain BARCLAY on a Testimony hereof his school Companions with other Loyal and Patrotic [*sic*][22] Canadians Voted FIFTY GUINEAS for this SWORD.

Today, the sabre is carefully kept and displayed at the Naval Museum of Québec. The hero's descendants have entrusted the museum with its safekeeping so that their ancestor's story never fades into oblivion. Few people know about the involvement of the Québécois in the War of 1812, and Frédéric Rolette's sabre and archives are relics from that era. They are therefore historically important and a source of interest for anyone curious about the subject.

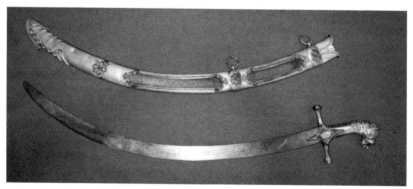

Honorary sabre presented to Frédéric Rolette.
(Chatillon family collection © Naval Museum of Québec)

Frédéric Rolette died on 17 March 1831, at the relatively young age of forty-six, as a result of his war injuries, from which he never completely recovered. He was survived by his wife, Luce Bouchette, who was given a pension by the provincial government,[23] and his five children. This career warrior's renown was never more celebrated than on 16 July 2015, when the Royal Canadian Navy announced with great pomp and circumstance that a new offshore patrol ship would bear the name HMCS *Frédérick Rolette.*[24]

It is not surprising that nineteenth-century Canadian authors, who sometimes embellished the actions of great men in the heady era when modern-day Canada was being built, attributed almost superhuman deeds and words to Lieutenant Frédéric Rolette; it seems as though his behaviour lent itself quite easily to such exaggerations. Under the light of Rolette's reconstructed history based on the above-cited primary sources, is it really necessary to inflate the military accomplishments of a person whose exploits are already so heroic? Don't these details make him even more historical, more realistic?

Rolette may not be exactly the man people have wanted to portray him as, but the real hero is perhaps the man Rolette truly was: the common man who faced war at the front lines, with all the suffering that entailed – suffering that got the better of him in the end. The Greek philosopher Diogenes said: 'I am looking for the Man'. To cautiously reconstruct the past of Frédéric Rolette, seeking the man rather than the superman, isn't it, in the end, the best way to pay tribute to him and show our respect?

Pathfinders: Front-line Hydrographic Data-gathering in the Wars of American Independence and 1812

Michael Barritt

The Seven Years War has been described as the first world war, and subsequent conflicts of the eighteenth century and the Great War of 1793–1815 were also played out on a global stage. Yet the eighteenth century was an era in Britain of 'small government' and reliance on the private sector, raising questions about the organisation needed to conduct such warfare effectively.[1]

Arrangements for the provision of navigational information to the fleet were criticised by senior officers, leading eventually to the appointment of Alexander Dalrymple as Hydrographer to the Board of Admiralty in 1795. Dalrymple and his successor, Captain Thomas Hurd, set in train the selection and supply of charts to the fleet, including those produced in-house and optimised for ongoing operations. They earned respect and proved able to elicit strategic guidance from the Admiralty Board. This top-level support included encouragement of enlightened commanders who deployed competent hydrographic practitioners to act as pathfinders for the fleet. By the end of the Napoleonic Wars, this network of enlightened interest had led to the receipt in the Hydrographical Office of a wealth of field data that belies the verdict in many historical studies that the Royal Navy of the period lacked interest and expertise in hydrographic surveying.[2]

This article will note the importance of experience on the North American coast in stimulating an appreciation of the operational importance of hydrographic surveying. The gathering of data during worldwide deployments in 1812–15 will be illustrated. The emergence from the conflict of talented men with the necessary higher-level skills and their subsequent employment in Hurd's new specialisation will be discussed.

The War of American Independence and the working of a network of interest

Richard Howe (later Admiral of the Fleet and 1st Earl Howe, 1726–1799) was amongst those who had lobbied for an improvement in the provision

92

of navigational information to the fleet, and proposed the establishment of a Hydrographical Office in the years immediately following the Seven Years War.[3] As conflict loomed once more in North America, he argued successfully for publication of the charts of the area which had been brought back by Colonel J F W Des Barres in 1774, after a decade of surveying effort under the auspices of the local flag officer. He also persuaded other officers working for the Board of Trade and Plantations to hand over their work for publication and use by the navy. The result was the great atlas entitled the *Atlantic Neptune*. The production of many of its sheets was accelerated at the outbreak of the War of American Independence.

When Howe was appointed to North America as commander-in-chief, he took a close interest in one of the midshipmen in the gunroom of his flagship. Thomas Hurd would claim in later life 'that in 1776 [...] from his knowledge of the American Coast, and his talents as a Draftsman and surveyor, [he] was taken by Lord Howe onboard the *Eagle* to that station'.[4] Also onboard was Major Samuel Holland, who could vouch that Hurd was one of the naval personnel who had been seconded to assist with surveys on the Atlantic coast of Nova Scotia and in the Bay of Fundy under his direction as Surveyor General of the Northern District of North America.[5] Deployed in small boats, Hurd had spent three years sounding along the coastal fringe of the deeply indented coast, fixing the position of offshore shoals by compass bearings and making a careful note of sunken ledges that would endanger a patrolling warship. He took astronomical observations for position alongside the land surveyors and also learnt their techniques for recording the work. The more detailed fair sheets were drawn by him.[6]

Hydrographic information was of the utmost importance to Howe during the subsequent amphibious operations against Washington's army on the rivers around New York. In December of that year he issued instructions to the ships on station for the covert gathering of soundings, and other pilotage and navigational information.[7] Hurd's manuscript record of service gives no indication of survey work, but there seems little doubt that his skills and local knowledge would have been exploited as newly arrived troops were landed in flat boats. Hurd was enabled to confirm his 'talents' and Howe promoted him lieutenant in January 1777.

Howe's patronage continued after the war. Now First Lord of the Admiralty, he secured Hurd a short-lived appointment as Surveyor General of the new colony of Cape Breton in 1785, and in 1788 nominated him to perform the hydrographic surveys for the development of a naval base in the

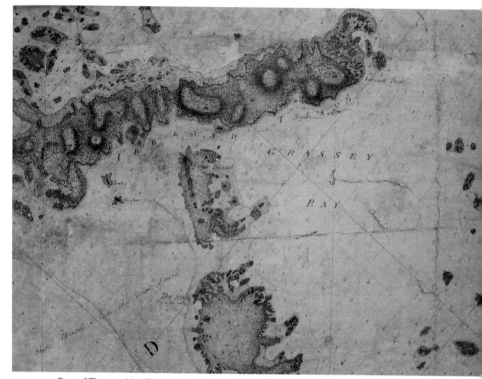

Part of Thomas Hurd's survey of Bermuda, showing Grassy Bay and the vicinity of the future naval base on Ireland Island. This extract shows the detailed record of depths and coral reefs that he achieved. (UK Hydrographic Office, reference A 124)

Bermuda archipelago to plug the gap between ports in the Caribbean and Canada. The importance of his work was underlined after the outbreak of hostilities with Revolutionary France, when French privateers received assistance in American ports that was extended only reluctantly to the British squadron on station.[8] Hurd was drawing up the results of his extraordinarily detailed large-scale surveys in the Admiralty a decade later, and this work commended him to the board for employment in an important front-line survey of the Bay of Brest.[9]

This task arose from the hydrographic output of another veteran of operations in North America. Like Hurd, John Knight had seen previous service as one of the naval volunteer assistants to the land surveyors at the end of the Seven Years War. Later, in May 1770 he had been appointed in command of the schooner *Diligent* in which Des Barres embarked to continue his work, bringing along no less than twenty-eight assistants.[10] In 1775 his sounding work offshore in the Gulf of Maine was terminated when the *Diligent* was captured by the rebels. Knight was placed on parole in Massachusetts, and exchanged at the end of 1776. Quite remarkably, his captors had failed to secure the survey data in his possession.[11]

Howe reappointed Knight to the sloop *Haerlem* (12), where he combined his survey skills with his warfare experience in a distinctive pattern of activity. When a French fleet under the Comte d'Estaing made landfall in the southern approaches to Delaware Bay on 6 July 1778, Knight's small ship was the first to sight them. As the enemy opened fire, Knight, with his inshore experience, immediately turned for the shoals to the northeast of Assateague, getting out sweeps and boats as the wind fell away. As he coasted northwards, one to two miles offshore, the French ships hauled their wind and gave up the chase. On 8 July Knight sounded his way round Sandy Hook and came to anchor near the *Eagle* off Staten Island. He had given the commander-in-chief time to make his dispositions, for it was not until 11 July that the flagship's log records: 'At noon a ship off the bar made a signal for a strange fleet in sight. At 2P.M. saw the French fleet at anchor without the bar.' Although his squadron was much inferior in force, Howe had positioned it brilliantly within Sandy Hook to enfilade the passage into New York Lower Bay. Knight had contributed 'soundings and nautical remarks' for the chart covering Sandy Hook and his work will have assisted the admiral's dispositions.[12]

Knight's hydrographic data-gathering again proved invaluable as Howe forestalled an attack on Newport and later attempted to head the French fleet off from their refitting base in Boston. A page headed 'Utility of the *Atlantic Neptune*' in the later editions of that book states that 'Earl Howe, on various critical occasions, greatly availed himself of the advantages given by this work, and particularly during the manoeuvres of the French Fleet under Count d'Estaing off Rhode Island, and the dangerous shoals of Nantucket, which not even the American pilots had it in their power to supply.' The charts in question were based on Knight's original surveys. Howe's flag captain's journal notes that 'His Lordship pushed our fleet with the greatest expedition through between Nantucket and St George's Bank in hopes of getting to Boston before them.'[13] Knight's pedigree as a pathfinder was very firmly established.

Throughout his subsequent career, including a crucial flag appointment afloat in the year of Trafalgar, Knight gathered hydrographic data and published many charts, some based on his own surveys. These included four sheets arising from work in the approaches to Brest during service with the advanced squadron in 1800. These were front-line reconnaissance surveys, produced in a tight timescale to satisfy a demanding commander-in-chief. They include specific intelligence of military use such as notes of the range of enemy shells. His old American experience came into play as lines of soundings were run to delineate the dangers and define safe tracks. Unfortunately, misleading information on some published French charts led him to misidentify the dangerous outlying Boufoloc rock on which the *Magnificent* (74) was subsequently wrecked. It was this disaster that led to Hurd's deployment to the scene.[14]

The examples of Howe, Hurd and Knight are not the only illustrations of the fruitful working of 'interest' arising from operations in the Americas. Hurd's work around Bermuda received very significant support from Rear-Admiral George Murray, who had a clear awareness of the importance of operational hydrography. Whilst in command of the sloop *Ferret* on the Jamaica station some three decades earlier in 1766, Murray had received orders to assist the surveyor George Gauld in the survey of the coastal waters of West Florida. The sloop and boats contributed soundings from Cape San Blas to Pensacola, further work off the bar and harbour of Mobile being interrupted by a hurricane.[15] One of Murray's protégés in the North American squadron was Captain Charles Penrose, who saw and commended Hurd's work at Bermuda and two decades later would champion the cause of William Henry Smith, Hurd's Admiralty Surveyor in the Mediterranean.

As a young post-captain, the later Admiral Lord Keith had conducted survey operations to assist the deployment of the fleet and landings of troops during the War of American Independence, assisted by Midshipman John Markham.[16] During his service as a naval lord, Markham would provide greatly valued support to Dalrymple and Hurd. In his commands in the waters of South Africa, the Mediterranean and the North Sea, Keith encouraged hydrographic practitioners and made collections of their work. He provided information on American harbours as the Admiralty watched developments in 1812.[17] One of the most active commanders in the War of 1812 would also recall early experience of surveying during global operations. Midshipman George Cockburn had drawn up several fair sheets whilst assisting Captain Robert Moorsom of the sloop *Ariel* (16), a practitioner who had been specially selected by the First Lord of the Admiralty as an 'expert surveyor' to examine harbours that might benefit the East Indies Squadron and the East India Company.[18]

Plate 1. The East Indiaman *Bridgewater* delivers a raking broadside on the New Hampshire privateer *Hampden*, 7 March 1779, Francis Holman (Courtesy Christie's). *See p20*

Plate 3. Commemorative stamps issued by the island of Nevis to mark the bicentenary of the marriage of Horatio Nelson and Frances Nisbet. See p35

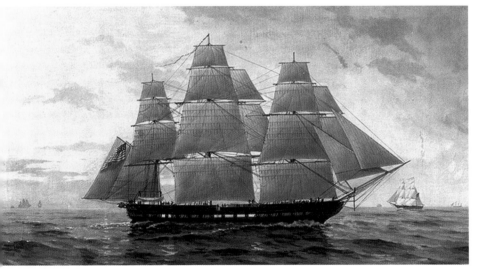

Plate 4. USS *Chesapeake*, from a painting by F Muller, about 1900 (US Naval History and Heritage Command). See p36

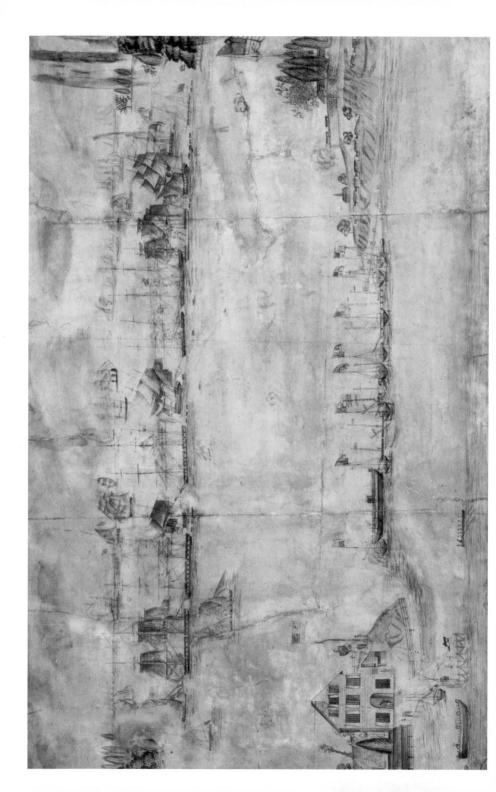

Plate 6. Bombardment of Fort McHenry, oil on canvas, by Alfred Jacob Miller, 1828–30 (1901.2.3, Maryland Historical Society). *See p71*

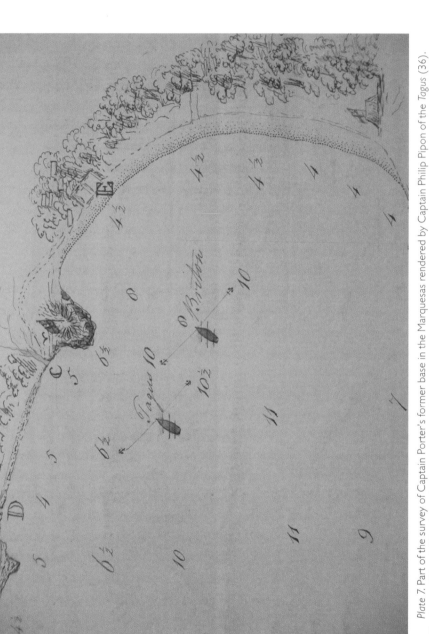

Plate 7. Part of the survey of Captain Porter's former base in the Marquesas rendered by Captain Philip Pipon of the *Tagus* (36). The letters 'D' and 'C' indicate the watering places for the two frigates, and 'E' marks the huts of the settlement that Porter had named

Plate 8. Bow view of author's 3-D model of HMS *Victory* at Trafalgar. *See p157*

Plate 9. Stern view of author's 3-D model of HMS *Victory* at Trafalgar. *See p157*

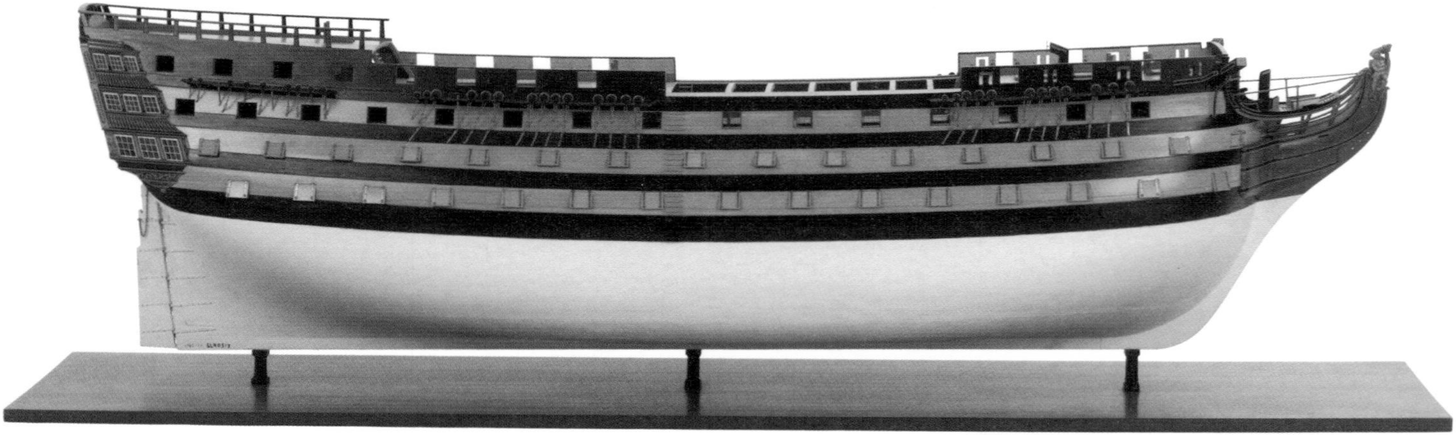

Plate 10. Profile of the of the National Maritime Museum model of HMS Victory *in 1805. (NMM photographs F2881-Series and I 3147-Series,*

Plate 11. Thomas Buttersworth, *Bombay Castle off Lisbon*, signed, c1820, oil on canvas, 17 × 23 in, private collection. Having spent years at sea in and around Lisbon, Buttersworth was very familiar with the coastline around the Tagus River. He used it as a background for dozens of paintings throughout his career (photograph courtesy of N R Omell Gallery). *See p161*

Plate 12. Thomas Buttersworth, *Royal Visit to Scotland, 1822*, signed, c1825, oil on canvas, 15 × 23 in, private collection. Numerous artists travelled to Scotland

Plate 13. Thomas Buttersworth, *Brigantine leaving Dover*, signed, c1820, oil on canvas, 17 x 23 in, private collection. Buttersworth, like many other artists, frequently used the cliffs of Dover as a background for naval and general shipping scenes (photograph courtesy of N R Omell Gallery). *See p161*

Paul Pry's Extrachan-airy Peep into Piccadillo

These are examples of how the requirement of commanders for hydrographic intelligence, including rapid reconnaissance survey, to support warfare in theatres worldwide, not least on the coast of North America, had given experience to a large number of officers and masters in the fleet, some of whom had shown that they possessed the necessary higher skills in mathematics and 'natural philosophy'.

Worldwide operations

This experience and promotion of talent was extensive by the outbreak of the War of 1812, which saw British forces deployed not just to the American coast but to the 'far side of the world'. Captain Peter Heywood, himself a distinguished hydrographic practitioner, was encouraging the master of his ship in a survey of the River Plate. From this station he monitored the reaction in Buenos Aires, and across the Andes in Chile, to British intervention in the Iberian peninsula.[19] He reported the efforts of the US consuls-general to spread the view that their country was much more likely than Britain to support moves towards independence. He urged the deployment of more British warships to the region, and in early 1813 passed on intelligence of enemy activity culminating in the appearance of the USS *Essex* (46) on the Pacific coast.[20] The destructive foray of Captain David Porter into the grounds of the British southern whale fishery, and subsequent reports that another large frigate had been sent to reinforce him, led to the diversion of several British cruisers to track them down.[21]

Captain Charles Malcolm, who had served with Heywood in eastern seas, was senior officer of a squadron sent out in 1814 in search of American units said to be operating on the Brazilian coast. Two of Malcolm's officers in the *Rhin* (38), the master, James Douglas, and Lieutenant George Crichton, had both been involved in hydrographic data-gathering earlier in their careers. When rendering his surveys to the Admiralty, Crichton commented that they 'were originally made by me [...] for practice, to enable me to fulfil that important duty assigned to the Commanders of His Majesty's ships, should I ever be fortunate enough to obtain that rank'. With Malcolm's encouragement, he had surveyed the harbour of São Luís de Maranhào and taken numerous soundings and astronomical observations whilst the ship patrolled the approaches. His work was attributed in three new Admiralty charts, and Hurd used this example to encourage another very competent young officer who submitted efforts from the same theatre.[22] Lieutenant William Hewett, a product of the Royal Mathematical School at Christ's Hospital, forwarded boat surveys, astronomical observations and substantial remarks, and volunteered for further hydrographic work.[23] In 1818 Hurd nominated Hewett to the Board of Admiralty as commander of the *Protector*, declaring him to be 'perfectly qualified both as a Draftsman and Mathematician'.[24] Hewett would spend the rest of his career surveying in the North Sea until the tragic loss of his second ship, the *Fairy*, with all hands in a great gale in 1840. Malcolm himself would go on to become Superintendent of the Bombay Marine and to encourage the work of its renowned surveyors, especially in the Red Sea where they opened the way for steam navigation.[25]

The *Essex* was located and captured off Valparaíso in March 1814 by Captain James Hillyar of the *Phoebe* (36), in command of a squadron which had been sent to support efforts of British traders from Canada to establish a fur trading depot on the Columbia River and to remove the American establishment at Astoria.[26] On return to England, Hillyar rendered to the Hydrographer manuscript charts and views made at Callao, Juan Fernandez and Valparaiso in the course of the hunt for the *Essex*. Hillyar's personal log from the deployment is preserved in the National Maritime Museum and the views and surveys pasted into it confirm his interest in gathering navigational data, whilst the journal of one of his midshipmen, Allen Gardiner, indicates that they were encouraged to exercise their powers of observation.[27] The bulk of the data-gathering had been performed by Mr Peter Brady, master of the *Phoebe*, a diligent observer whose higher skills are apparent in his 'trigonometrical survey' of Callao.[28] Flag officers would subsequently deploy his survey skills in other theatres.

Next on the scene were Captain Sir Thomas Staines of the *Briton* (38), and Captain Philip Pipon of the *Tagus* (36). They would follow up a fresh report that a squadron of French and American frigates had rounded Cape Horn.[29] They visited the Galapagos group where Porter had found the British whalers, and followed in his footsteps in reporting deficiencies in the published chart based on earlier running surveys of the archipelago.[30] They then sailed on to another remote island group, the Marquesas, where Porter had selected a refitting base in a sheltered anchorage described in Vancouver's *Voyage of Discovery*.[31] The bay was surveyed and both captains rendered fair sheets to the Admiralty.[32] They were stowed away in the Hydrographical Office, and no chart was ever made from them. The activities nonetheless inspired at least two young men. In due course, Midshipman Francis Crozier of the *Briton* would distinguish himself as a polar explorer, whilst his shipmate William Skyring would develop his skills under the tutelage of the Admiralty Surveyor in the Mediterranean and earn respect as an outstanding surveyor of his generation in the *Beagle*, working once again in the Pacific.[33]

These operations, taking British warships into unfamiliar waters, had indeed encouraged hydrographic awareness. The Hydrographer welcomed the published charts which the captains had gathered and brought back, bringing him the results of good Spanish surveys, and he supplemented them with the views and remarks that the naval observers had made during their high-paced deployment. These reflected a philosophy expressed by Captain Basil Hall:[34]

> Officers are too apt to undervalue the nautical knowledge which they acquire in the ordinary course of service; and to forget, that every piece of correct information which they obtain, especially on distant stations, is essentially valuable. If it be new, it is a clear gain to the stock already accumulated; if not, it is still useful as a corroboration.

In 1820–22 Hall commanded the *Conway* (20) on the South America Station, and encouraged his officers to follow his precepts. He was immensely proud of the achievements of Master's Mate Henry Foster. He already had extensive experience on the South American Station and had made a survey of the entrance to the Columbia River whilst serving in the *Blossom* (18) in 1818. With Hall's encouragement, he made a series of surveys whilst his captain assessed the commercial potential of ports in Chile, in Peru, at Guayaquil and in Mexico. Five of the surveys would be published as Admiralty charts. He classified his work carefully, ranging from 'Eye Draught' through 'sketch surveys' to 'trigonometrical surveys'. Foster would be an early recruit to Hurd's new cadre of surveying specialists with higher skills.

Higher skills

Other recruits emerged from front-line service in North America during the War of 1812. The defence of the frontier line on the Great Lakes had been hampered by want of information on the tortuous waters where Lieutenant Newdigate Poyntz made a sketch survey of the area around a proposed base at Penetanguishene.[35] In May 1815 the conduct of a formal Lakes Frontier Survey acquired impetus with the arrival on station of Captain William Fitz William Owen. He formed a team that included some of Hurd's most competent practitioners, Lieutenants Henry Bayfield, Alexander Vidal, and Alexander Becher, and a master, Mr John Harris. The first season of work in 1815 was largely occupied in urgent reconnaissance surveys to secure information on the coasts and harbours

 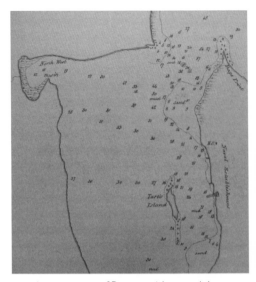

Part of Lieutenant Poyntz's wartime reconnaissance survey of Penetanguishene and the larger-scale work of Lieutenant Bayfield of the Lakes Frontier Survey after the establishment of the naval base. (UK Hydrographic Office, references 191 on Aa2 and L3210 on Aa)

of Lakes Erie and Huron and Georgian Bay, where Vidal's journal from Lake Erie shows how river mouths were checked for suitability as bases for gunboats, whilst an accompanying expert recorded timber of use for naval purposes. More detailed survey work was necessary along the most vulnerable sector of the border with the USA: the Detroit River, Lake St Clair and the St Clair River.[36]

From an early stage, Owen had entrusted Vidal with the painstaking work on 'shores and measures', detaching him inshore in a canoe, whilst the other assistants undertook the soundings.[37] Such activity, especially so soon after the recent conflict, was almost bound to prompt adverse attention from the Americans in the narrow Detroit waterway. Furthermore, William Owen's prickly personality guaranteed a robust response to any provocation. This was to cost Vidal five weeks' detention in Detroit when Owen despatched him in pursuit of some deserters and thieves.[38] Owen was a tough taskmaster, sending his men out early each season to commence their survey measurements whilst the lakes and rivers were still frozen.

Survey effort was also required during the campaign in Chesapeake Bay in which the Royal Navy went onto the offensive. As units under the aggressive command of Rear-Admiral George Cockburn scoured the subsidiary rivers, taking or destroying vessels, batteries and stores, they earned the grudging admiration of local mariners for knowledge better than their own pilots. Mr George Thoms, who had followed Cockburn as master of his flagships, was prominent in this work, which included surveys of the Middle Ground and Horse Shoe Sand and the buoying of the channel to Hampton Roads.[39] Thoms would remain with Cockburn in the *Northumberland* (74), conveying Napoleon to exile, and he made surveys around Ascension and St Helena.

In the summer of 1814 Vice-Admiral Sir Alexander Cochrane and Major-General Sir Robert Ross planned a major offensive which would lead to attacks on Washington and Baltimore. Cochrane, another officer who had been familiar with Thomas Hurd's work in Bermuda and who had subsequently encouraged hydrographic efforts when in flag rank, had applied for two surveyors to be employed under his command in North America. Hurd was only too ready to support the proposal. He was pleased by Cochrane's identification of the need to correct the errors in the charts of Des Barres. This work was allocated to Cochrane's protégé, Mr Anthony Lockwood, who had conducted surveys off the Spanish coast and in the Caribbean whilst under his command. Hurd secured the appointment of Mr Anthony De Mayne, his preferred candidate, to the second position, to survey the coast from Rhode Island southwards.[40] An operational survey in the entrance to the Great Belt in 1807 had first brought De Mayne to the Hydrographer's attention. He subsequently achieved some fame when, as master in the *Amelia* (38), he took command of the vessel when all the commissioned officers were killed or wounded during a drawn battle with a French frigate.[41] During the same commission on the west coast of Africa in 1811–13, when Captain Irby commanded a reinforced anti-slavery squadron, De Mayne rendered three coastal sheets which Hurd would declare to be 'by far the most correct of any that had been made' on that coast.[42] After the war, De Mayne would be a prominent member of Hurd's cadre, carrying out extensive surveys around Belize, Jamaica and in the Gulf of Florida and the Bahama Islands and adjacent channels. At least one present-day chart is still based solely on his work.

It was De Mayne who supervised the sounding of the River Patuxent as Cochrane entered to land Major-General Ross and his troops at Benedict for the advance on Washington.[43] The boats and men were furnished from the *Royal Oak* (74) by Rear-Admiral Pulteney Malcolm, a commander who had encouraged the early efforts of Peter Heywood and had always shown an appreciation of hydrography. De Mayne also rendered plans of Tangier

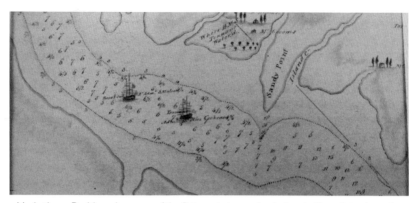

Mr Anthony De Mayne's survey of the Patuxent river extended up to Benedict, where the troops were landed. He defined the shoal water areas and confirmed the navigable channel for the troop transports and the major units, including the two flagships illustrated in this portion. (UK Hydrographic Office, reference 303 on Ra)

Island, where the British established a fortified base, and the soundings in this area are noticeably more complete on the chart of Chesapeake Bay which he compiled in 1814, and which Hurd described as showing 'an entire new arrangement of the eastern side of that bay particularly about the Tangier islands and banks'.[44] De Mayne may also have obtained and used the soundings taken under the direction of Admirals Warren and Cockburn in the Patapsco[45] and the rivers of Chesapeake Bay. He certainly used some published material, including Edmund Blunt's *Coasting Pilot* and an enlargement of an American map of part of Maryland. In addition to soundings and natures of the seabed, his chart includes indications of tidal streams, recommended anchorages, and lighthouses and prominent marks. It would be the best depiction of the areas that had been surveyed that was available until the work of the US Coast Survey got underway later in the nineteenth century.[46]

Conclusion

Thomas Hurd's vision for a surveying specialisation sprang from his early experiences in the Americas, his own front-line hydrographic data-gathering, and his oversight of worldwide activity as Hydrographer to the Board of Admiralty. Despite post-war retrenchment, it was on a firm footing by the time of his death in April 1823. His arrangements enabled it to weather a period when his successor Edward Parry was frustrated by the limitations of his remit and revealed his ambivalence by frequent absences in the Arctic. Francis Beaufort is generally credited with launching the golden age of the Royal Navy Surveying Service in 1829. Hurd's foundations had been reinforced, however, by the close and informed interest of a Naval Commissioner of the Admiralty with credentials as a field surveyor, an enlightened commander, and an American veteran. His name was George Cockburn.[47]

Tagus map, see colour plate 7

Charting the Waters: The Emergence of Modern Marine Charting and Surveying during the Career of James Cook in North American Waters, 1758–1767

Victor Suthren

When James Cook arrived at Halifax in the spring of 1758, he was a capable but undistinguished sailing master in the Royal Navy, serving in *Pembroke* (64). Over the next nine years, as his active professional life developed in the waters of coastal Canada and Newfoundland, he was transformed from a simple warrant officer into a competent navigator, innovative chartmaker and surveyor, whose superior skills led him to be selected to command the first of three epic voyages of oceanic exploration, and a role in the forefront of European scientific and philosophical investigation of the Pacific. Cook's experiences on the coasts of Nova Scotia, the Gulf and River St Lawrence, and on the coast of Newfoundland, and his exposure to the work, instruments and methods of Samuel Van Hollandt, J F W Des Barres and others were, it can be argued, the basis by which he and others developed the first reliable marine chartmaking methodology in Western experience. Cook's achievements in North American marine cartography led not only to his selection for the later Pacific voyages but provided a secure navigational basis for the post-1763 settlement of British North America and the development of inshore fishery. Cook's success in this regard, and in the Pacific, would lead him to be later recognised as one of the most competent participants in the eighteenth century's European burst of seaborne exploration and scientific inquiry into the Pacific after the close of the Seven Years War.

Cook's emergence as a surveyor and chartmaker began with his chance encounter with the Dutch-born military surveyor, Samuel Van Hollandt, at Louisbourg in the summer of 1758. Cook learned from Van Hollandt the techniques of land surveying using the telescope- and compass-equipped plane table, Gunter's chains, field tables, and the creation of triangulation diagrams on a set baseline to allow calculation of exactitude in distance and location by geometry. He was instrumental in combining the use of those instruments with existing naval chartmaking usages utilising box compasses, horizontal octants and lead lines to produce chartwork and marine surveys of a wholly new level of accuracy. His participation in the ascent to Quebec in 1759 by the Royal Navy fleet carrying James Wolfe's troops, his key role in the success of that ascent, and his preparation of charts resulting from that voyage, and other survey work on the Nova Scotian and Newfoundland coasts in the closing years of the Seven Years War, led to his selection to undertake a major survey of the west and south coasts of Newfoundland. The extraordinary quality of this work, coupled with concurrent demonstrations of his astronomical observation skills, led to his selection in 1768 to command HM Bark *Endeavour* on her Pacific voyage, on behalf of the Royal Society and the Royal Navy, when both parties could not agree on another suggested commander.

The examination of James Cook's period of North American service arguably reveals that the development of Cook's innovative chartmaking and surveying skills, and other qualities which led to the selection for the Pacific voyages, came as a direct consequence of his North American adoption of land surveying technology and its marriage with existing naval usage, and that the period 1758–67 was not only the most significant advance in Western marine cartography and hydrography since the Renaissance, but also laid the basis for a dramatic expansion in settlement and commercial shipping in colonial Canadian and Newfoundland waters, and arguably for British and European exploration of the Pacific in the remainder of the eighteenth century.

Cook had entered the navy in 1755, for reasons of his own, and much to the astonishment of both the Walker brothers whose employ he left, and the Royal Navy, who were only too pleased to receive him into pay. At the time of his entry into the navy he was a highly competent coastal mariner who had learned his trade in the Walkers' colliers along the treacherous North Sea coast and on a few passages to Ireland and Norway. His practical seamanship was unmatched, and combined with his physical and personal qualities to produce promotion out of the ranks of the common seamen within a month of his joining the navy. His scholarly self-instruction in mathematics and the scientific bases of navigation were not yet developed to a similar degree, however, and it would only achieve an equal level of competence with his physical seamanship when he had had the benefit of additional encouragement from perceptive commanders such as Hugh Palliser of *Eagle*, and, in particular, John Simcoe of *Pembroke*, under whom Cook first came to North American waters.

The arrival of *Pembroke* at Halifax in the spring of 1758, with over twenty of the ship's company ill with scurvy, brought Cook to a harbour that arguably he was to know better than any in his career, save his collier home port of Whitby, as from 1758 until 1762 Cook was based at Halifax, first as the master of *Pembroke*, and then of *Northumberland* (64). The latter vessel remained on station at Halifax with a small squadron when the armada that had carried James Wolfe to Quebec returned to Britain. The transatlantic passage had been Cook's longest, and *Pembroke*'s ship's company had been so incapacitated by scurvy that the ship had remained at anchor in Halifax, as the remainder of the squadron with which she had crossed sailed northward for the assault on the Fortress of Louisbourg.

Pembroke finally embarked her convalescent seamen from the hospital at Halifax and sailed north along the iron, evergreen-clad coastline of Nova Scotia to join the fleet under Vice-Admiral Richard Boscawen which had carried the assault troops of General Jeffrey Amherst to Louisbourg. *Pembroke* arrived at the fleet's anchorage in Gabarus Bay, south of the fortress, on 12 June 1758, to learn that a successful landing had been made on 8 June, and a slow but steady investment of the fortress was underway. The task of the fleet was largely to provide support to the troops ashore, which proved a challenging task in the abnormally squally and tumultuous weather that swept over the anchorage. Over a hundred boats from the various warships and transports were lost in the powerful surf that swept the single landing beach, at what later came to be known as Kennington Cove.[1]

It was just off this beach that the most significant event in James Cook's transformation of the marine cartography process took place. On 27 July 1758, one day after the French garrison had surrendered, Cook came in to Kennington Cove beach with *Pembroke*'s longboat, on unrecorded business ashore. As Cook arrived, his attention was drawn to the figure of an engineer officer in the grasslands just off the beach, employing a strange device and apparently making some kind of observations of the cove. Intrigued, Cook approached him, and asked what he was about. He soon found himself in conversation with a pleasant man of about his own age, Samuel Holland – more properly Van Hollandt, as he was Dutch in origin – who explained that he was carrying out a survey of the cove using a plane table.

A plane table had a small, square flat surface supported on a tripod; Holland would sight over the top of the table at distinguishing marks using a rotating telescope fixed to the table's centre, and make notes of those observations. Cook learned that the process allowed the creation of an accurate diagram in which all physical features could be placed in correct relation to one another, and to a baseline with a known magnetic heading, obtained from a box compass affixed to the table. It was a concept that grasped Cook's imagination immediately, and he extracted from the agreeable Holland a promise to instruct Cook in the technique the next day.

On returning aboard *Pembroke*, Cook reported his encounter to Captain John Simcoe, who not only approved of Cook's initiative, but requested that Holland be brought on board the vessel to impart the instruction to Simcoe, as well as Cook. Although Cook would later benefit from association with other highly competent surveyors during his stay in Canada, such as J F W Des Barres, author of the *Atlantic Neptune*,[2] it was this contact and period of learning with Holland that was instrumental in launching Cook toward his own apogee of achievement as an innovative maritime surveyor and cartographer.

Through instructions that all masters and master's mates had to observe in 1758, Cook was required as a matter of duty to produce charts and sailing directions for any harbour his ship visited. The quality of these drawings and writings varied as greatly as the capacities of the men who undertook them. For Cook, the electrifying realisation which emerged out of the instructional sessions with Holland was that a combination of land surveying methods and accuracy with these established methods of marine sounding, surveying and chartmaking would offer the prospect of new exactitude in the heretofore very inexact science of marine charting. Cook's signal contribution to the state and competency of marine hydrography was in this innovative exercise of two traditions of observation as a single art with a uniform standard of precision, which raised chartmaking and the recorded basis of navigation to a whole new level. The importance to Cook's career, and to the history of western exploratory hydrography and chartmaking, of that chance meeting on the windy beach of Kennington Cove near the Fortress of Louisbourg, Cape Breton Island, cannot be overstated.

As *Pembroke* rode at anchor within the harbour of Louisbourg in the waning summer of 1758, Cook continued to develop his surveying skills under Holland's tutelage, until the demands of war called him to put them unexpectedly to use. *Pembroke* was dispatched with a small squadron to carry troops into the Gulf of St Lawrence, where the army was to carry out the inglorious work of burning and destroying French settlements that might send supplies to the colonial capital at Quebec. One of these was the town and harbour of Gaspe, on the mainland. Cook's reaction to the business of carrying war to a defenceless civilian population is unknown, but he busied himself on the Gaspe expedition with observing, sketching

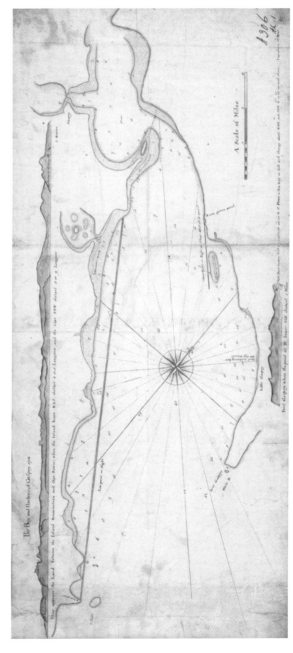

Draught of the bay and harbour of Gaspe, 1758, Cook's first published map. (Canadian War Museum)

and sounding, doing the latter from *Pembroke*'s boats, and possibly exercising his new land survey skills as well.

On the return of the squadron to Louisbourg, Cook appears to have secured from Simcoe permission to spend time penning a chart and survey of the harbour of Gaspe. The result was a carefully drawn two-sheet effort in a scale of 2in to the mile, and Cook was successful in obtaining its publication in London by Mount & Page in 1759.[3] The publication of this chart of a small, beleagured Canadian port marked Cook's emergence into the serious realm of surveying and charting beyond the ordinary duty of a sailing master.

The bleak days of late autumn fell over the captured fortress, and the Royal Navy vessels were ordered back to Halifax, to secure themselves for the long northern winter. *Pembroke* came to anchor in Halifax harbour on 19 November 1758, below the muddy, rough-sawn town and its palisaded hilltop citadel. The campaign of the following summer would, according to a grand strategy ordered by Prime Minister William Pitt, be an ascent of the St Lawrence with an army like that which had taken Louisbourg, but with orders to capture Quebec itself. Cook's production of the Gaspe chart, and his increasing competence in charting and survey work, led to his being ordered, along with Holland, to busy themselves in *Pembroke*'s great cabin under Simcoe's encouraging eye in the compilation of all known French and other charts of the Saint Lawrence into a folio that could be used to guide the great fleet up the treacherous passages of the river.

The coming of spring led to the arrival of troop transports from Britain and a sizeable escort of warships, all under the command of Vice-Admiral Charles Saunders, who had replaced Boscawen. Cook's *Pembroke* was assigned to an advance squadron under Rear-Admiral Durrell that sailed from Halifax on 5 May 1759 and attempted to work its way into the Gulf and River St Lawrence, which was choked by an unusually heavy ice pack. With the main force halting at Louisbourg to pick up additional troops for the attack on Quebec, Durrell's force busied itself penetrating the river and allowing for the discovery of the safe channel – the French had taken up what marks there were – and the completion of a workable chart of the river.

In *Pembroke*, Cook soon found that the compilation of French charts was insufficiently accurate to be relied upon, and took the initiative in forming a sounding flotilla of ship's boats from the squadron, each carrying that ship's master or master's mate, which sounded ahead of the fleet as it advanced up the several hundred miles of the river in stages, depending upon whether the winds were fair or foul. The greatest challenge to this technique came just below Quebec, at the eastern end of the Isle d'Orleans, where the safe navigation channel was known to cross from the northern side of the river to the southern for entry into the wide basin below Quebec, in a swooping track known as the Traverse. Cook's boats sounded diligently while the squadron waited at anchor downstream, and discovered that the Traverse was a narrow channel no wider in some places than the extreme beam of some of Saunders's largest ships. Cook devised a method of marking the channel whereby the flotilla of boats moored themselves as buoys on either side of the channel, marking a clear if constricted passage into the wider anchorage of the Basin. With a favourable east wind, all 140-odd vessels of the fleet sailed one by one in slow majesty through this remarkable assemblage. By 27 June 1759 all of Saunders's fleet, including his flagship *Neptune* (90), had come to anchor in the basin below Quebec, and the assault could begin.

The siege, however, would last all summer, as the army's commander, Major-General James Wolfe, could not decide on a method of attacking the very formidable French defences, and the towering rocky citadel of the heights of Quebec themselves. Cook was kept busy in sounding those waters that were safe to operate boats in – Indian warriors and Canadian militia would frequently race out in swift birchbark canoes to attack naval longboats engaged in sounding – and had some controversy attached to his name when an abortive assault landing on the Beauport shore below Quebec went awry, at least in part because the assault transports and boats had gone aground on a ledge Cook's surveys had not reported. Cook's energy in continuing with the sounding and chartwork, when his other duties would allow, nonetheless had brought him by this point, scarcely a year after first asking Samuel Holland what his strange instrument was called, to be referred to as the 'Surveyor of the Fleet'.

Cook played no direct role, as far as is known, in the 12 September night assault by troops under Wolfe that scaled the heights to the Plains of Abraham by means of the pathway at the Anse au Foulon. At the successful conclusion of the siege, when Saunders's main force was preparing to return to Britain bearing with it the body of James Wolfe, Cook was transferred into *Northumberland*, which would remain at Halifax over the coming winter and return to Quebec in 1760 to support the garrison the British were leaving behind.

Cook used the descent of the river to complete observations made on the way up by both himself and Holland, and on arrival at Halifax was able to complete *A New Chart of the River St Lawrence*,[4] which was a huge work of some twelve sheets, in dimensions each 35in by 90in, with a main scale of one inch to two leagues [six miles] and an inset scale of one inch to one league. In April of 1760, Vice-Admiral Saunders recommended to the Admiralty that Cook's application to publish this enormous chart folio be granted.[5] Cook's charts brought a new level of reliable navigation to the great river, just as its new custodians needed such reference; but it had been Cook's leadership in the trying work of finding the passage up for the huge fleet that had provided James Wolfe and his troops the opportunity Pitt wished them to have: the capture and retention of the heart of Canada.

Northumberland lay at Halifax over the winter of 1759/60, cocooned against the ice and snow, and Cook continued his personal studies of mathematics, navigation and astronomy, 'bringing in his hand' as he completed the great work of the St Lawrence chart.[6] Cook would return again to Quebec the following summer, albeit briefly, but now entered into a period where his life and activities were centred on Halifax and the routine of the squadron. He nonetheless produced no less than four superb charts of Halifax harbour, and worked with the accomplished military surveyor Des Barres, who like Cook had made land surveying and marine charting into a composite science, and would produce the masterful charting of the Nova Scotian and adjacent coasts entitled the *Atlantic Neptune.*[7]

In 1762 a last French attempt to secure bargaining power in the peace treaty which was to end the Seven Years War led to their attack and capture of the port of St John's on the rocky eastern shore of Newfoundland. *Northumberland* took part in the combined force that successfully forced the French out of Newfoundland, and during this service Cook produced charts of Placentia, on the west side of the Avalon Peninsula, of St John's harbour, and of two fishing ports, Harbour Grace and Carbonear. In addition, he now produced a compendium *Description of the Sea Coast of Novascotia [sic], Cape Breton Island, and Newfoundland,*[8] along with detailed sailing directions which would be published in several editions of the *Newfoundland Pilot*, produced by Thomas Jeffreys in London.[9]

So extraordinary was the quality of this work that, at the end of the war when *Northumberland* was paid off and Cook might have expected to re-enter the struggle for survival in the civilian world, he was retained as a result of requests made by Thomas Graves, governor of Newfoundland, to do further survey and charting work of that island. His first task was to complete, in the summer of 1763, a speedy but reliable survey of the islands of St Pierre and Miquelon, which were being turned over to the French. Cook completed the work, to what was now his customary standard of excellence, while the newly appointed French governor paced fuming on the quarterdeck of his ship.[10]

Thomas Graves was replaced as governor of Newfoundland by Hugh Palliser, who had commanded Cook in HMS *Eagle* before Cook had come to Canada. Palliser now continued Cook's work as a surveyor and chartmaker by having him undertake a detailed survey of major portions of the coast of Newfoundland, in a pattern that would see Cook spend the summer on the island's coast working from his small command, the schooner (later brig) *Grenville*, and returning to Britain for the winter to work up fair copies of his charts and sailing directions. From 1764 to the end of the summer of 1767, Cook managed a survey of the west and south coasts of Newfoundland to such exacting detail that his charts remained in use within living memory. He demonstrated an additional and important skill during this period, one that would bear heavily on his career. On 5 August 1766, aware that an eclipse of the sun was predicted, Cook observed it carefully from the Burgeo Islands off the south coast of Newfoundland, and wrote up his observations. These he presented in the autumn to Dr John Nevis of the Royal Society, who in turn read them to a meeting of the society. Bevis went on to report that Cook's observations allowed another astronomer to compare them successfully with a set taken at Oxford, and to deduce accurately the longitude of both places of observation. Cook's expertise was duly noted by the gentlemen of the society.[11]

In April 1768, as Cook was preparing for another summer on the Newfoundland coast, he was informed that the Admiralty had decided to send another individual in his place, the highly competent Michael Lane, and to employ Cook elsewhere. Cook had therefore completed a remarkable four years of surveying and navigating on one of the most varied and challenging coastlines in the world, and the products of all this work were four extraordinarily detailed, accurate, and carefully penned charts of Newfoundland, with accompanying sailing directions. They joined the enormous chart of the Gulf and River St Lawrence as a striking advancement in the professional standards of marine surveying and charting in waters of North America which were vital to Britain's interests.

It had not been lost on both the Admiralty and the Royal Society that Cook, though technically still at the warrant rank of master, had effectively commanded a minor war vessel in a lengthy and distant commission, had produced superlative chartwork and surveying, and had also demonstrated a professional capability as an astronomical observer and mathematician. When the Royal Society and the Admiralty could not agree on the appointment of Alexander Dalrymple to command a small vessel which was to set off for the South Pacific to carry out astronomical observations and survey new coastlines should they be found, it was not

Replica armed ship's boat of Cook's era, rigged as a cutter, on a Gulf of St Lawrence shore, Canada. (Photo © Peter Rindlisbacher)

long before the name of Cook came to the fore. Before 1768 closed he had become Lieutenant Cook, in command of HM Bark *Endeavour*, and bound off on a world-girdling voyage of scientific observation, exploration, and discovery.

The shaping of Cook's fine metal into the instrument selected for this task had taken place in the waters now known as Canada, in the River and Gulf of St Lawrence, the Nova Scotian coast, and on the rocky shores of Newfoundland. As much as his growth and development in the world of the North Sea colliers, it was his exposure to the instruments and procedures of the eighteenth-century land surveyor, and his marriage of their use with that of existing marine surveying instruments, that turned a competent but undistinguished warrant officer into the seaman and surveyor capable of the Pacific voyages, and the greater destiny they would hold for him.

Captain Archibald Kennedy,
an American in the Royal Navy

Byrne McLeod

Captain Archibald Kennedy was born in New York, son of the Scottish peer of the same name, who had emigrated to New York in 1722 to be customs collector and receiver-general for the province of New York. Archibald Kennedy amassed a great deal of prime real estate. In 1745 he bought No. 3 Broadway, which he left to his daughter Catherine in his will. In 1746 he bought Bedloe's Island in New York harbour (later known as Kennedy Island) for £100. He sold the island to the Corporation of the City of New York for £1,000 in 1759, and the Statue of Liberty was erected there in 1876. His son Captain Archibald Kennedy bought the lot No. 1 Broadway in 1756, and later built his mansion on the site.[1]

First commissioned in 1744, Archibald Kennedy sailed as a lieutenant in the sixth-rate *Centaur* (22) with Captain Henry Cosby for New York in June 1751. Cosby fell ill soon after they arrived, and for nearly two years the responsibility fell more and more on the young Kennedy's shoulders. As early as April 1753, Kennedy was writing to the Admiralty in the role of captain, telling them of his proposals for over-wintering *Centaur* in Turtle Bay, and having her refitted as soon as the weather permitted. Captain Lloyd, the senior officer on the New York Station, appointed Kennedy to act as captain from the death of Captain Cosby in October 1753 until May 1754, when he was superseded by Captain Dudley Digges, sent out by the Admiralty to replace Captain Cosby. Although Kennedy hoped to have his acting rank confirmed, as he had been in charge of the vessel for the whole period of Crosby's illness, he was disappointed, and told that he had return to his duty as lieutenant and 'await another opportunity of being provided for.'[2] The Admiralty was not totally heartless, however, and ordered Kennedy to be paid at the rank of captain for the days from Cosby's death until Digges's arrival. Kennedy was not being victimised: in the years before the Seven Years War was declared, the Navy appointed very few new captains.

As the preparations for war progressed, Kennedy was not forgotten, but he had to wait until March 1756 to be made master and commander of the brigantine *Halifax,* on Lake Ontario.[3] In this appointment the Admiralty was taking advantage of Kennedy's local knowledge, but showed that they were unaware of the belligerence of the French, who already had a superior force on the lake.

While he was waiting to get back to America to take up his new command, the Admiralty appointed Kennedy as the transport agent responsible for getting a fleet of transports ready to sail. He sent in reports on a daily basis, enumerating all the delays involved in the very complex task of fitting out and loading the transports, which were prepared at Deptford and then sent down the Thames to Gravesend to embark troops. Kennedy showed during this period tenacity of purpose, attention to detail, an ability to write clear and succinct reports, and a huge amount of patience.

With his understanding of the local conditions, Kennedy thought ahead about the problems that would be faced when the transports reached New York. He appreciated that his new command was many difficult miles from experienced dockyards and asked for a set of armourer's tools to be sent with the other stores. He also asked for an armourer and a sailmaker to travel with him from England, along with the crew for *Halifax.* The Admiralty appreciated the wisdom of this request, and Kennedy was told that he could have the two specialists if he located and engaged them.

Eventually, Kennedy's eleven charges were safely in the Downs and got under way in May 1756, arriving in New York in August. The ships were all discharged, the only problem being the fact that demurrage was charged for those ships which had carried powder, as the magazines ashore were full and there was nowhere to put the new supply.

Kennedy and his fellow American Joshua Loring were entrusted by the Admiralty with responsibility for local shipping once they arrived back in New York. They worked together as far as possible in the confused situation on land and sea in 1756. Kennedy's report of their situation lost the dispassionate calm with which he had acted as an agent in the Thames. He appealed to the Admiralty to give him leave to act independently of the army. He could see that there was no possibility of a naval action against the French until the land forces had recovered control of the territory then denied them by the French possession of Lake Ontario, and Fort Oswego had been rebuilt. He begged to be saved from 'the hands of land officers who are heaping favours upon their own corps while we lye by neglected.'[4]

Before a reply could be expected, he was ordered into the brigantine *Prince of Orange* to transport troops to Halifax, and he used his own resources to feed his *Halifax* crew, whom he took on board. This independence of spirit is typical of the man. Kennedy was confident that his actions would be supported by the Admiralty, explaining that he had acted according to the best of his judgement. The Admiralty had no idea how to resolve this unusual situation and referred the matter to the Victualling Board 'to consider where he sits further and to report their opinions thereon.'[5] They must have been sufficiently impressed by his willingness to take independent decisions to reward him with promotion, and he was appointed to the sixth-rate *Vestal* (32) in April 1757, and for once it does appear as though Charnock is right, and the appointment was made to give him the rank of a post-captain.[6]

Kennedy was commissioned into the sixth-rate *Flamborough* (20) in March 1758, and spent the next six months in action in the St Malo, Cherbourg and St Cas operations.[7] The concern he showed for his crew in the confusion of 1757 was repeated in November 1758, when Kennedy wrote to the Admiralty asking for his crew to be paid, as they had received no pay since June 1756. He reported that before he sailed from Spithead there were 'great murmurs' amongst the crew about going to sea again without receiving any part of their wages, then twenty-seven months overdue. The crew's grievance was compounded by the fact that a neighbouring ship had been mustered for pay. Kennedy expressed hope that the order for the men to be paid could be given before the wind changed, when he would be forced to take a resentful crew to sea. The Admiralty ordered the ship's books to be sent by express for the essential signatures so that the crew could be paid.

Kennedy went back to convoy duty across to Amsterdam and to Lisbon, where he described the local merchants' practice of enticing English sailors to desert while protecting them from coercion.

After this period of working up his crew, he began to have success. He wrote to the Admiralty to report his first capture, a ship under Spanish colours which had a French crew and a French cargo. Shortly afterwards, while cruising off Vigo, Kennedy took *Vermudian*, a privateer which had 'for long infested this coast', having taken thirty-two English vessels in the previous three years. The British consul at Lisbon wrote to the prime minister, telling him of Kennedy's success.

Kennedy and Captain Skynner of the sixth-rate *Bideford* (20) were involved in a joint action against the much larger French frigates *Malicieux* (36) and *Opale* (32) in April 1759. After 'inviting her to action', the encounter lasted from mid-afternoon, through the night until the morning light showed the French frigate setting what sail she could, and by noon she 'had so much the advantage of sailing better than the *Flamborough* that

The inconclusive battle, with Kennedy's *Blonde* second from left.

she had almost run us out of sight'. *Bideford* arrived safely in Lisbon, but Launcelot Skynner had been killed at the outset of their battle against *Opale*, and the first lieutenant mortally wounded.

Thomas Stace, the master of *Bideford*, was the most senior surviving officer:[8]

> Everyone was sensible of the very superior forces of the two ships now standing towards us, besides that several other ships were coming in view, to whom the enemy was seen to make signals. No questions passed, *shall we engage*, the word was *Now for Honour*. We saluted each other with three cheers and stood in a line for the enemy who upon seeing this hauled up and obliged us to make the attack.

By chance, a British naval officer was witness to the engagement. The French *Malicieux* and *Opale*, mounting much heavier guns, had captured the sixth-rate *Penguin* (20) on 28 March. Her crew had been sent in to Vigo, and the vessel burnt, but her captain, William Harris, had been kept on board. On his return to England after his exchange, Harris was able to relate the explanations given by the French captains for the considerable damage they had suffered. Despite being much bigger than the British sixth-rates, they claimed that they had escaped from attack by two ships of the line. Kennedy learned when he returned to Lisbon that *Malicieux* had lost twenty-one men killed and thirty-two wounded. The public's enthusiasm was sparked by the resolution shown by the two small frigates, despite the inconclusive nature of this encounter, and the engraving shown below, immortalising the engagement, had wide sales.[9]

The original of this image, Francis Swaine's painting of the encounter, 'was reproduced on an enormous silver salver presented to Captain Kennedy by the British businessmen of Lisbon for preventing the sacking of their businesses by the French.'[10]

The portrait of Archibald Kennedy shown below, also hanging in Culzean Castle, is the only image of him in a naval setting, and in the original, the battle scene in the background is recognisably that of the engagement between *Flamborough* and *Bideford* and the two French frigates.[11] The artist, Mather Brown, has inserted two of the vessels into the available space.[12] He did not copy *Flamborough* taking on the larger of the two French frigates. The British sixth-rate portrayed is flying a flag hoisted in her mizzen rigging, signifying that the captain has been killed. There is little doubt that Archibald Kennedy would have put the artist right, so there is a possibility that this is a posthumous portrait.

Portrait of Captain Kennedy, as 11th Earl of Cassillis.
(National Trust of Scotland, Culzean Castle)

As a reward for his achievements, Kennedy was commissioned into the fifth-rate *Blonde* (32), the French frigate taken by John Elliott off the Isle of Man in February 1760. This was the beginning of a very happy time for Kennedy. Most unusually, he was permitted to take with him all his men

119

from *Flamborough*, and was given a cutter and a sloop under his command to assist in his work against privateers off the Portuguese coast. Kennedy had the highest regard for the sailing qualities of *Blonde*, and recommended that her lines be studied by the Navy Board. He described her as fast, and together they made many captures. In January 1761 he took a large vessel of eighteen guns from Bordeaux. In February he took 'a large French ship laden with wine flower and brandy', and repeated his success within days by taking a privateer out of St Jean de Luz. In June he captured *St Gregory* from Martinique, and he retook a variety of ships which had been captured by the French. In February 1762 Kennedy captured *Boutin*, an East Indiaman loaded with coffee and paprika. In April he took a smaller brigantine, as well as a succession of retakings of French captures.

Archibald Kennedy must have been a very wealthy man by this time. *Boutin*'s cargo was worth £150,000, before the ship itself was sold. There were always expenses, deductions, and other 'drawbacks', before what remained of the prize money could be divided up, and in this case Kennedy would have shared the benefit of this and the other captures with his little squadron. Once the prize and its cargo had been sold and the expenses settled, the prize money was divided amongst the ship's company in a fixed proportion: one-eighth went to flag officers; one-quarter to captains, who received an additional one-eighth if there had been no flag officers; one-eighth to lieutenants and the higher-ranking warrant officers; one-quarter for the remaining warrant and petty officers; one-quarter to the seamen.[13] The great benefit to Kennedy of this independent commission was that there were no deductions for flag officers, and each member of the crew would have worked very hard to make sure of his share.

Blonde was too fragile to be easily careened, which was typical of a French-built ship. She could not be put on shore to be cleaned at low tide, unlike the command of one of Kennedy's colleagues, who used to careen his ship on an out-of-the way French beach, knowing that he could do it in twenty-four hours and leave long before any French retaliation could get near him.[14] Eventually, Kennedy had to ask for leave to return to Plymouth for her to be cleaned. *Blonde* was paid off in February 1763, and by 9 April Kennedy received a commission for the sixth-rate *Coventry* (28).[15] He sailed for New York in July 1763 with reinforcements for the forces in New England, and for the first time had sickness aboard, brought in his opinion by the soldiers 'whose fevers are of a very malignant nature spread much'.[16]

In New York, Kennedy was back in the confused and confusing arena between the army and the navy, with the added complication that the civil authorities on land had to be placated as well. He was well placed to be able to send back detailed, articulate letters about matters on the waterfront at New York. At the beginning of 1765 it was the severe winter which concerned him. The River Hudson had frozen, and he had had to haul alongside the wharfs for the security of the ships, which made it impossible to stop the seamen from deserting. Kennedy was dispassionate about the inducements offered by the merchants, which tempted the seamen to desert. He knew that after the winter he would impress the seamen who had deserted, if he could get them before the merchant vessels left. He had planned to hire a small vessel which could stop the merchant ships and impress their crews. But it was the desire of the merchant ships to leave legitimately with their cargoes which provoked an outburst of feeling on the waterfront.

The Stamp Act of 1765 had been intended by the authorities in England as a means whereby the colonies could begin to pay for their own defence. All legal transactions were to be concluded on 'stamped paper'. This was commonplace in England, where every document such as a carpenter's warrant in the navy was issued on paper stamped with the value of the document. The furore which ensued in the colonies was not anticipated. In the colonies, all trading activities were concentrated in the ports where the goods coming into and leaving the country were absolute essentials: manufactured or trade goods coming in and materials produced in the hinterland from which an income could be derived going out. The customs house was the centre of this trade, as every vessel coming into or going from the port had to have a certificate of clearance – on stamped paper.

In 1765 supplies of stamped paper for New York had run out, and many clearances had been granted on unstamped paper. This concerned Kennedy, as it was his responsibility to have all vessels stopped and their cargoes checked to make sure that they were not smugglers. If some clearances were on unstamped paper, how could the validity of the cargo be checked?

In the meantime local feeling against the imposition of these dues was becoming inflamed. Ten boxes of stamped paper arrived from England, and were instantly seized and burned by a local mob. This action further encouraged the mob, and provoked threatening letters and menacing advertisements. In retaliation, the newly arrived Governor, Sir Henry Moore, offered a reward of £100 to anyone who could identify any of those concerned in the burning of the paper.

When the next consignment of stamped paper was expected, Kennedy was asked by Cadwallader Colden, who had been acting governor of New York, to guard the boxes on board *Coventry*. Kennedy refused. He could not safeguard a wooden vessel alongside the wharf against a mob of several

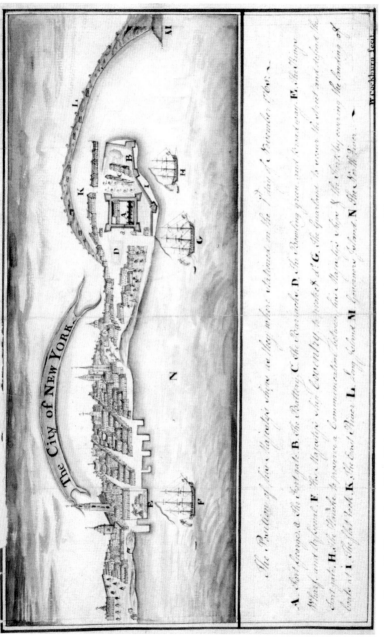

Kennedy's 'Perspective of New York across the North River showing the positions of HM ships "where [sic] stationed on the 1st day of November 1765"'. The drawing is signed 'W Cockburn'. (TNA MPI1-168 extracted from ADM 1/2012)

A – Fort George and the Fort gate; B – The Battery; C – The Barracks; D – The Bowling Green and Broadway; E – The King's Wharf and Arsenal; F – His Majestyss ship *Coventry* to protect the above; G – The *Guarland* to scour the street and defend the Fort Gate; H – The *Hawke* to preserve a communication between his Majesty's ships and the Fort by covering the landing boats at I – The Flat Rock.

thousand people determined to do harm, and while the river was frozen he was not able to take *Coventry* out into the stream. Even more to the point, he said that the interior of the vessel was wet and the papers would be spoiled. His refusal was taken as evidence that he was not prepared 'to act with the zeal of his Majesty's service which, as captain of the Kings ship I should have shown at such a conjunction.'

To explain his decision Kennedy drew a map of the position of his vessels in relation to New York, as they were before the impending winter's ice forced them to the wharfs.

In December 1765 Kennedy was superseded as captain of *Coventry*. At his own expense, in the fastest packet boat, he immediately returned to England to clear his name with the Admiralty, and succeeded in doing so. Kennedy insisted that he must be reinstated in *Coventry* to show the world that he had the support of the Admiralty. He returned to New York in October 1766, and on the death of Vice-Admiral Durell took over the responsibilities of the senior captain on the station. His letters are full of the necessary administrative detail that accompanied such a position, with all of which Kennedy dealt with supreme confidence.

Kennedy had two schooners built during this period for service in Jamaica. A great deal of the work was done by *Coventry*'s crew, and they sailed the two craft down to Jamaica. However, Kennedy had some explanations to make when he arrived in Spithead in January 1768, having been ordered to join Commodore Samuel Hood in Halifax. *Coventry* was shorthanded, with a substantial part of his crew away in Jamaica. The weather was typical for that time of year, with strong northwesterly winds which prevented his sailing toward Halifax. He also had a packet of letters from the Governor Sir Henry Moore for the minister. *Coventry* was paid off, and Kennedy went on half-pay.

Archibald Kennedy built for himself and his family a beautiful mansion at No. 1 Broadway, the most prestigious region of New York, on ground first occupied by his father.[17] His first wife was the heiress Katherine Schuyler, from whom he inherited large estates on her death in January 1768, and the family home of his second wife, Ann Watts, was next to his mansion. Their three sons, Archibald, John and Robert were born in New York. Kennedy lived in America, on his estates in New York and New Jersey, and every year asked with formal politeness to have his leave from England renewed.

During the War of Independence, Kennedy was targeted by leaders of the rebellion and taken prisoner. He was held for three years, moved from place to place to prevent his being rescued, and eventually freed and allowed to return to England, having given his parole 'not to take part against the rebel states'.[18] After the war, Kennedy lived quietly in New York, managing his estates.

In 1781 he wrote a formal 'Memorial' to the Admiralty, asking to be reinstated in the navy:[19]

To the Right Honourable the Lords Commissioners of the Admiralty
The Memorial of Captain Archibald Kennedy Humbly sheweth
That your Memorialist having served in the Royal Navy, during the whole course of the last war, and for four years after the close of it, settled in North America, where he possessed very considerable property, especially in the colonies of New Jersey and New York. That his known principles of Loyalty to his sovereign and attachment to this country as well as his avowed abhorrence of the seditious practices of the leaders of the Rebellion, very early attracted their jealousy, and provoked their resentment, and upon the approach of the Kings Fleet and Army to Staten Island in 1776, he was apprehended by an armed party, dragged out of his bed and forced into the interior parts of New Jersey, where he was detained as a prisoner. That during his absence from home his houses at Second River were plundered and his property, to a considerable value taken away or destroyed; A plan for effecting his release concerted at New York and patronised by the Commander in Chief having miscarried and every effort for procuring his exchange having been rejected by those who held him in confinement.

That after being restrained of his liberty for upwards of three years, in the course of which he was removed from place to place, to prevent his being rescued by the Kings Troops, your Memorialist at length obtained permission to come to England, but not till he had been compelled to give a parole 'not to take part against the rebel states'.

That your Memorialist after his arrival in New York and his friends by his direction since he came to England used every method to get him exchanged, that he might be enabled to offer his services in the Line of his profession; but although his Excellency Major General Robertson has declared his readiness to acceded to the exchange yet the attempt has been rejected by the Rebel Governor of New Jersey, while his property has again been invaded, his estate stripped of every necessary for the use of the Rebel army, and his family by this violence and outrage exposed to the utmost distress.

Animated by the most ardent desire of exerting himself in the cause of his King and Country he feels himself peculiarly unhappy under

Kennedy Mansion, No. 1 Broadway, New York, before the American War of Independence: Archibald Kennedy built a cupola on the house to provide a rooftop look out over the harbour, artist Horace Baker. (Art and Picture Collection, New York Public Library)

his present embarrassments to which he has been compelled to submit by a usurper power, from which besides numberless personal injuries and Insults, he has sustained losses in his property at different times and on various occasions to the amount of upwards of £25,000. But in as much as he may probably soon be extricated from his present restrictions, he most humbly prays that he may not be exposed to any disadvantage from them, should any promotions in the navy take place, which might otherwise benefit him in his rank, before his exchange is accomplished.

This impassioned plea may well have been prompted by the achievement of flag rank by Richard Kempenfelt in 1780, the first of his cohort of captains. The other four captains of his seniority awarded flag rank were all serving officers, whereas Captain Kennedy's request for further employment was not granted.

In 1792 when the 10th Earl died without male heir, Kennedy was recalled to Scotland. He succeeded to the titles of 11th Earl of Cassilis and 13th Lord Kennedy on 18 December 1792 and died on 29 December 1794.[20]

Admiral Sir Isaac Coffin:
Nelson's American Pallbearer[1]

Peter Turner

Admiral Sir Isaac Coffin was born on 16 May 1759, in Boston, Massachusetts, the fourth and last son of Nathaniel Coffin, the Paymaster of the Customs in Boston, and Elizabeth, the daughter of merchant Henry Barnes of Boston. Isaac attended Boston Latin School.[2] Nathaniel Coffin was a descendant of Tristram Coffin (1605–1681), a member of the landed gentry in England and one of the founders of Nantucket, who had sailed from Plymouth, England, to Massachusetts in 1642, thus escaping the English Civil War. Tristram Coffin first settled at Pentucket (now Haverhill), Massachusetts, where he prospered. In 1659, with a number of other investors, Tristram Coffin bought the island of Nantucket from Thomas Mayhew (for £30 and two beaver skin hats), the Coffin clan populated the island and when in 1827 Sir Isaac Coffin founded the Egan Maritime Institute, with its emphasis on nautical skills, to educate the descendants of Tristram Coffin, that meant nearly all the children on the island.[3]

Isaac's father was a Loyalist who left Boston in 1775 and briefly took refuge in Halifax during the build-up to the American Revolution, not long before the American Declaration of Independence, before settling with his family in Quebec.[4]

The first record of young Isaac Coffin in the Royal Navy is probably spurious, as he was entered in the books of *Captain* (74), Captain Thomas Symonds, in 1771 while she was stationed at Boston, when he would have been just twelve. It is more likely that he was entered in order to get sea time whilst still at school – in a similar way that the names of prospective pupils' names are 'put down' for public school in England, to reserve their future place at that school.[5] He did join the brig *Gaspée* (6), Lieutenant William Hunter, at Rhode Island in May 1773. Hunter apparently thought so well of his young charge that he regretted it when Isaac was ordered to join the sloop *Kingfisher* (14), commanded by Captain George Montagu, who was the son of Rear-Admiral John Montagu, then commander-in-chief on the North American Station. Later Isaac followed George Montagu into *Fowey* (24).

Sir Isaac Coffin, 1759–1839, Admiral of the Blue.
(RMGMN 0072, © National Maritime Museum, Greenwich, London)

Coffin was commissioned lieutenant on 18 August 1776, when serving aboard the ex-mercantile schooner *Diligent* (6), Lieutenant Edmund Dod, at Halifax but he was unable to take up the rank immediately, so he transferred to *Romney* (50) as a midshipman in September 1776 – *Romney*

127

then being at Newfoundland – and in June 1778 he moved to *Europe* (64), Captain Francis Parry,[6] still serving as a midshipman. Eventually, in October 1778 he achieved his first appointment as a lieutenant, aboard the armed cutter *Placentia*. After a brief period as a volunteer aboard *Sibyl* (28), Captain Thomas Pasley, in June 1779 he moved to command the armed ship *Pinson*, or *le Pinçon*, stationed on the Labrador coast. *Pinson* was wrecked in August 1779, owing to the negligence of the master: at the subsequent court martial at St John's, Coffin was found to be free from blame. In the following November he came to England – no record has been found of Coffin being aboard on any earlier trip eastbound across the Atlantic, so this may have been his first visit to the Old Country – and transferred to *Adamant* (50), Captain Gideon Johnstone, where he served as second lieutenant. *Adamant* was still under construction at Liverpool, Coffin was needed to help oversee the work, and he was involved in a number of minor accidents during the final phases of work, but she was able to sail under a jury rig in June 1780 for Plymouth.

Coffin returned in *Adamant* to North America in July 1780 as a convoy escort. On her passage she escaped the combined French and Spanish fleets, through the good fortune of having been warned by a Dutchman who had seen the enemy fleet just the day before. In February 1781 Coffin transferred briefly to *London* (90), Captain David Graves, flagship of Rear-Admiral Sir Thomas Graves, but moved again in March to *Royal Oak* (74), Captain William Swiney.

Royal Oak was the flagship of Vice-Admiral Mariot Arbuthnot at the Battle of Cape Henry in March, where Coffin acted as Arbuthnot's signal lieutenant. Arbuthnot's squadron chased de Ternay's French fleet, which had managed to get out of Rhode Island on 14 March, and two days later were found about fourteen leagues off the cape where they were partially engaged at 2pm by the three leading British ships, *Robust*, *Europe* and *Ardent*, until the rest of Arbuthnot's squadron caught up. The action became general until 3pm, when the French escaped to leeward. The much-damaged condition of the three van ships prevented Arbuthnot's pursuit of the French and on the next day, 17 March, his squadron anchored in Lynn Haven Bay to effect repairs. *Royal Oak* had sustained little damage and relatively few wounded (just three), although the British overall had suffered thirty killed and seventy-three wounded. It must have been somewhat irksome for Coffin, serving in his first sea battle, to watch the enemy escape.

Royal Oak then returned to New York, but she ran aground while passing from the North to the East River and was so badly damaged that she had to sail to Halifax, attended by *Medea*, for repairs, when Arbuthnot returned to England. Coffin remained in New York, where the body of his father arrived in a ship from Bristol in the middle of June 1781, he having died of gout the day before, and where he was buried with due honours: presumably Isaac made the arrangements.[7]

Royal Oak set sail, intending to return to New York in July, but when she fell in with the British North American fleet, now under Admiral Samuel Graves, the mails gave news of Coffin's promotion to master and commander dated 3 July. So he served on in the fleet as a volunteer until arriving in New York. There he was given the sloop *Avenger* (14), initially based in the North River, but in January 1782 he exchanged ships with Alexander Cochrane and took command of sloop *Pacahunter* (14). *Pacahunter* was present during a great fire which swept through St John's, Newfoundland, and Coffin earned the thanks of the House of Assembly for his part in helping to fight the fire.

Coffin had made many moves between ships and had not enjoyed a prolonged stay in any of them: a process that was to continue when he and all his *Pacahunter*s volunteered to join Rear-Admiral Samuel Hood's flagship, *Barfleur* (90), Captain Alexander Hood, in Barbados, to which they were transported in *Prince William*. Hood was temporary commander-in-chief during Rodney's absence in England, and he was hoping to recover the situation caused by the attack and invasion by the Comte de Grasse on Saint Kitts and Nevis. Consequently, Coffin was present at Hood's attack on the much larger French fleet at Basseterre, known as the Battle of St Kitts, on 25 January 1782.[8] The French fleet were anchored until attacked by the English, when they unmoored and moved away from the land in order to give themselves more sea room for the imminent battle, only for the wind to change, allowing the English to take their place and anchor in an 'L' formation in the bay at Basseterre, thereby cutting de Grasse off from the French troops ashore. De Grasse made three vigorous counter-attacks on Hood on 26 January, without success and sustaining severe loss of men and damage to his ships. Hood was able to stay in position for two weeks, but was unable to relieve the siege of the fort on Brimstone Hill or to prevent the island surrendering to French troops ashore, so he withdrew and rejoined Rodney, who had returned from England.

On 12 April 1782 Rodney again attacked de Grasse, this time in the large basin of water lying between the dangerous shores of Guadeloupe, Dominique, the Saintes and Marie Galante. De Grasse in *Ville de Paris* had been battling with *Canada* (74), Captain William Cornwallis, for some time when *Barfleur*, who had been becalmed at the start of the action, joined in at dusk, pouring fire into *Ville de Paris* and forcing her to strike to Hood with just three uninjured men on deck. Hood was despatched to pursue other escaping French ships, of whom he captured four. *Ville de Paris* was carrying thirty-six chests of money to pay the French troops and was said to be the only first rate to have been captured and carried into port by the commander of another fleet. The Battle of the Saintes, as it became known, was one of the first battles to see the tactic of breaking the line used: Rodney was made a peer of England, Hood a peer of Ireland, and Admirals Affleck and Drake were made baronets.

It is unclear whether Coffin was in *Barfleur* and so present at these actions, but we know he was aboard as a volunteer at St Kitts, and no record has been found of his transfer elsewhere, until he is found soon afterwards in 1782 as a supernumerary in Captain Hugh Cloberry Christian's *Fortunee* (40) and in company with *Convert* (32), Captain Henry Harvey, when these two ships met the French ship of the line *Triomphant* (80) in company with a frigate. The French fired on the smaller British ships, but they were able to escape and arrived safely at St John's.

Coffin then proceeded to Jamaica, where his friendship with Hood led to his promotion to post-captain on 13 June 1782 and an appointment to the command of *Shrewsbury* (74); he was just twenty-three years old. Prior to impressing Hood, Coffin had apparently progressed in the navy simply by his wits and abilities, without enjoying any particular 'interest'. Perhaps he had not attracted patronage because, as a colonial, he had been raised in an ambience of free spirits, and was clearly maintaining his links with family and friends in what had become an enemy country. It seems Hood may have seen something the others missed.

However, promotion to post-captain seems to have heralded a series of clashes with the naval authorities which blighted Coffin's career. One of his first duties was to transport Guy Carleton, 1st Baron Dorchester, and his family to and from Quebec. It has been said that Canada could not have been held for the Crown in 1775 without Carleton, and it is clear that the Coffin family were supporters of the Carletons. Isaac's cousin, Sir Thomas Aston Coffin, was Dorchester's secretary when governor of Canada. However, when the commander of the fleet, Admiral Sir George Rodney, ordered Coffin to take Dorchester's three sons aboard as lieutenants, Coffin refused, arguing that as the boys had respectively only five, three and two years' service, they were unqualified to serve as lieutenants, not having reached the required six years. When Coffin learned that it was Rodney himself who had issued the order, he reluctantly agreed, but when in turn Rodney heard of Coffin's initial refusal he called him before a court martial on charges of disobedience and contempt. The trial was held at Port Royal, Jamaica, on 29 July 1782, just six weeks after Coffin had received his commission. He was acquitted of both charges, the court determining that 'the appointment of these officers by commission was irregular and contrary to the established rules of the service'. Despite the verdict, the court did not have the power to suspend appointments made by the commander-in-chief, so Coffin needed to write to the Admiralty on 20 September 1782, requesting the lieutenants' commissions be suspended. The Admiralty issued the recall of the commissions on 14 December, by which time Coffin had moved from *Shrewsbury* to take command of *Hydra* (20).

Coffin sailed *Hydra* back to England and after a stormy passage paid her off in March 1783, when a general peace was declared between Britain, France, Spain and America. One imagines Coffin was glad for this episode to fall below the horizon astern – little did he know what was in store for him.

During the peace, Coffin remained without a ship and lived in England for the first time. A large part of his family had also relocated to London, England, so he was able to enjoy the usual benefits of a handsome, young naval captain at large with plenty of prize money in his pocket. However, the joys of such a life can lead one astray, so, rather than risk too much, he went to France to study the French language. Presumably it was easier for one to go astray when in France, without it becoming generally known.

Returning to England in May 1786, he took command of *Thisbe* (28), in which he again took Lord Dorchester and his family to Quebec, taking his departure from the Scilly Isles on 9 September, arriving in the Gulf of St Lawrence on 10 October, and anchoring off Quebec thirteen days later. He sailed for Halifax two days later, reaching there on 9 November for the winter.

In 1787 he returned to the Gulf of Saint Lawrence and took an interest in the Magdalen Islands, or Les Îles-de-la-Madeleine, where he found that New Englanders were exploiting the fisheries in the gulf and were trading illegally with the inhabitants of the islands, which he reported to the governor's council. Later, after he had been deprived of his patrimony by the government of the newly independent USA, Coffin was appointed seigneur of the islands in 1798, but his attempts to attract settlers and to evict French-Canadian squatters failed. One scheme created by Coffin in 1815 to assert his authority was to issue one-penny tokens, manufactured for him in Birmingham, England, but the British government took a dim view of this, considering it an unwarranted extension of his authority, and revoked the grant.

An incident occurred in 1788, whilst Coffin was in command of *Thisbe*, that was to have a profound effect on his immediate future: at the request of colleagues he entered four young people on the ship's books as captain's servants, as was normal practice at the time, though prohibited, as they did not actually serve on board and were probably still at school. This was a widespread irregularity that had been used by many serving officers at the start of their naval careers, including Coffin himself, of course.[9] On this occasion, Coffin was accused by the ship's master of signing false musters and was tried by court martial. The court had no alternative but to find him guilty, but the court considered there were mitigating circumstances, including that they concluded he had not set out to defraud His Majesty, and sentenced him to merely be dismissed from his ship. All seemed well, until Coffin returned to Britain and Lord Howe, who was First Lord of the Admiralty, was made aware of the case and insisted that Coffin suffer the full punishment required under the 31st Article of War.[10] When Coffin's name was duly struck off the Navy List, he lodged an appeal, and whilst waiting for his appeal to be heard, he emigrated to Europe and travelled about unsuccessfully seeking work as a mercenary in Denmark, Sweden and Russia. He did, however, join the Brabant Patriots, serving as a captain of artillery, in the short-lived Belgian Revolution of 1789/90 against Austria.

Meanwhile, the appeal lodged by Coffin, on the basis of whether or not the Admiralty had the right to set aside a judgement by a court martial, was put before the King, who called upon the Admiralty judges to look into it without delay. Their swift and final decision was that it could not. The original judgement by the court martial was deemed not to have been legal, but Howe's later overruling of it was not permissible, so Coffin was reinstated in the navy, with full back pay. This case defined the limits of the Admiralty's powers over courts martial, and was frequently used as a precedent in later cases.

It was not until the Spanish Armament, or Nootka Crisis, in 1790 that Coffin was called back into active service, taking command of *Alligator* (28), in which he was injured when diving overboard at the Nore to rescue a sailor who had fallen in high winds, without having taken the trouble to learn to swim beforehand.[11] The seaman made a full recovery, but Coffin suffered a serious hernia, from which he never fully recovered. Following this, *Alligator* was sent briefly on a number of duties: Spithead, Ceuta – briefly bearing the flag of Admiral Sir Philip Cosby until superseded by *Fame* – and finally to cruise off western Ireland before being sent to Canada in 1791 to bring home Lord Dorchester.

Later in 1791, whilst stationed at Halifax, Coffin went on leave in Canada, spending a year in Quebec, where his cousin, Thomas Aston, and his Uncle John and their families lived, and he stayed amongst these family members, which he found much to his pleasure.

Following this long break, Coffin returned to England where, on arrival in 1792, *Alligator* was paid off for a refit at Deptford and Coffin was cast ashore, unemployed.

Coffin again visited Denmark, Sweden and Russia seeking a commission, but was recalled to British service at the outbreak of the French Revolutionary Wars in 1793, when he was appointed the command of *Melampus* (36) at Plymouth. His first order in *Melampus* was to take Lord Dorchester back to Canada, but this was soon cancelled and, instead, Coffin was ordered to transfer most of his crew to *Severn* and then to re-man *Melampus*. With just twelve seamen and 120 landsmen, *Melampus* was able to get to Liverpool, where Coffin managed to complete a full crew. Next, she was used to transport men and field guns to Guernsey, where she remained attached to Earl Moira's ultimately unsuccessful expedition to Ostend. There followed a spell in the English Channel Fleet. One time, when in company with frigate *Active* (32), Captain Edmund Nagle, and hired lugger *Argus* (10), they came across a French squadron comprising five frigates, a corvette and a cutter, from which they were lucky to escape. Soon after, Coffin was sent cruising in the chops of the Channel in company with *Monarch* and *Active*, but in this he over-exerted himself, became seriously ill from his hernia and a fistula, and was obliged to resign his command. For the next four months Coffin suffered badly and, in fact, never again enjoyed a seagoing command, although, unknown to him, an important part of his service life was about to begin.

During his years of sea service, Coffin had accrued a considerable amount of prize money, which he entrusted to a cousin in America, who doubled his money for him.

In early 1795 Coffin was appointed Regulating Captain[12] at Leith and, later that year he was made Navy Commissioner[13] at Corsica with duties in Naples, Florence and Leghorn. Corsica was a dangerous place to serve at that time, as commented by Collingwood in a letter to his father-in-law.[14] When Corsica was evacuated in 1796, Coffin went to Lisbon, where he remained for two years, until he was appointed to Menorca for some months, followed eventually by Sheerness.

In May 1797, an example of Isaac Coffin's daring and sense of fun is given by Lord St Vincent, when he was at Gibraltar and in need of a courier to go to Lisbon to warn Lord Keith, blockading Cadiz, that the Brest Fleet had entered the Mediterranean. St Vincent's first courier was driven back by bad weather, so Coffin cheerfully volunteered to pass overland through Spain as a merchant carrying letters to Keith from Lisbon. When his first courier returned, having failed to get through:

> St Vincent at once cried out, 'Then nothing remains but to rummage the Rock and try how much gold is wanting to raise up the man who will brave a sentry's bullet, and maybe a spy's halter.' As the secretary was about to start off in search of a messenger, Sir Isaac Coffin exclaimed, 'Stay! I will go.' 'You will go?' 'Yes, on plea of proceeding on my appointment to Halifax the Governor of San Roque will give me a passport to Lisbon; but, once in Spain, I shall travel as a merchant of the country, and, if I can't send off to Lord Keith from Cadiz, I certainly shall be able to do so from Faro. So cypher the despatches while I go and dress. You see, this thing must be done!' Although the risk involved was considerable, Sir Isaac's courage and address, and his perfect mastery of the Spanish language, were not to be rejected – and he left the room in the highest spirits, singing a bolero, and infecting everybody with his light-heartedness. 'Good-bye, Coffin!' said St Vincent laughingly, 'you'll be hanged to-morrow.' Happily, this prophecy was not fulfilled, for Sir Isaac got through quite safely, and by daybreak of the earliest morning on which it was possible for Lord Keith to appear, his fleet was reported as rounding into the harbour. On their arrival [his secretary] Tucker remarked that Sir Isaac had not been hanged after all. 'That's by no means certain yet,' replied the chief, laughing; 'though, to tell the truth, I never imagined any Spaniard of our day would prove a match for an American like Sir Isaac – an Indian hunter, every inch of him. But now, Tucker, tell Mr Jackson to hurry on the watering of the fleet, and that we'll all sail as soon as possible.'[15]

No other mention has yet been found of this incident, but it seems that Coffin succeeded in his dangerous mission.

An appointment to Sheerness was delayed by a six-month period during which he temporarily replaced Henry Duncan at the Halifax yard, whilst Duncan fulfilled Coffin's role at Sheerness – clearly the result of an administrative muddle. It was Coffin's understanding, given directly to him by Lord St Vincent, that he was to clean up the corruption of the existing civil officers at all these dockyards, so he enthusiastically set about to impose the Admiralty regulations. This has never been the way to win people over and become popular; Coffin did neither, nor did he seek to.

Coffin's six months in Halifax, from mid-October 1799, were mayhem, caused by his efforts to bring things into line, by issuing orders – not done before by the commissioner; by instructing yard officers to not take orders from naval captains – who often exceeded their authority; by counter-manding some of the vice-admiral's orders to the naval storekeepers – for unauthorised fuel; by accusing all ships' warrant officers of embezzlement – without first checking the facts; by accusing captains of twice storing their ships without going to sea – which they denied; by preventing the yard officers from offering immediate succour to any ships struggling into harbour – their usual, kind-hearted, practice, and by generally suspecting everyone in the yard of fraud and embezzlement, including suspending the master shipwright and the foreman of the yard – both of whom were reinstated after Coffin had left Halifax.

Wherever he went, Coffin's strict and energetic imposition of regulations, and his effectiveness at it, made him extremely unpopular with dockyard workers, and in April 1801, when he impressed a yard worker for insolence and disobedience, a large number of artificers, riggers, and labourers threatened his life, forcing him to revoke his order.[16] But he never lost the support of the Admiralty and the Navy Board: in fact, he applied himself with such efficiency and energy that he was brought back to the sea service (not normally allowed in the case of civil commissioners) and Lord St Vincent remained confident in him, promoting him rear-admiral on 23 April 1804, and he had the honour of being created a baronet of Great Britain less than one month later. Soon after this, Coffin was appointed Admiral-Superintendent at Portsmouth Dockyard, hoisting his flag in *Gladiator* (44).

When Lord Nelson arrived in Portsmouth, England, at 6am on 14 September 1805, immediately prior to embarking aboard *Victory* for the culmination of the campaign of Trafalgar, Coffin joined him, together with George Rose and his wife and George Canning, at breakfast at the George Inn. Coffin was also one of those who helped sneak Nelson out of the George through the rear livery entrance at about 10am, and through the back ways to the beach, near the bathing machines, from where he and hundreds of others (the subterfuge clearly having failed) waved him off.

Just a few months later, on 9 January 1806 he was a pallbearer at Nelson's funeral.[17] Coffin remained at Portsmouth until being promoted vice-admiral on 28 April 1808, following which he retired, and once again started yet another new life.

In the early nineteenth century it was the vogue to be an inventor, with Coffin taking out a patent on what he called his Perpetual Oven. This oven was designed by him to bake sea-biscuits for the navy, and would be familiar to users of some hotel bread toasters, as it made use of a continuous mesh belt on cast-iron rollers, on which the unbaked biscuits were perpetually transported through the oven chamber, to come out baked. This design anticipated the industrial ovens developed later during the Industrial Revolution.

On 3 April 1811 Coffin married Welsh-speaking Elizabeth Browne at Titley, Herefordshire. Elizabeth was the heiress of William Greenly, the local Lord of the Manor, and Coffin briefly changed his surname to Coffin-Greenly on 11 February 1811. The marriage was not a great success and was without issue, the family being more comfortable with propriety than with the rumbustious ways of a sea officer. Lady Greenly, as she styled herself, was very religious and enjoyed writing sermons as a hobby; it seems Coffin had other interests – at one time Coffin offended his father-in-law when he arranged for the local sexton to ring the church bells to call the villagers to join him for a drink. Coffin and his wife remained friendly, but they led independent lives – they rarely met and he reverted to the simpler Coffin surname on 13 March 1813. However, when shipwrecked in 1829, after *Boston* had been struck by lightning on her way from Charlestown to Liverpool, Coffin gave his watch to the captain, with whom he shared a lifeboat for several days, to send to Lady Coffin should he himself not survive. While in the crowded boat, with no shelter and little covering, and the scantiest supply of food and water, his cheerfulness, interesting conversation, and 'ebullitions of good humour kept his companions in heart and courage'.[18]

Another story illustrates Coffin's character and his continuing connections to empathy for his countrymen:

One day an American ship sailed into Portsmouth, or Plymouth, before the War of 1812, when Sir Isaac had charge of the naval fleet. An English officer was sent on board. The master having gone ashore, the mate being in charge, did not receive the officer with the etiquette required upon such occasions. The officer gave the first salutation as he reached the deck by saying : 'What d[amne]d kind of a Yankee lubber has charge here, who don't know his duty to properly receive his majesty's officer?' The mate said not a word, but, seizing his visitor by the collar and slack of his trousers, threw him overboard for his own crew to pick up. Soon after an armed boat came alongside to take the mate on board the flag-ship, where he was arraigned before Sir Isaac, who soon became aware that the culprit was a kinsman, whose father he had been familiar with in boyhood. He tried to get the mate to acknowledge that he was ignorant 'of the laws and customs, that he might dismiss the case with a caution not to do so again'; but the Yankee was obdurate. 'He'd be d[amne]d,' he said, 'if any man should insult him on his own deck and under the flag of his country.' The offender was remanded to be regularly tried the next day. In the meantime the admiral sent a messenger to privately assure the mate that a suitable apology would relieve him from any further trouble in the matter; but on the trial the same defiant manner was assumed. The admiral drew out some expression, however, which he accepted as satisfactory, and dismissed the offender with suitable admonitions. Later in the day, from the shore, the admiral sent a message to the young man, stating that, as his father was an old friend and relative, he would be happy to meet the son and enjoy a bottle of wine with him at the inn. But the young man replied that the admiral might go to h[el]l with his wine. He'd see him d[amne]d first, before he'd drink with any d[amne]d Englisher, especially one who would approve of an insult to an officer under his own flag, upon his own deck. The admiral used to relate the above incident with much gusto, as he admired the spirit of independence exhibited by the Yankee mate.[19]

Coffin was promoted full admiral on 4 June 1814 and was elected Member of Parliament for Ilchester, Somerset in 1818, a seat that he held until 1826. He acted generally in the Whig interest against Lord Liverpool's ministry on major issues, including parliamentary reform and Catholic relief, but he usually spoke on naval matters, and when he started out on his parliamentary career he was not always popular. In fact, once he had 'learnt the ropes', Coffin was still inclined to not always pull together with his allies and to even push on them from time to time. Coffin exhibited an obsession with the fraudulent importation of American timber identified as Canadian produce, and when supporting a British merchants' petition for redress, on 27 March 1821, he wished Canada 'at the bottom of the sea'. Opposing Maxwell's slaves removal bill, on 1 June, he maintained that they 'would rather have their throats cut than be removed to Demerara', and he believed that nothing short of a declaration of war against every guilty nation would put an end to the foreign slave trade. When debating parliamentary reform, on 15 February 1822 Coffin observed that 'the best qualification [for a Member] consists in the possession of talents and property ... the sooner the House is weeded of those who, like myself, have neither one nor the other, the better'. On 14 February 1825 he approved the substitution of tea for a portion of the naval rum ration and reiterated his view that a war could not be fought without impressment. Coffin retired from Parliament at the dissolution in the summer of 1826, having amused many and many others not.[20]

In 1821 Sir Isaac Coffin set off for Tripoli, North Africa, as a passenger aboard survey ship *Adventure*, on which his nephew Henry Coffin was a volunteer lieutenant (what a family for sticking together!), but Isaac left the ship early when he heard that the plague was prevalent at his intended destination.

It was in 1827 that Coffin instigated the creation of the Sir Isaac Coffin's Lancasterian School in Nantucket (see note 3).

Coffin was created a Knight Grand Cross of the Royal Guelphic Order in 1832. He also came almost within touching distance of a peerage, thanks to his friendship with the Duke of Clarence (later William IV), and during the 1832 reform crisis he was placed on the King's private list of those to be made peers, but this came to nothing. Coffin had continued to maintain a close association with friends, relatives and business associates in New England,[21] which was the cause of several government ministers opposing his appointment as a peer.

Coffin supported many charities, and shortly before his death donated £100 to the Royal Naval Charity, with the note that he did so 'fearful it might suddenly slip my mind, and in the hurry of my departure forget to order ... £100 to be set aside'.[22] Elizabeth Coffin died on 27 January 1839 and Admiral Sir Isaac Coffin died sixth months later, eighty years old, on 23 July 1839.

He was buried at Cheltenham, Gloucestershire, and without heirs the baronetcy became extinct. He bequeathed the Magdalen Islands in the Gulf of St Lawrence, granted to him in recognition of his services in the American war in 1787, to his nephew Captain John Townsend Coffin (1789–1882), the son of his elder brother John of New Brunswick. He directed that when his property at Boston, Massachusetts, currently worth £11,500, had increased by investment to £20,000, the interest should be paid to his nephew and the principal given to John's son Isaac Tristram Coffin. The interest on his funded property was left to John, as he had been unable to make a distribution of his holdings because of obstacles created by his late wife's trustees. His personal property was sworn under £25,000, but the heavy annotation of the estate duty register suggests that administration of his estate was far from simple.

Coffin had been Resident Naval Commissioner at Sheerness, when Matthew Flinders' ship *Investigator* was fitted out for this voyage of exploration, and so twenty-five miles west of Port Lincoln, South Australia,

Coffin Bay and Greenly Island are named in honour of Sir Isaac Coffin and his then fiancée, on 16 February 1802.

History seems to have Sir Isaac Coffin written up as an irascible and eccentric martinet, but his own family loved him, his officers valued him and his crews followed him, so it seems his personal history may have been written more by those who crossed his hawse and by his wife's family, rather than by those who knew him well as a competent, courageous, fun-loving and charitable naval officer.

What Did HMS *Victory* Actually Look Like at the Battle of Trafalgar?

John Conover

The question of what HMS *Victory* looked like at the Battle of Trafalgar has challenged artists, ship-modellers and historians who have pored over old plans, official records, and history books in an effort to develop their representations of HMS *Victory* at the Battle of Trafalgar accurately. However, few of these efforts include study of some of the most useful sources of data, such as models of the ship at the National Maritime Museum at Greenwich, and drawings and sketches made by artists shortly after the battle, nor take into account that the great ship, launched in 1765, had been extensively modified in 1800–1803. This modification and modernisation substantially revised the external configuration of the ship, but with the exception of brief Admiralty orders and two partially conflicting dockyard models, no drawings or details of the refit are available.

The victory of the British fleet over the combined French and Spanish fleet on 21 October 1805, and the aftermath of the battle, is documented in hundreds of major publications and first-hand accounts by eyewitnesses of both sides. The battle itself is a fascinating event, but has value in this analysis as a source of information on the damage to *Victory* that was recorded by artists after the battle. What post-battle artists recorded in their drawings and sketches is essential to understanding the pre-battle configuration of the ship that is the subject of this analysis. The damage itself will be the topic of a future analysis that will define what *Victory* looked like *after* the battle.

Contemporary Models of HMS Victory

Three models of HMS *Victory* exist at the National Maritime Museum at Greenwich, England. The earliest, an Admiralty model of the ship as launched in 1765, is of no real significance for this analysis, and the second, a half-hull model of *Victory* made circa 1800–1803, which is of little value to this analysis because it lacks sufficient bow and stern detail. The third model, a block model, which was created in 1805, after the 1803 refit and before Trafalgar, exhibits less detail and precision than the older Admiralty model, yet has great significance and excellent detail as regards the 1803 refit and is a primary element in this analysis. The museum catalogue documents it as 'created circa 1805, source unknown'. The catalogue notes read: 'depicted after extensive refit (her so-called 'large repair') completed in 1803, prior to the Battle of Trafalgar. Model also shows further modifications which were proposed after Trafalgar which were not carried out.'

This large repair was conducted from February 1800 through April 1803 and incorporated many modifications and updates to the ship. An Admiralty directive of 27 October 1798 abolished open stern galleries that were subject to structural failure. This modification and the replacement of the ornate figurehead of 1765 were substantial changes to the outward appearance of the ship at Trafalgar. Other changes to external configuration were also directed, including the raising of the channels serving the fore and mainmasts from below the upper deck gun ports to above them, removal of the stern davits (in accordance with a 1798 Admiralty directive), the addition of two new gun ports forward on the main gun deck, and the elimination of two of the original four gun ports on the stern counter.

The degree to which the dockyard actually performed these modifications is the question of primary interest, since it established the appearance and configuration of the ship at Trafalgar. A comparison of the NMM model with drawings of *Victory* made by the Royal Academician J M W Turner in 1805 and early 1806, prior to the repair of its battle damage, provides insight into the actual configuration of the ship at Trafalgar.

Commentary on NMM block model of HMS Victory, 1803

The profile of the 1805 model, Figure 1, provides valuable information regarding modifications that were accomplished in the 1803 refit and equally valuable information about what was not modified in 1803, but may have been planned for later refits. Eight gun ports are shown on each side of the quarterdeck. Four of these eight are within the captain's quarters. All the ship's gun ports are spaced nearly equally to conform to the hull frames. The break of the poop deck is between the fourth and fifth quarterdeck gun ports. A fifteenth gun port appears on the main gun deck at the bow. No decorative entry port is depicted and the side ladder of the model is simple. No fenders or chess trees appear on the 1805 model, but most of the other fine details on a large ship's hull, such as D-blocks, anchor rests, hammock cranes, mouldings, and so on, also do not appear on this simplified model. There are new bulwarks for the model's forecastle deck, each with a large gun port forward for a 68pdr carronade and two ports for 12pdr cannons or smaller carronades, along with four timber head access

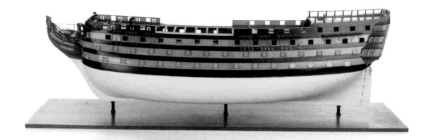

Figure 1. Profile of the National Maritime Museum model of HMS *Victory* in 1805.
(NMM photographs: F2881-Series and L3147-Series
© National Maritime Museum, Greenwich, London)

Figure 2. Port quarter view of transom of the National Maritime Museum model
of HMS *Victory* in 1805. (© National Maritime Museum, Greenwich, London)

ports, designed to provide support points for the stowed anchors. Shallow slots in the forward ends of the forecastle bulwarks suggest a location for the conventional bow snatch blocks and provide access to the timber heads of the upper head rails. Except for these slots, the forecastle bulwarks are joined with the forecastle rail above the beakhead bulkhead.

The transom, Figure 2, provides valuable information, both about details that the Admiralty papers do mention and others they do not mention. The Admiralty called for the removal of the stern jolly-boat davits and two of the original four stern gun ports, and they are missing on the 1805 model. A poop deck railing, fitted for a single gun port on each side, is present, which was not mentioned in the Admiralty instructions. The transom displays a facade, about 8in thick, surrounding the upper two rows of transom windows and balustrades. This three-dimensional feature creates a distinctive set of mouldings around sunburst arches and a painted arched panel above the quarterdeck windows. Badges of arms and flags decorate the aft faces of the middle deck quarter galleries. Hances (mouldings) on the periphery of the transom at the upper and middle deck level define a distinctive shape of the transom. These changes to the original ship comply with Admiralty general instructions to remove the decorative, but structurally weak, transom and its balconies on older ships.

The model's bow, Figure 3, suggests that major revisions to the bow structure were conducted during the 1803 refit. The forward forecastle pin rail (1) has no timber heads and has a continuous pin rail cap. Three sets of cheeks (2) are shown, spaced more or less equally apart, with the upper cheek lying just below the most forward port on the middle gun deck. The lower (third) cheek terminates on the knee of the head. The hawse holes (3) are located between the middle and the lower cheeks. The gammoning knee on the top of the beakhead (4) extends well above the upper cheek. The forward slot for the model's gammoning (5) appears below the upper cheek. The aft gammoning slot lies above the upper cheek but is not visible on this view. There is a middle bow rail (6), but no eaking rail from the cathead support to it, and the cathead support (7) is shown vertical with no bend forward in its foot. The knight heads (8) are a substantial assembly of timbers but modernised so they lack the classic timber head at their tops. Three trestles (9) support the head timbers. The false rails (10) atop the upper bow rails are depicted as little changed from the 1765 ship. The catheads (11) have the classic cat head decoration on their ends.

The seats of ease on the bow gratings are elongated to provide for more seats. The model's figurehead is depicted with the legs of the figurers uncrossed and it is not painted. The typical heraldry details, such as the

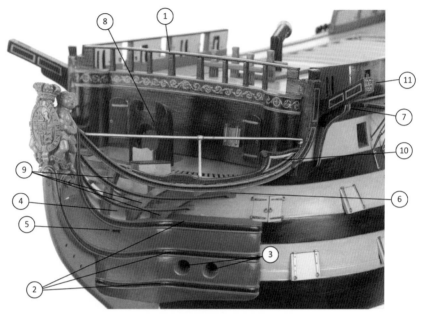

Figure 3. Port bow view of National Maritime Museum model of HMS *Victory* 1805.
(© National Maritime Museum, Greenwich, London)

garter ribbon, are not depicted, and many other fine details are omitted. The thin hance plates that cover the bow rails where they cross the trestles supporting the head timbers are not shown, but there are painted decorations on the trestle edges. These relatively minor features are not annotated on Figure 3.

HMS Victory at Trafalgar versus the 1805 model

After the battle and the ensuing storm, *Victory* received emergency repairs at Gibraltar and began a difficult voyage to England, arriving at Portsmouth on 5 December 1805, where she received additional emergency repairs and supplies, departing on 11 December, and arriving at Sheerness and Chatham on Christmas Eve.[1] There she was stripped for repairs, decommissioned on 14 January 1806 and, presumably, was dry-docked soon thereafter. The repaired and re-coppered *Victory* undocked on 3 May 1806 and was placed in ordinary at Medway. At some time after her repairs, *Victory* was downrated to a second-rate ship of the line.[2]

Figure 4. Exploded transom structure, author's 3-D rendering.

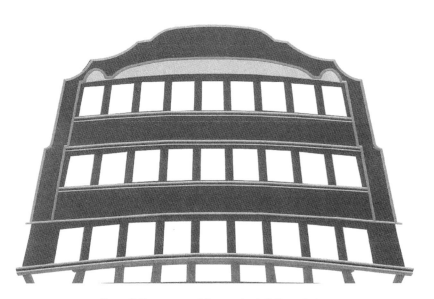

Figure 5. Transom mouldings, author's 3-D rendering.

There are no known high-quality renderings of *Victory* following her 1803 refit to verify what changes were actually incorporated in the ship, and there are no construction plans for the multiple changes to her that occurred

145

during the 1803 refit that might give clues as to her true configuration at the battle. There are, however, a large number of sketches of *Victory* by J M W Turner, the renowned landscape and nautical artist, made after she arrived at Portsmouth and before she entered the repair dock at Chatham. These sketches included one watercolour sketch, though it is of questionable accuracy, and a wonderful view of the quarter and forecastle decks. Although the sketches are precise in some details, many of them require careful interpretation. The 1805 model is nevertheless of great value in explaining some of *Victory*'s features that Turner illustrated.

The unique characteristics of a three-dimensional transom structure are important to making the case that the 1805 model represents what Turner sketched. The typical transom of large warships of the period consisted of two or three layers of structure of differing thickness, upon which detailed decorations were fastened. An exploded view of the transom components (Figure 4), and a stern view (Figure 5) illustrate the significant characteristics of a multi-layer transom of the early nineteenth century.

The layers of structure in Figure 4 from right to left are the transom primary timbers, the first planking layer, the three-dimensional horseshoe element, the moulding, and the encapsulating taffrail and its unique moulding extensions. Figure 5 is a stern view of the assembled layers. Major mouldings separated and delineated the various segments of the structure. One of the most important of these is the triple arc moulding which separates the horseshoe of thick upper structure from the lower thinner structures and caps the blue coloured panels used for decorative paintings. The existence of this moulding in Turner's sketches is strong evidence for *Victory* having such a multi-layer transom.

In all of Turner's sketches, the taffrail and its port and starboard extensions, as well as major portions of both upper quarter galleries, and some transom windows, were obscured or partially obscured by what he noted on one drawing as 'white'. This was no doubt sailcloth used to keep the weather out of a badly damaged stern structure.

Commentary on Sketches of HMS Victory in 1805 by J M W Turner: Tate Britain Collection

The first reference in any of Turner's sketches that are relevant to post-Trafalgar *Victory* is a relatively crude, combined image of the bow and the stern of a warship he annotated as '*Victory*'. The sketch was likely made at Portsmouth upon *Victory*'s arrival there after Trafalgar. It is not presented in this paper, since any details shown in it are better reflected in later sketches Turner made of *Victory* at Sheerness and Chatham. The upper

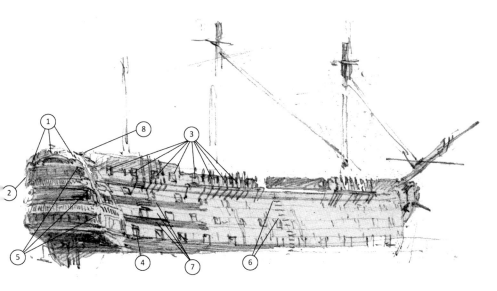

Figure 6. Starboard aft view of *Victory*. (Tate Britain, London)

sketch of the bow is certainly that ship, based on the figurehead. This sketch is within a sketchbook entitled 'Shipwrecks' that includes a number of drawings of the sterns of two-decker men-of-war, but no other drawings of the *Victory*.[3] The upper image of *Victory*'s bow provides further evidence of battle damage. This image appears to confirm that the two legs of the port cherub in the figurehead were shot away, as described by a visitor at Dover.[4] The starboard cathead is missing, as reported by the crew.[5]

Later, in December 1805, he travelled to Chatham, where he began a new sketchbook more focused on the *Victory*, her crew, and the Battle of Trafalgar. The later sketchbook seems to be dedicated to images of ships of Trafalgar, the men who sailed them, the battle events as he heard them from the crew, and images of the people and animals near Portsmouth, Chatham and Sheerness.[6] Several of the images represent early sketches for large paintings by Turner and other artists (not shown in this paper).

Turner's relatively detailed sketch, Figure 6, recorded hull, transom, and quarter gallery features and damage.[7] The triple arches (1) of the three-dimensional transom appear surrounding the recessed arc of the decorative painting surface. The extension of the taffrail (2) is present on the port edge of the transom and helps confirm that the transom is of the multi-layer type as on the 1805 model. Eight gun ports (3) on the quarterdeck conform to the 1805 model. A sixteenth main deck gun port (4) is shown that does not appear on the 1805 model, but which did exist on the ship in 1765. Considerable damage to the starboard transom and quarter galleries (5) is indicated but partially obscured by the white cloth (8), noted by Turner on Figure 7. Damage to the starboard transom windows of the admiral's quarters seems obvious and consistent with prior sketches. The faint traces of window frames on the quarterdeck and middle deck suggest that the dead lights may have been in place where they were not damaged. Simple entry steps (6) without a decorative entry port on the middle gun deck conform to the 1805 model. The colour scheme for the hull (7) is clearly the bumblebee pattern of black and light colour stripes.

The details of the transom decorations shown by Turner in Figure 7 verify that the 1805 model transom, or one very similar, was installed at Trafalgar.[8] The triple arch features and the taffrail extension (1) are obvious and cap the recessed painting panel (6). The clutter at the taffrail (2) probably is composed to some extent of the driver boom rest and the centre

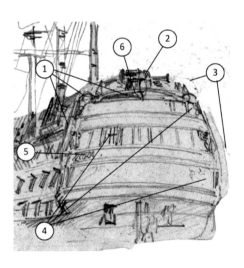

Figure 7. Port aft quarter view of stern of *Victory*. (Tate Britain, London)

lantern, but the decorative details of the national badge at the peak were likely obscured by the white cloth (3) that Turner notes at the upper right. Port and starboard stern lanterns are not indicated. The damage (4) to the admiral's transom windows, the captain's starboard windows, and the starboard middle deck windows shows clearly. The lack of window frames and details may be artist's licence, raised dead lights, destroyed windows, sailcloth weather protection, or all of these. Turner also illustrates what must be damaged balustrade trim elements (5) on the port end of the admiral's windows, but none of the many others that decorate the transom. Turner indicated 'wooldings' (tarred rope bands) on the mainmast and mizzenmast in this drawing that support the reports that the mizzenmast had been replaced and the mainmast had been fished with splints.[9] Prior to the battle, Nelson had directed all British ships in his command at Trafalgar to paint their black mast bands the same colour as the mast to aid in identification of friend and foe.[10]

In the marvellous sketch of starboard bow, Figure 8, Turner details additional facts establishing the historical validity of the 1805 model.[11] It

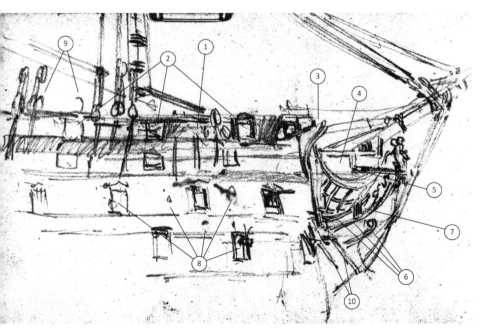

Figure 8. Starboard bow detail of *Victory*. (Tate Britain, London)

clearly shows the existence of a forecastle bulwark (1) at Trafalgar. Turner drew three gun ports (2) in the bulwark, aligned precisely as shown on the 1805 model. The four timberhead openings in the model's bulwarks are not obvious because of battle damage, but some do appear in the port side views. The starboard cathead (3) is missing as is consistent with battle damage reported.[12] The drawing also illustrates that the false rail (4) had been replaced with a bulkhead to the hand rail in the bow works which obscures the bowsprit. This feature was likely further evidence of the trend to improve crew protection in weather and battle. The boomkin (5) projects through this new bulkhead. A third cheek (6) terminating in a circular decoration is represented on the knee of the head. The forward gammoning slot (7) lies below the upper cheek and the rear slot is not visible in this view. Gun port frame (8) and hull damage is shown. Numerous pencil or pen marks that were often employed by Turner to represent shot damage appear in the bow and some of the gun ports, as reported in other sources. Bent hammock cranes (9) suggest that the starboard forecastle hammocks and covers had been blown away. Two anchor cables (10) for deployed anchors are visible. The starboard sheet anchor had been damaged at Trafalgar and was replaced at Gibraltar.[13]

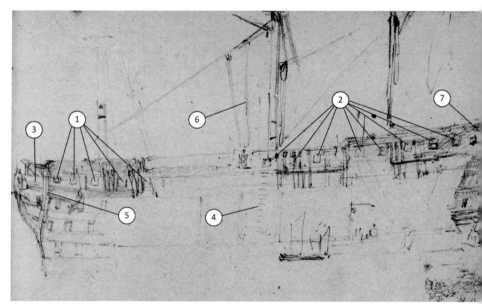

Figure 9. Port side view with smaller vessels. (Tate Britain, London)

In this drawing, Figure 9, Turner shows five openings (1) in the forecastle, with two in use by the bower anchor (5) and at least eight gun ports and openings on the quarterdeck bulwarks (2) of the port side.[14] The port hammock covers are shown in place on all of the weather decks. The false rail bulkhead (3) obscures the bowsprit, as on the starboard side. Again, the entry steps (4) are minimal and no obvious entry port is indicated. The port bower anchor (5) is stowed. Stay pendant lifting tackle (6) is deployed from the mainmast forestay for unloading of guns, shingle ballast, and other heavy loads. Damage to the quarter gallery roof and windows (7) is suggested. Vertical lines shown fore and aft of the boarding ladder are likely tackle used to manage platforms used to assess damage and make temporary repairs to the damaged wales and planking.

Turner probably made a sketch he used as a basis for this drawing, Figure 10, before *Victory* went to the Chatham dock, but after the guns had been removed on 1 January 1806.[15] The sketch has not been found in the Tate

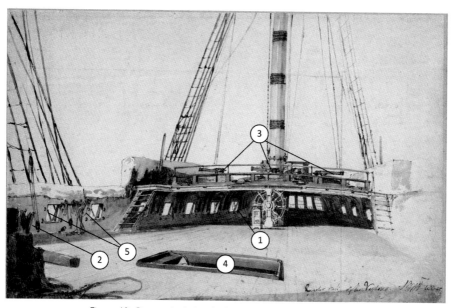

Figure 10. Quarterdeck detail of *Victory*. (Tate Britain, London)

records. This later watercolour wash is remarkably detailed and confirms many reports derived from the battle. As far as the artist was concerned, this scene would have been the location where any painting of Nelson's mortal wounding would be based, but it tells far more. An ensign staff is not depicted, nor is an ensign visible in the drawing. This could set the date of sketch used for this picture as after decommissioning on 14 January 1806.

This drawing helps confirms the quarterdeck gun port configuration of the 1805 NMM model is accurate, if we forgive Turner the error of showing a fifth starboard gun port (1) in the captain's quarters. In fact, there can be only four, with the fifth likely being the door to the starboard quarter gallery which had been shot away (or removed) with the damage to the quarterdeck quarter gallery. Turner's notes on the drawing indicate that a 12pdr gun was used at the 'fifth gun port', which would be unlikely considering the lack of gun tackle fittings for a door to the captain's head.[16]

It shows the damage to the fore brace bitts (2) at the base of the mainmast that spawned the fragments that historically hit Captain Hardy on the foot, early in the engagement.[17] It clearly shows three pivot guns (3) on the poop pin rail that do not seem to be mentioned in any published record. There is no evidence of other guns on the poop.

It shows that the railings for the quarterdeck companionway (4) were removed either before or after the battle, and that Turner pictured the quarterdeck companionway descending from starboard to port. That orientation is not consistent with all other companionways on the ship, according to copies of the original plans for the ship in 1765. Wooldings on the mizzenmast are consistent with the temporary mast installed at Portsmouth in December 1805. The starboard quarterdeck kevel and staghorn (5) that are crucial for securing the tacks and sheets from the mainsail are missing. They were either cleanly shot away (unlikely) or missing at Trafalgar (impossible). It also shows probably accurate construction details of the poop rail that do not exist elsewhere except in this sketch, Figure 11. This drawing also shows the temporary, undersized replacement binnacle and the new ship's wheel installed at Gibraltar after the battle.

Other than possible lost glass, there is no obvious window damage to the transom window panels, which slide down into their frames. There is no evidence of other serious damage to the interior of the captain's spaces, other than the missing door to his bathroom. This image does indicate the use of deadlights on the quarterdeck transom windows. The overall spartan nature of the captain's quarters is probably standard for British warships of the period. The drawing does not indicate any sign of the poop deck railing present on the 1805 model. Other information suggests that 1½in planks were fixed to the exterior of the poop hammock cranes in 1780 for additional protection to poop deck hammocks and covers from the poop deck cannons muzzle blasts, and these were retained during the 1803–1805 refit.[18] This feature was probably intended to protect the crew on the poop from small-arms fire, since there were no guns located on the poop deck after 1803.

An interesting (and cryptic) comment noted on the sketch by Turner is 'Guns 12 used in Vic ports marked: X.' There appear to be at least eight quarterdeck ports (including the captain's bathroom door) labelled with an 'X', including two transom windows. This may suggest that the 'hidden' gun ports in the transom were employed. However, opening any of these stern port lids would have damaged the transom balustrades, but such major damage to the balustrades is not indicated at the location of any of the nine port lids in any of Turner's other sketches. The most likely explanation of these inconsistencies is that Turner made an initial sketch on the ship at Chatham and produced this detailed wash later for sale to artists producing images of the scene where Nelson was shot. As a result, artistic licence is likely present in some elements of this drawing.

For the sketch in Figure 11,[19] Turner climbed the mizzen rigging to capture this unique view of *Victory*'s quarter and forecastle decks, specifically for a painting he made later, entitled *The Battle of Trafalgar, as Seen from the Mizen [sic] Starboard Shrouds of the Victory*. The sketch was done on 10in by 16in paper, much larger than the 4in by 7in sketchbooks he used for most of his other *Victory* sketches, and offers more detail than most of the others. The badly damaged mainmast is shown as fished, splinted with boards and wrapped with black wooldings, as is described in damage reports.[20] The foremast has similar black wooldings confirming that it is a jury rig to replace the original foremast that had been badly shot through. (1) The bowsprit is obscured and the sketch depicts the structure at the fore edge of the forecastle deck as a bulkhead, and not the railing shown on the 1805 model. (2) Two gun ports are visible in the same locations of wide spacing of the railing on the model, suggesting that the bulkhead shown in the sketch is simply the boarded-up railing shown on the model. The sketch suggests the usual low railing at the after edge of the spar deck (3), but does not depict the forward spar deck rail with its important rigging tie points for the bowsprit and foreyard. No ship's bell cupola is shown, but the galley stovepipe (4) is. Brian Lavery states that cupolas were not installed on British ships after 1800 and that the ship's bell was relocated to two fore and aft beams to support the bell support beam, which would likely have been done in the 1803 refit.[21] No such beams

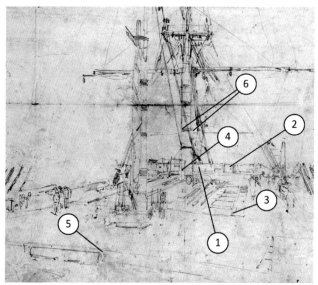

Figure 11. View forward from mizzen shrouds,
by J M W Turner. (Tate Britain, London)

appear in this view of the forecastle, but the bell may have been relocated to the break of the poop or shot away. The poop deck forward rail base (5) is shown in the foreground, but there is no representation of anything on it.

An interesting rigging fact is shown in this drawing. The main and preventer stays (6) are clearly shown passing on either side of the foremast, over the forecastle forward rail, where they are obscured by the bulkhead, and on to the bowsprit, vice the conventional both to starboard routing.[22] This may have been a transitional configuration to one established in 1810 where the main and preventer stays passed on either side of the foremast, but were affixed to eyes in the deck at the base of that mast.

Comparison of 1805 block model transom with 110-gun HMS Queen Charlotte, launched 1810

The transom configuration and decorations of the 1805 block model, Figure 13, compare favourably with a sketch, Figure 12, made in 1824 by John Christian Shetkey, the drawing master at Portsmouth, of the transom of the HMS *Queen Charlotte*, a 110-gun ship launched at Deptford shipyard in 1810.

Queen Charlotte displays most of the same decorative features as the 1805 *Victory* model. She has a three-dimensional structure with the three-arc moulding that the 1805 model exhibits. The peak transom decorations consist of the same lion, arms badge, and unicorn on both ships. Even the side-panel trim is virtually the same on both ships. *Queen Charlotte*'s carved details are more elaborate than *Victory*'s and they are situated lower on the transom. She has stern jolly-boat davits and the poop deck railing that *Victory* lacks, and has slightly more rounded corners on her taffrail and its extensions. Otherwise, *Queen Charlotte*'s configuration and decor suggests that the transom of the 1805 NMM model of *Victory* is highly likely to be fully representative of *Victory* at Trafalgar.

Evaluation of differences between the 1805 model and HMS Victory at Trafalgar

Turner's sketches provide the firmest evidence of the degree to which the 1805 model reflects the appearance of *Victory* at Trafalgar. The principal

Figure 12. Transom of HMS *Queen Charlotte*.
(© National Maritime Museum, Greenwich, London)

155

differences between the NMM model and Turner's sketches of the ship are as follows:

- There was a sixteenth aftermost gun port on the main (lower) gun deck which had not been removed in 1803.
- The 'break' of the poop deck on the ship at Trafalgar was between the fifth and sixth gun ports on the quarterdeck, but port and starboard gangways were extended to ladders between the fourth and fifth gun ports.
- There was no railing on the poop deck except at the forward edge or break.
- The false rails over the main (upper) bow rails were replaced with planked bulkheads through which the boomkins projected.

Figure 13. View of transom of National Maritime Museum model of HMS *Victory*.
(Photo Series L3147 © National Maritime Museum, Greenwich, London)

- The support brackets for the catheads were curved forward and may have continued as an eaking rail to the middle head rail.
- The railing above the beakhead bulkhead at the forward edge of the forecastle deck was planked as a bulkhead with two gun ports.

There is little doubt that the items on this list were on *Victory* at Trafalgar. What would have been planned for later modifications, according to the NMM description of the 1805 model? The sixteenth gun port was obviously not removed at Trafalgar and its removal was a planned future modification, yet it still exists in an 1884 photograph. Moving the break of the poop deck forward 4ft would have required moving the steering gear as well: not a likely modification just to expand the captain's quarters, although it may well be one of the planned future modifications. The railing on the poop deck periphery is a reasonable modification that would have been in line with the trend of the period as it was on the *Queen Charlotte*, and it may well have been planned for a future modification of *Victory*. An interesting etching of *Victory* in 1828 by Edward William Cooke shows the ship's poop deck with bulkheads, but no railings.

The author's computer model of HMS Victory at Trafalgar

A very important part of working with limited data to accurately define *Victory*'s appearance at Trafalgar is not just assuming that the NMM 1805 block model is accurate, but in proving that the features it depicts are actually consistent with the internal structure of the ship. For example, do the modification features on the block model match the hull structure as defined in the early drawings of the ship? Using a combination of the ancient drawings, John McKay's beautiful plans, and Bugler's incredibly detailed description of the modern ship's structural components, the keel and stem was fitted with frames, deck beams, and planking in a 3-D computer model using TurboCAD. Every detail down to the scuppers and individual pieces of the decorative trim was modelled.

Once in the computer, a scratch-built wooden model of the ship was constructed to validate the computer version. Most of the critical structural junctions where the hull components met at the bow and stern had to be adjusted from the plans available in order to match reality.

Figure 14 and colour plates 8 and 9, taken from the 3-D model with the gun port lids open, are consistent with all of the data available to the author as to what HMS *Victory* actually looked like before her damage at Trafalgar.

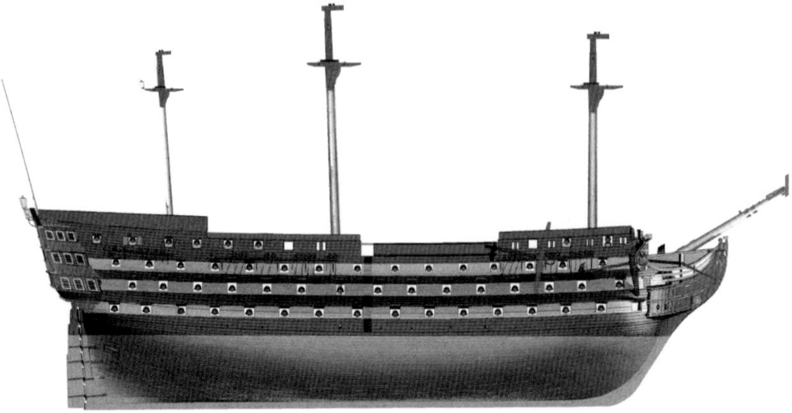

Figure 14. Profile of author's 3-D model of HMS *Victory* at Trafalgar.

Limitations of the analysis

The use of artists' sketches and drawings to define details of structure and details has inherent weaknesses. The evaluator must constantly make judgements about what the artist saw, or thought he saw, when he put pencil to paper 210 years ago. That problem is largely mitigated in this case by the existence of a relatively detailed contemporary model of the ship. One can be reasonably confident if the major structural elements Turner drew can be related correctly to the museum model and the data regarding the 1765 ship. The evaluator faces two other problems: first, when the artist drew a feature that does not appear on the reference model; and secondly, when the artist failed to see or image some detail that does appear on the museum model. Examples of these circumstances are the poop deck railing which Turner did not draw, and the new bulwark on the bow replacing the classic false rail over the upper head rail that he did draw. Turner drew a sixteenth main gun deck port in all of his drawings of the ship that showed the stern gun ports. An evaluator would find it hard to ignore this as artistic licence. Conversely, his depiction of swivel guns on the forward poop rail is not consistent with the arming of three-deckers of the period, nor with their existence on the ship after all other guns had been removed, and which the author has rejected.

Other issues arose when trying to correlate basic ship frame structure and gun port locations in Bugler's data and the computer model with the museum model's exact locations and configurations of the channels. Without adjusting those, the guns of a ship built to the model would have been tearing up some of the deadeyes and shrouds. This adjustment was not risky because the museum model was a block version that did not have the internal framing structure that defines the true locations of the ports, whereas the computer model did. The 1805 model served well to help define *Victory*'s appearance at Trafalgar, but fell somewhat short of what actually happened in the 1803–1805 refit. The issue of incomplete source investgations is also a problem, but most of the source data for this evaluation is at least consistent, if not complete.

A relatively hot topic for *Victory* today is her paint scheme. According to some recent reports in the British press, the bumblebee pattern of black and yellow ochre has been called into question by paint scientists who examined old wood from *Victory*. While this author's evaluation shows conclusively that the *Victory* was bumblebee at Trafalgar, until recently the true colours remained a mystery. Andrew Baines, Head of Historic Ships at the National Museum of the Royal Navy, has supervised a technical analysis of the old paint from shards of wood stored from early repairs of the ship. Crick Smith, a company that specialises in antique restorations, conducted a detailed investigation and determined that the black colour at Trafalgar was actually a very dark grey, that the yellow ochre was actually a pinkish tan, the masts were painted a light cream, and the red on the gun ports and lids was actually a darker hue of red than previously thought. Thanks to their work, accurate colour value codes are now available for all four colours and Portsmouth's *Victory* has been repainted.

For ship-modellers, the issue of hull trim always nags historical purists. They are always looking for decorative trim such as the planksheer, channel, and main mouldings and functional fenders. As far as this researcher can determine, such decorative devices were virtually eliminated on major British warships during the early nineteenth century. The fancy trim was relegated almost exclusively to the transom, quarter galleries and bows, where complicated mouldings and carvings were diminished or eliminated over time. HMS *Victory* was no exception. After she was returned to active service from ordinary in 1808 as a second-rate ship, her transom decorations were apparently simplified from those at Trafalgar, but those details will be dealt with in a future article.

Conclusions

The author, a dedicated ship-modeller, decided to construct a scratch-built model of HMS *Victory* after a trip to visit the ship at Portsmouth about fifteen years ago. In an effort to get it right, existing plans of the ship were secured from multiple sources, including the National Maritime Museum in Greenwich. NMM and other museums and historical records were searched on line, and construction began on a set of computer-generated plans. During the process of defining the ship's details, a search of NMM online images disclosed two strange-looking models of the ship bearing historically well-known features of the 1803 major refit. One of the models, the principal subject of this analysis, bore a transom that looked nothing like expected based on the Portsmouth visit. A vigorous search for the truth resulted in discovery of period images of the ship by J M W Turner held by the Tate Turner galleries.

Turner's sketches of *Victory* made a few weeks after the Battle of Trafalgar provide an excellent source by which the NMM block model of the ship made just before the battle can be evaluated. The model not only provides high quality details of the decor and configuration of the bow and stern, but also displays structures and characteristics that the Turner sketches refute as historical truth. Nevertheless, the 1805 model has long been overlooked as a largely accurate source for nautical historians, ship-modellers, and artists looking for facts about the world's most famous ship. Additionally, Shetkey's detailed sketch of *Queen Charlotte*, a contemporary three-decker, adds confidence that the details of the transom and the decor of the 1805 model are accurate.

With the following exceptions, the 1805 NMM model should be considered an accurate representation of *Victory* at Trafalgar:

- The bulkheads at the bow above the beakhead bulkhead and atop the upper bow rails on the ship are not present on the model as Turner recorded them.
- The model shows a poop railing, but only the forward poop railing was on the ship Turner sketched just after the battle.
- A sixteenth main gun deck gun port that existed aft on the ship is not on the model.
- The break of the poop shown on the model is too far forward.
- The configurations of the model's channels are not completely accurate.
- The colour scheme of the model, including the figurehead, is probably not accurate, based on modern evaluation of paint chips from the period.

The author's computer model has incorporated all of these adjustments, and likely presents the most accurate information to date regarding what HMS *Victory* actually looked like at Trafalgar.

Bow and stern views and profile, see colour plates 8, 9 and 10

Thomas Buttersworth:
A Biographical Note of a Sailor Turned Artist

Kathryn Campbell

Naval records referred to Thomas Buttersworth as a 'celebrated marine painter.'[1] And indeed he was. By the time he died, Buttersworth had been painting for well over forty years and had produced hundreds of oil paintings, watercolours and prints which, in their entirety, represent a history of the Royal Navy and merchant shipping. While some have criticised Buttersworth for producing paintings which were flat or lacking in atmosphere, the years he spent at sea lent his paintings a degree of detail and accuracy which not all artists achieved. Whether one is viewing a painting of a battle, a shipwreck or a fishing scene, there is no doubt that Buttersworth knew his ships and knew how they moved through the sea.

Thomas Buttersworth was born on the Isle of Wight in 1768 and grew up in Cowes. He was the fifth child of James, a butcher. Although not much is known of his early life, it is clear that he spent some time at sea before he entered the Royal Navy in 1790. He was rated able-bodied seaman and served on the sloop *Flirt* for three months. He was discharged, and, according to his service record, did not join another ship until 1795.[2] Interestingly, *Flirt*, under Captain William Luke, had been stationed off the Isle of Wight from 1783–86. When Buttersworth rejoined the navy, he signed onto Captain Luke's ship *Caroline* (36), perhaps suggesting that he knew Luke. It is not clear how he was supporting himself between 1790 and 1795, but he was clearly doing some painting.

One of his earliest known oil paintings shows the Coronation Fleet Review of 1794. It is signed and dated 1795. Given the quality of this painting, it is very unlikely it was his first attempt at oil painting. Buttersworth painted at least two watercolours of the same scene. It is very likely that he witnessed the review in person and painted the watercolours first, using them later as reference for the oil painting.

By the summer of 1795, Buttersworth was in London. There are at least eight prints published by the firm of Laurie and Whittle, Fleet Street, between July and November of that year. Buttersworth seems to have learned early on that producing prints was a good way to reach a larger audience with his paintings. He must have completed the watercolours, turned them over to the printers and then entered the navy again. There is large disparity in technique and skill when one compares these watercolours to those he completed just a few years later. The earlier watercolours are somewhat naïve. They have little to no background and the sea is very stylised, almost primitive. At least two of the watercolours were not dated, unlike the later ones. This leaves the possibility that some of them were done much earlier and that Buttersworth took them to London that summer to be engraved, even though he had completed them earlier. However, one of the watercolours depicts *Apollo* (38), a ship which was only ordered in 1793.[3]

The 'Return of men raised at the Port of London' for 1795 gives Buttersworth's occupation as seaman, even though he had already begun his alternate career as a marine artist.[4] Buttersworth served on the newly-commissioned *Caroline* (36) for almost five years. He signed on as able-bodied seaman on 16 August 1795, but was promoted to master-at-arms on 26 November. Many of Buttersworth's known watercolours date from this five-year period in the navy, all of which he spent in *Caroline*. It is not surprising, given the conditions onboard a relatively small frigate, that Buttersworth would have worked in watercolours, not oils. Many of the watercolours in the collection of the National Maritime Museum are done on the pages of signal or log books, and represent major actions of the time, such as the Battle of Cape St Vincent and the Battle of the Nile, blockading Cadiz, or the fleet at the mouth of the Tagus. These paintings are far more skilled than his earlier watercolours, and are almost always signed and dated. It suggests the possibility that Buttersworth had received some instruction, although there is no proof of this.

It has been suggested that Buttersworth painted scenes he witnessed first-hand. While this is certainly true in some cases, it was by no means always true. If one compares the position of *Caroline*, according to the log book, with the dates of the actions, it is clear that Buttersworth was often nowhere near the action on the day. For example, during the Battle of Cape St Vincent on 14 February 1797, *Caroline* did not arrive at Cape St Vincent until 2 March.[5]

During the Battle of the Nile, *Caroline* was off Cape Bellum, on the northern coast of Portugal. An intriguing coincidence is that Buttersworth's younger brother, George, was at both actions.[6] Similarly, Buttersworth painted at least six views of the sinking of *Bombay Castle* in the mouth of

Thomas Buttersworth, *Royal Fleet Review 1794*, signed and dated 1795, oil on canvas, 29 x 42in, private collection. This is one of Thomas Buttersworth's earliest known oil paintings. (Photograph courtesy of N R Omell Gallery)

the Tagus, many of which show people being rescued. According to the lieutenant's log, *Britannia* (100) 'sent our boats to assist the Bombay Castle' on 24 December 1796. On 28 December, the log indicates that the sea was breaking over *Bombay Castle* and the people were taken off.[7] The log book from *Caroline* puts her 111 miles off Cape Finisterre on 28 December. Thomas Buttersworth almost certainly did not see the rescue first-hand, but George Buttersworth was serving onboard *Britannia* at the time and presumably saw it all. In 1804, a published engraving indicates that Buttersworth did the original painting from a sketch by 'an officer.'[8] This shows that he was able to use his first-hand knowledge of ships to execute accurate paintings from descriptions or sketches supplied by others.

Many of the watercolours Buttersworth completed during his time on *Caroline* were views which he did see first-hand, and for days at a time. For example, there are at least eight watercolours of the Blockade of Cadiz, many of them dated 1797. *Caroline*'s log book indicates that for all of June 1797, she was with the fleet off Cadiz. No doubt many of these paintings were done on the spot. Similarly, there are numerous paintings of the fleet in the mouth of the Tagus River in Lisbon, where Buttersworth spent months during his years on *Caroline*. After he left the navy and began to paint more oil paintings, Buttersworth returned to the scenes he knew so well. There are at least sixty-nine views of Lisbon and almost as many miscellaneous Mediterranean views.

In March 1800 Buttersworth was promoted to midshipman. It was a short-lived promotion, because at the end of May he was sent to hospital in Port Mahon, and subsequently invalided out of the service. It has been suggested that there is some mystery about this, but that seems to be confusion about the dates involved.[9] William Bowen, then captain of *Caroline*, noted in his log book on 28 May, 'sent 2 men to the hospital.' At the time, the frigate was moored in Port Mahon.[10] There is a corresponding entry in the muster book from Port Mahon Hospital, which indicates Buttersworth was admitted with an ulcered leg, then discharged to *Resource* (28) to be sent home.[11] Finally, the muster book from *Resource* lists Thomas Buttersworth under the supernumeraries for passage to England and states that he was discharged on 16 August 1800.[12]

Thomas Buttersworth, *Wellesley (74) off Cape Town*, signed, c1815, oil on canvas, 16 x 25in, private collection. There is no evidence to suggest that Buttersworth was ever in Cape Town, but this view of Table Mountain was well-known and often used as a background for ship portraits. (Photograph courtesy of N R Omell Gallery)

Having been discharged at Spithead, Buttersworth eventually made his way to London, rather than returning to the Isle of Wight. By 1800, both his parents were dead. His sister Mary had inherited all the properties in Cowes, and presumably Buttersworth decided his best chance of making a living from his artwork was to go to London.[13]

The first certain date that places Buttersworth in London is 28 October 1801, when he married Martha Snelgrove in Lambeth. Almost a year later, his daughter Martha was baptised at St Mary's, Lambeth, implying that the family was still living in Lambeth. Dated watercolours from 1800 and 1801 indicate that Buttersworth was painting. As yet, there is no evidence that he had any other source of income. It is difficult to know exactly how many paintings Buttersworth produced in any given year, as he rarely dated his oil paintings. Of roughly 550 known oil paintings, only 3 per cent are dated. He dated almost 50 per cent of his watercolours, but there are far fewer of them, only sixty-seven identified so far.

By 26 November 1802, Buttersworth had moved his new family to Little St Martin's Lane, in the parish of St Anne's, Soho.[14] Little St Martin's Lane ran north off St Martin's Lane, an area which had been very popular with artists in the eighteenth century. The street had been home to an artists' academy where the likes of Hogarth, Gainsborough and Reynolds had worked. Rudolph Ackermann started his engraving business in nearby Long Acre, Thomas Chippendale ran his furniture business on St Martin's Lane, and Old Slaughter's Coffee House was a regular meeting place for artists.[15] By the time Buttersworth moved there, the academy was gone and Ackermann had moved to the Strand, but it is clear that he was trying to position himself in a better place from which to conduct his new business. He may have had prize money and back wages from his time in the navy, but he almost certainly could not afford a more fashionable address.

On 11 July 1803 a second daughter, Mary Caroline, was baptised at St Anne's. Buttersworth appears to have run into financial trouble in the following months and by May of the next year, it appears he was in debtors' prison. A burial record for his daughter Martha, at St George the Martyr, Southwark, describes Buttersworth as being 'of the Marshalsea.'[16] No commitment books for this time period have been found for the Marshalsea, but there is not much doubt. Buttersworth struggled financially for his entire life, and ended up in debtors' prison on at least two more occasions.

There are few sources which pinpoint Buttersworth's addresses over the years, but everything that does exist places him in London, mostly south of the river. From about 1809 to 1818 the family had a relatively settled existence, living for three or four years at a time at two different addresses,

Glass House Yard and Goldens Place, both in Lambeth. By 1820, there had been at least eight children, though two had died quite young. Buttersworth's wife, Martha, ended her days in the workhouse, and it is those records which indicate that after leaving Goldens Place, the family entered another time of instability.[17]

Moving around so frequently must have made it difficult for Buttersworth to work, but he continued to paint. All indications are that he maintained naval connections, or even developed new contacts with various naval personnel, including Admiral Nelson. There are three engravings, published in 1802, which show clearly that Buttersworth had some dealings with Nelson. The first, published on 16 March 1802, shows a profile of Nelson's head, surrounded by twenty-six different ships. Along the bottom are four small battle scenes, the last being the Battle of Copenhagen (1801).[18] It is this print, drawn, painted and partially engraved by Buttersworth, which is the subject of notes which Nelson wrote, probably in 1801 or early 1802, describing the number of guns on each ship, how the ships should be positioned and which portrait of himself to use.[19] These notes have been described as a letter written to Buttersworth, but there is no salutation, no signature, and it is part of a collection of manuscripts sent to Emma Hamilton. It is more likely that Nelson sent these notes to Lady Hamilton and had her pass along the information.

In July 1802 Thomas Williamson published an engraving of the Blockade of Cadiz, 'taken from an original drawing by T Buttersworth now in his Lordship's possession.'[20] Similarly, in August 1802 Williamson published another engraving of a Buttersworth painting, 'in the possession of his Lordship.'[21] Nelson is known to have been interested in promoting himself and it seems he found a willing collaborator in Buttersworth.

Perhaps the clearest indication of Buttersworth's contact with Nelson comes from 1805. On 6 November 1805, the day Londoners were reeling from the news of Nelson's death, Buttersworth and George Andrews published two engravings. One, depicting the battle of El Muros Fort in June 1805, was dedicated to Nelson, 'by permission of his Lordship previous to his going to attack the combined fleets by his much obliged & humble servant T Buttersworth.'[22] In some ways, this dedication raises as many questions as it answers. Nelson was not involved in the action of El Muros, and it is not clear why Buttersworth would have asked for permission to dedicate the print to him. Also, it implies that Buttersworth met with Nelson in the few weeks that Nelson was back in England before Trafalgar. This is further suggested by a note from Nelson to his bankers, dated 13 September 1805, which directs Marsh and Creed to pay

Buttersworth fifteen guineas when he delivered the 100 prints of 'my ships and head' to Lady Hamilton.[23] The other engraving which Buttersworth and Andrews published on 6 November was a second version of Nelson's head surrounded by ships. Clearly, there had already been an agreement to publish a new edition of the 1802 engraving. Buttersworth was no doubt devastated by the news of Nelson's death, but businessman enough to know that the sooner the prints were published, the better.

Another interesting point about the note to Nelson's bankers is that it mentions a price. It is the only information yet found about what Buttersworth was paid for any of his work. It is quite possible that because it was Nelson, and because it was a large order, the price may have been low. In his book on the business of art in nineteenth-century Britain, James Hamilton cites an example where artist and engraver John Buckler charged a guinea for an uncoloured engraving and one and a half guineas for a coloured one, in 1800.[24]

It is impossible not to speculate about how Buttersworth's life might have differed if Nelson had lived. Much of naval life and the artistic world in London was based on personal connections. There is nothing to suggest that Buttersworth had any really powerful connections in either world. The art world was very much dominated by the Royal Academy, and maritime art was not terribly popular. In 1813 Buttersworth exhibited a painting of Trafalgar at the Royal Academy's annual exhibition. There were 766 pictures on show that year, but only twenty-three were marine paintings. Most of those were not done by artists, like Buttersworth, who painted primarily maritime scenes.

This bias against marine paintings was even more evident in 1825 when Buttersworth exhibited at the British Institution. That year, the institution put out a call for paintings of Trafalgar and the Battle of the Nile. Even so, there were only thirty-seven paintings of the two battles, out of a total of 375 paintings in the exhibit. A notice of the exhibit in a Manchester paper reveals what may have been a common attitude toward marine paintings. 'This absurd superabundance of sea fights arises from the Directors having had the folly to propose no less than four premiums for the best representations of the victories of the Nile and Trafalgar.'[25] In addition to a lack of interest from the general public, Buttersworth also faced stiff competition from other marine artists. Some of the more well-known include Thomas Whitcombe, William Anderson, William J Huggins and J T Serres, all of whom were in London. There were also a number of artists outside London, such as Thomas Luny in Devon.

In spite of this, it appears that Buttersworth worked on commission

Thomas Buttersworth, del, Plate of Ships Captured by Nelson 1793–1805, published by G Andrews and T Buttersworth, 6 November 1805. (Sim Comfort Collection)

through his naval connections. For example, he produced a painting of Admiral Troubridge's squadron leaving Spithead, a painting which still belongs to the family and was no doubt a commissioned work.[26] Through the years, both watercolours and oil paintings have come up for auction with established provenance back to people such as Earl St Vincent and Captain Montgomerie Hamilton.[27] At the same time, he also followed current events and produced paintings which would have a wider potential audience. In those cases, he often did numerous versions of the same event. In addition to famous battles like Trafalgar and Cape St Vincent, Buttersworth produced multiple paintings of events like the shipwreck of the East Indiaman *Kent* in 1806. The heroic rescue of most of the passengers captured the public's attention and Buttersworth no doubt saw potential sales. He painted at least thirteen views of the wreck of the East Indiamen *Britannia* and *Admiral Gardner*. Similarly, he painted at least twelve versions of King George IV's arrival in Leith in 1822. Even an artist

Thomas Buttersworth, *Smugglers' Cutter engaging Customs brig off the Isle of Wight*, signed, c1810, oil on canvas, 17 × 21in, private collection. Buttersworth painted various smuggling scenes more than any other marine artist. Almost all are off the Isle of Wight and many show armed conflict with customs men. (Photograph courtesy of N R Omell Gallery)

Thomas Buttersworth, *Wreck of Bombay Castle off Lisbon 1796*, signed, c1810, oil on canvas, 12 × 16in, private collection. Contemporary accounts of the wreck of *Bombay Castle* indicate that the ship was in trouble for days before the decision was taken to abandon her. In this view, Buttersworth shows the crew being rescued. (Photograph courtesy of N R Omell Gallery)

as successful as J M W Turner considered the royal visit significant enough to warrant a visit to Scotland to record the event, so Buttersworth was in good company. During the War of 1812, Buttersworth produced at least fifteen paintings of various battles.

When he was not working on commission, or recording famous battles and shipwrecks, Buttersworth painted general shipping scenes, showing vessels off Spithead, Dover, the Seven Sisters and other backgrounds which would be well-known to the general public.

In addition to the many paintings of Lisbon and the Mediterranean, there are a few themes to which Buttersworth returned again and again. In addition to the famous shipwrecks already mentioned, Buttersworth painted numerous versions of a ship foundering off the southern coast of the Isle of Wight. The ship is not identified and the paintings found so far have never had a name associated with them. In all, he did over fifty paintings of shipwrecks, not counting those in Lisbon.

Another theme he returned to frequently was smuggling. There are over fifty different paintings of various smuggling scenes. Many show revenue or customs boats chasing smugglers or smugglers firing on customs officials. Having grown up on the Isle of Wight, it is certain that Buttersworth knew as much, if not more, about smuggling as any marine artist. Along with Cornwall and Kent, the Isle of Wight was a hotbed of smuggling activity, particularly in the latter half of the eighteenth century. It is not clear exactly what connection Buttersworth had and, although no records have yet been found, it is not impossible that he worked for the customs or revenue service at some point. His father, James Buttersworth, served as a churchwarden with Thomas Francis, who worked for the customs service as a tide surveyor. Such a connection would have made it easier for Thomas Buttersworth to get a job. Interestingly, one of the largest private collections of Buttersworth's paintings identified so far belonged to a man named Thomas Watson, who worked in the London Customs House. After his death, his wife donated thirty-two Buttersworth paintings to the Royal United Services Institution. The collection was later broken up and auctioned off through Sotheby's in 1973 and 1974.

In 1837, at sixty-nine years old, Thomas Buttersworth was old and not well, all but one of his children had left home, and his daughters were married and raising families of their own. Both his sons, Thomas (1807–1842) and James Edward (1817–1894), inherited their father's skill and became well-known marine artists. James Edward in particular is regarded among the foremost portraitists of American nineteenth-century ships. In May 1837 Buttersworth was granted a place at

Greenwich Royal Naval Hospital. His brother George had become a pensioner there two years earlier.

For many years, there has been some confusion about when exactly Thomas Buttersworth senior died. This confusion stemmed from uncertainty whether there were two marine painters named Thomas Buttersworth.[28] A careful examination of the relevant records allows the record to be set straight. Thomas Buttersworth senior was baptised on 6 May 1768, and recent research shows that Thomas Buttersworth junior was baptised on 1 May 1816. Indeed, Thomas junior's baptismal record shows his birth date as 7 November 1807 and his father as Thomas, a painter.[29] Both Thomases painted and their style was similar, but both were inconsistent about how they signed their paintings, if they signed at all. The 1841 census records show Thomas senior living at the naval hospital in Greenwich, and Thomas junior living with his family in the town of Greenwich. Again, recent research shows that Thomas junior died in his prime on 25 November 1842,[30] while Thomas senior died at old age in the hospital on 19 August 1841 and was buried there on 27 August 1841.[31]

Bombay Castle off Lisbon, see colour plate 10
Royal visit to Scotland, see colour plate 11
Brigantine off Dover, see colour plate 12

Thomas Buttersworth, *Battle of Cape St Vincent*, signed, c1805, oil on canvas, 16 × 24in, private collection. Buttersworth did numerous versions of this famous battle, in both watercolours and oils. This version is somewhat unusual in that it shows a very late stage of the battle, after *San Josef* and *San Nicolo* have been captured. (Photograph courtesy of Vallejo Maritime Gallery)

Port Mahon under
Admiral Fremantle 1810–11

Tom D Fremantle

After Trafalgar

After Trafalgar, Admiral Collingwood's attention most immediately focused on Cadiz, before recognising that he had to change himself from being second in command of a fleet to being a major player in the complex diplomacy of the Mediterranean. His treatment of the Spanish prisoners after Trafalgar had been commended and appreciated for its humanity and he had struck up a warm relationship with the Marquis de la Solana, Captain General of Andalucia,[1] which must have contributed subsequently to Anglo-Spanish relationships. Towards the end of the decade when the Spanish rebelled against the French, Cadiz became the base of the Spanish Junta and therefore a very important point of diplomatic contact.

During 1808 French fleets had escaped from Rochefort and Toulon, and the Spanish from Cartagena, but after causing Collingwood a few months of frantic activity and worry, the French had returned to Toulon, and the Spaniards were found in Port Mahon secure but unready for sea.[2] Collingwood returned to blockading Toulon, but took a strategic decision to lay his ships further away from Toulon, on a line from Menorca north-northwest to the Spanish Cabo San Sebastian. Meanwhile, the Spanish Junta in Cadiz had given command of the Balearics to the seventy-year-old General Cuesta, based in Majorca. Port Mahon would, once again, become a valuable base from which the British could sustain their blockading fleet.

The small island garrison, of doubtful loyalty, was threatened by the French army which dominated mainland Spain, but nonetheless the friendly population of the island made the British ships welcome and provided a valuable haven for Collingwood, whose name is greatly revered there even today. He is said to have lived ashore in a house, now converted into an hotel, which overlooks the Isla del Rey and the naval hospital.

The strain of the Toulon blockade and the responsibilities for diplomacy placed upon him by the British government took its toll on Collingwood's health as his repeated requests to return home were refused. Three days after permission arrived, he died in March 1810. Admiral Sir Charles Cotton succeeded Collingwood as commander-in-chief.

Fremantle returns to the Mediterranean

Meanwhile, Captain Thomas Fremantle had remained in *Neptune* (98), on station off Cadiz until ordered home, and arrived in Portsmouth in October 1806. He had become MP for Sandwich and had been appointed a Lord of the Admiralty, although turmoil within the government following the death of William Pitt meant that his appointment only lasted a few months. He was then given command of one of the royal yachts, the *William and Mary*, a more or less nominal post but one which secured an extra £500 a year.[3] In July 1810 Fremantle was promoted rear-admiral and on 27 August was ordered to embark in the *Fortunee* and report to Sir Charles Cotton in the Mediterranean.[4] Arriving on station in early October, he hoisted his flag in *Ville de Paris* (110), previously Collingwood's flagship; his ten-year-old son Charles accompanied him (later to be responsible for the family name being used for the port of Western Australia – see also 'A Boy in Battle' in this edition of the *Trafalgar Chronicle*).[5]

As early as 20 October, Fremantle is writing home asking his wife, Betsey, to inform Lord Buckingham that 'Cotton is incapable of governing his fleet, jealous of Hood, led by his secretary – Hood is led by Hallowell who abuses Cotton publicly'.[6] The Fremantle archive contains letters which describe the problems of keeping station during the winter gales, maintaining a fleet ready for battle, and harassing French armies in Catalonia, Naples, and the Adriatic, and negotiating with governments and rebels throughout the Mediterranean. There are also many orders, specific and general, which were issued by Cotton and provide a fascinating insight into the practical administration of the fleet. Cotton, in *San Josef* (114), spent some time at Mahon, which had become the main base for the fleet blockading Toulon, and provided support to the Spanish army in its fight with the French.

After only a week or two with the blockading fleet, Fremantle must have requested permission to take the *Ville de Paris* for much needed repairs, but found himself rebuffed by Cotton on 29 October 1810:[7]

I have the honour to acknowledge receipt of your letter of this date, representing the state of his Majesty's ship bearing your flag; I have to state in return thereto that your wants shall be supplied as far as the services in the fleet will admit, until the stores demanded shall arrive from the dock yards. I must at the same time remark that the state of the enemy in Toulon renders it impossible that the services of the Ville de Paris can be dispensed with at the present moment however desirable and necessary her defects may make her proceeding to one of the dockyards in this country.

In his letter off Toulon to his wife on 30 October, he blamed Cotton for lack of clothing for his men, and 'we are without a nail, a foot of plank or a fathom of rope spare in case of accident.'[8] His own journal records that on the same day he 'wrote again to Cotton' and that '*Temeraire, Resistance* and *Invincible* have sprung their main masts.'[9]

Arriving in Port Mahon

Notwithstanding Cotton's letter above on 5 November, he took *Ville de Paris* through the 150yd-wide channel into Port Mahon in a gale, and using ropes and cables warped up to a position 150yds from either shore for a refit. He found several Spanish battleships in harbour and gave dinner to two admirals and twenty-six captains. He told Betsey, his wife, that he had found half a dozen tolerable Spanish ladies to visit ashore (to learn the local language!) including a Madame Bourke, a general's wife from Galicia. He and his fellow officers tried their hands at dancing the *contradansa espanola* (ie *contradanza española*) at the Posada Alexandre, but were like 'logs in armour', compared with the graceful and beautiful Spanish ladies, but he was shocked by their conversation![10]

Fremantle found the island lacking not only a reliable garrison, but a skilled dockyard workforce, and the raw materials to keep the ships in good repair, particularly timber. Shortly after arriving in Port Mahon, he issued an order for operating the dockyard, covering the hours of work and the required behaviour of the dockyard workers.[11] In summer, workers' hours were 6–11.30am and 2.30–7pm, whilst in winter work ceased at sunset. The orders make it clear that the work in the dockyard must be devoted entirely to English vessels: 'Care is to be taken that none of the men are employed on the Spanish Ships lying near the Dock Yard or in any Store house, or at any work whatever for the Spanish Government unless expressly ordered by the Admiral'. Although far briefer than the sort of orders which might be issued today, there are some detailed points, such as the prohibition on 'the practice of boats crews landing at the mast house to spread their wet clothes to dry etc. on the top of the Sheds'. Furthermore, neither 'workmen nor water Casks from any of the Ships to be landed without an Order from the Admiral, unless the case shall be deemed urgent, when it is to be left to the discretion of the Builder'. It is apparent from another order issued by Fremantle on 11 April 1811 that the 'Builder' is a Mr Josh Jay who was 'required to take upon [him] the entire management and control of all the work to be conducted in the Dock Yard'.[12]

The island's defence

From the outset, Fremantle was very concerned at the lack of loyal land-based defences against the possibility of insurrection or even invasion. In a letter to his brother on 5 January 1811, he bemoaned the fact that 'there are not more than 600 Spanish troops here and melancholy to say one half of these are French men who have been made prisoners, and now serving in the Walloons (Walloon Guards)'.[13]

Defence of the island against attack by French forces from Catalonia was a constant worry to Fremantle. He doubtless was aware of the ease with which Commodore John Duckworth, leading a combined operation, had taken the island in November 1798. General Charles Stuart, described by Sugden as 'one of the few senior army officers whose energy, talent and volatility were comparable with the admiral's [Nelson's] own',[14] landed at Addya Creek (Port d'Addaia) on the northeast coast of the island on 7 November, and Colonel Paget took the formidable Fort San Carlos north of the entrance to Port Mahon with a force of only three hundred men. Within ten days the island had fallen, and some four thousand Spanish troops had surrendered, together with four frigates and their crews.[15]

Amongst other things, he had responsibility for guarding the French prisoners on the island of Cabrera, southeast of Palma, Majorca (now an uninhabited national park), as well as ensuring the overall defence of Menorca. The questionable loyalty of the Walloon garrison was but one issue, for in a long letter dated 4 January 1811, Fremantle cast doubt on the loyalty of the governor, Commodore Posada, who had fought against Admiral Howe in 1782, and was influenced by his French secretary, de May, whose brother was captain of the port at Barcelona under French occupation. Fremantle urged Cotton to ask Henry Wellesley, British ambassador to the Spanish Junta at Cadiz, to get the governor removed and to reinforce the garrison with British troops.[16]

Relationships with the Spanish authorities in Menorca generally appear to have been good, but in January 1811 Fremantle complained that 'riding yesterday with Captains Blackwood and Otway to the mouth of the harbour to the fort near St Phillips the centinel presented his musket with an intention of impeding the entrance of the said officers, though in their uniform at the time.' Cotton wrote a firmly worded letter to Major-General de Villava, whose reply was apologetic and cordial, promising to chastise 'the centinel with the rigour he deserves, as well as the commanding officer of the post, for not having obeyed his repeated orders of respect and every liberty to the gentleman officers of his Britannic Majesty.' Villava excused the behaviour, explaining 'the troops of that detachment are of the militia of Majorca, little instructed, and of a very poor military education, as they never have left their firesides before.' A closing letter from Cotton backs off and concludes, 'I far from wish that the man should be punished but only admonished against a recurrence of such conduct.'[17]

In April 1811 Major-General Samford Whittingham, who had been sent by the Spanish to Majorca to raise troops, wrote at length to Cotton, drawing attention to the dangers presented by the eighty-five French officers:[18]

> Confined in the Castle of Bellver, and who find ways and means to visit constantly their friends in this town ... These men at the head of 4000 prisoners at Cabrera would I fear find a considerable support in the country.

Whittingham's letter also makes reference to a food shortage, and begs help from Cotton in respect of the arms provided by the British government:

> Not having received ammunition with the arms sent by the British Government for the use of this army, I take the liberty of requesting you will have the goodness to inform me if it be in your power to supply me with any quantity of powder, as in such case, I can order the cartridges to be made up under the direction of the Commanding Officer of the Artillery, and as the musquets [sic] are some English and some foreign, and consequently of different calibres this would be the most convenient mode of passing the ammunition.

Activity in Port Mahon

The dockyard at Port Mahon must have been a very busy place. On 5 January Fremantle noted that there were '18 sail of the line here.' It is unclear whether this number included the 'eight good Spanish ships of the line', and he again expressed his anxiety that the French, having established themselves in Catalonia could, whilst the British fleet was elsewhere, 'take this island by a coup de main and turn all this force against us.'[19] He had plans in place to destroy the Spanish ships if an invasion were to take place.

By March 1811, Cotton seems finally to have recognised the value of having Fremantle based at Port Mahon. On 22 March he wrote:

Vice-Admiral Sir Thomas Fremantle, by Edmund Scriven. (Lord Cottesloe)

Whereas I think it expeditious that you should remain here with his Majesty's ship bearing your flag [in] the *Bombay*, until further order, for the purpose of the cooperation by all means in your power, to the governor, for the safety and defence of the island of Menorca against any attempts the enemy. You are hereby required and directed to continue here for the above-mentioned purpose.[20]

On 15 May, as the east coast of Spain fell to the French under General Suchet, Fremantle ordered the Agent Victualler to load the transports *Maria* and *Augusta* with 52,976lbs of bread, plus rice and oatmeal, for the relief of Tarragona, and on 31 May he offered *Warspite* (76) (Captain Blackwood) to General Cuesta in Majorca to carry more troops and supplies, but by 11 June the ship was back in Mahon, having failed in that mission. Fremantle predicted to Cotton that the city would fall and that he would need three ships of the line and a frigate to protect the island. Fremantle had written anxiously to Cotton on 3 June about the 'inundation of poor creatures' fleeing from the city and that the threat to the island was exacerbated, because 'the regiment of Walloons seem daily to be more disinclined to the English'. Nevertheless, when Tarragona fell on 28 June, the French massacred men, women, and children, and set the town on fire.[21]

The day after the fall of the city Thomas wrote to his brother William, again criticising his boss, 'I confess I am somewhat surprized that none of our Naval heroes who have been there have had a single seaman in the batteries, I am quite assured there was a field for a Man of enterprise to have done something, but the want of energy on the part of our chief certainly dampens the ardour of others.'[22] The 1,350 British troops under Colonel Skerritt, who had been sent too late from Gibraltar to assist in the defence of Tarragona, arrived there too late for the action and arrived instead in Menorca to replenish their water. Skerrit agreed to land seven hundred men, but the following day it was decided that Wellington had a greater need for them, and they re-embarked and returned to Gibraltar.[23]

Timber, spars and water
Fremantle was very aware of the need for good quality timber, not only locally, but back in the English shipyards which had been denied Baltic supplies as a result of the Napoleonic Continental system. So when the Spanish Commodore Posada announced a sale of timber in order to be able to buy victuals for his sailors, Fremantle believed that two valuable ends could be satisfied at once by buying the timber and sending it home, and thereby helping to ensure the loyalty and friendship of Posada. He

reported the purchase to Cotton on 10 May from *Rodney* (96), to which he had shifted his flag. He received a frosty reply: 'Nothing could induce me to sanction a proceeding which has already been refused us by the Government of Spain, upon application of His Majesty's Minister at Cadiz to purchase the stores in the arsenal at Carthagena for British purposes.'[24]

Despite this, the purchase seemed to go ahead. (Timber was still an issue after Sir Edward Pellew had assumed command from Cotton in July, and he wrote to Fremantle on 2 August stressing the importance of maintaining good relations to reassure the 'Spanish Commodore [Posada] may be perfectly satisfied that no interference on our part has been intended.'[25])

Mr Felton, the agent victualler, and Mr Jay, the dockyard superintendent, were the two people who were most likely to be carrying out the detailed instructions regarding the repairs, re-equipping and stocking the ships which regularly passed through Port Mahon. Mr Motta, the consul, was also deeply involved, and specific mention is made of arranging payments and generally looking after the Spanish artificers sent from Cartagena. A detailed list of merchant vessels shows spars, planks and anchors to be loaded, and another order concerns the need to cut a 'safe port' in a vessel, 'to admit of her receiving the largest sized spars now remaining at Carthagena 75 to 97 feet in length and from 24 to 36 inches in diameter.'[26] Spars were self-evidently of critical importance; a letter from Cotton to Fremantle mentions that the mast which had been provided for the *Temeraire* (98) had, in fact, been used for the *Warspite*, and requiring a rapid replacement.[27] A later communication encloses a list of spars and timber required which lists main topsail yards for *Bombay* (84), *Rodney* and *Ville de Paris*, and adds 'a quantity of oak and elm board to repair boats.'[28]

Supplies of fresh water were, not surprisingly, a major concern to the captains of the ships on blockade off Toulon, and there was a continual flow of transports and brigs between Mahon and the fleet, carrying despatches and casks of water with other supplies, and returning with empty casks to be refilled. On 6 November Cotton wrote to Fremantle:

> The agent victualler shall be directed to provide Coopers for the repair of the water casks of the Ville de Paris in addition to your own Coopers. And if it should be necessary to land casks, the same must be done at the dockyard with previous permission of the Spanish Commodore.

A letter from Cotton six months later suggests that Posada had not been as obliging as Fremantle would have expected concerning the filling of water casks: 'I hope the reply you have given Commodore Posada regarding the casks will have the effect of convincing him that we are not to be trifled with: and that the remaining casks will be filled in readiness to forward by the first opportunity to the fleet.'[29] Again, on 9 June, Cotton complained about water: 'Of the last supply of water several of the casks had leaked partly, and some entirely out, owing to their defective state. You will be pleased therefore to give particular directions that the casks sent in lately may be effectually repaired and as possible before they are filled.'[30]

The recruitment of skilled men for the dockyard was also discussed and it is evident that a number were recruited from Cartagena, initially under a two-month contract to the Royal Navy. At the end of the period it was suggested that the Spanish might take over their employment, or that they might be diverted to the repair of merchant vessels. But Cotton was careful to add a caution: 'Should however any difficulty arise in the payment of these artificers by the Spanish authorities as aforesaid it is desirable that the present measures should be again resorted to, rather than they should be disencouraged, and have reason to complain of their removal from Carthagena.'[31]

Naval personnel

Matters of personnel did not escape attention. A general memorandum from Cotton criticises the practice of appointing boys, sent to sea by the Marine Society, as personal servants to junior and non-commissioned officers, and then holding them in that role rather than allowing them to be rated 'landsmen'. Cotton wrote: 'It is my positive direction that practices so prejudicial to the public service be discontinued [...] that the boys may be brought forward to seamen's duties as early as may be.'[32]

Other papers include detailed description of three allegedly American seamen taken from a French privateer, but suspected of being deserters from British ships. A twenty-year-old is described as having 'flaxen hair cropped, grey eyes, a little freckled common nose, ears pierced.'[33] In March, Cotton orders Fremantle to convene a court martial of the lieutenant of a sloop *Philomel* (18), who whilst officer of the guard at Malta was alleged to have committed 'disorderly conduct unbecoming the character of an officer and having been discovered in a disgraceful state of intoxication.'[34]

Amongst the course of the business of keeping a fleet at sea, Fremantle's rather patchy journal records brief details of other activities, some of which are clearly recreational. 'Dined at Madame's ... played whist late. A young Lt. of the Kent was stabbed at a masquerade.' (19 January); 'gave a ball onboard to 350 people which went off very well.' (11 February); 'Dined with the Duchess of Orleans, rather pleasant.'(26 March).[35]

Change of commander-in-chief

It was considerably to Fremantle's relief that Admiral Sir Edward Pellew arrived on 10 July, and succeeded Cotton as commander-in-chief on 16 July. Fremantle reported spending a whole day showing Sir Edward around Port Mahon, and discussing Mediterranean matters more generally, during which he was told to await the arrival of the new second in command, Vice-Admiral Sir Richard Keats, and then to take command in Sicily with the Adriatic squadron. On 2 August Pellew gave Fremantle orders to hand affairs in Menorca to Admiral Pickmore and concluded his letter: 'In relinquishing the charge of the naval services at Port Mahon I cannot refuse myself the satisfaction of expressing my sense of your zealous and uniform attention to the public interests confided to your superintendence there, which had obtained the fullest approbation of my predecessor in this command.'[36] And to the Secretary to the Admiralty he wrote: 'On arriving at Menorca, I have found Rear Admiral Fremantle in charge of the Port duties, and every thing under his authority in such excellent order, that I have not interfered in any manner with his arrangements.'[37]

Whilst this ended Fremantle's engagement with Menorca, the island and Port Mahon clearly continued to be a valuable resource to the Royal Navy until the end of the war in 1815. Once there was no need to support a blockading fleet off Toulon, the dockyards at Gibraltar and Malta were able to satisfy British demand for repair facilities, and the significance of Port Mahon to the British declined.

Sir Richard Strachan

Mark West

Cape Ortegal

Of the ships which fought at Trafalgar, only two survived until the twentieth century, one the *Victory* (100), and the other a vessel which had fought in the Combined Fleet under the French tricolour on 21 October 1805.[1] The *Victory*, of course, rests in dry dock at Portsmouth. Of the other vessel, all that remains is her stern gallery on the wall of the Neptune Gallery at the National Maritime Museum, and her capstan in the naval museum at Rochefort. That other ship was the *Duguay-Trouin* (74) (Captain Claude Touffet), which was part of Rear-Admiral Dumanoir le Pelley's van squadron at Trafalgar, and which escaped the annihilation of the Combined Fleet in the company of Dumanoir's own flagship, the *Formidable* (80) (Captain Jean-Marie Letellier), the *Scipion* (74) (Captain Charles Berrenger) and the *Mont Blanc* (74) (Captain Guillaume-Jean-Noël de Lavillegris). Yet on 4 November 1805 all four of the French ships were brought to battle off Cape Ortegal by a squadron of four ships of the line and four frigates, commanded by Commodore Sir Richard Strachan (mounting a total of 444 guns to the French 287), and all were captured, Captain Touffet being killed in the battle. The British lost twenty-four men killed and 111 wounded, the French, 730. The four captured ships were duly commissioned into the Royal Navy, the *Duguay-Trouin* as HMS *Implacable*.[2]

Under her new colours, the *Implacable* served in the Baltic in 1808 and captured the Russian ship *Vsevolod* (74). She saw service off France, Spain, Cuba and Mexico, and took part in the bombardment of Acre in 1840, finally being converted into a training ship for boys in 1860. In the aftermath of the Second World War, and given the post-war austerity, the British government decided against the cost of her restoration, which was estimated at £150,000, with another £50,000 for re-rigging (in today's terms, £4.58 million and £1.53 million for rigging).[3] The *Implacable* was offered back to France in 1947, but the offer was politely declined by the equally cash-strapped French, although the ship's capstan was removed and taken to the naval museum in Rochefort. On 2 December 1949 the last but one

184

survivor of Trafalgar was towed out, under British and French ensigns, into the English Channel to a position five miles off Ventnor and scuttled at 1.45pm with 500 tons of pig iron in the hold as ballast.[4] Yet for three hours she still would not sink, and was finally sunk only after the tug *Alligator* rammed her repeatedly. Parts of the ship eventually washed up on the beach at Dunkirk. The outraged public reaction to the 'criminal action against the maritime history of Britain' did, however, force the government to support the preservation of the *Cutty Sark*.[5]

The man and his naval career

Sir Richard John Strachan[6] was born in Devon on 27 October 1760, the eldest son of Lieutenant Patrick Strachan and Caroline Susanne, the daughter of Captain John Pitman.[7] His uncle was Sir John Strachan, the 3rd Baronet, who had captured the French privateer *Télémaque* (20) off Alicante on 8 July 1757 with the loss of 235 French and forty-eight British sailors.[8] He entered the navy in 1772 aboard *Intrepid* (64), in which he sailed to the East Indies, and then moved to *Orford* (70), commanded by his uncle. He was on the North American Station with Commodore William Hotham in *Preston* (50), *Eagle* (64) with Lord Howe, and in *Actaeon* (28) off the coast of Africa and in the East Indies. On the death of his uncle on 26 December 1777, he succeeded to the baronetcy. He was made lieutenant on 5 April 1779. Early in 1781 he was appointed to *Hero* (74) with Captain James Hawker, and fought in the abortive action against Suffren at Porto Praya, moving to *Magnanime* (64) and then *Superb* (74), in which he was present in the first of four of the actions between Suffren and Sir Edward Hughes, the Battle of Sadras, on 17 February 1782. Hughes appointed him to command the cutter *Lizard* (28) in January 1783, and on 26 April of that year to be captain of the frigate *Naiad* (38).

He took the ambassador to China, the Hon Charles Alan Cathcart, to his post in *Vestal* (28) in the spring of 1788, but Cathcart died en route and *Vestal* returned to England. The following year, *Vestal* was sent to the East Indies to join Commodore William Cornwallis's squadron, and in 1790 Strachan was appointed to command *Phoenix* (36). In November 1791, after a sharp action at Tellicherry off the western coast of India, he captured the French frigate *Résolue* (32) which, with a convoy of merchant vessels, was believed to be carrying military stores to Tipu Sultan. French losses totalled twenty-five men killed and sixty wounded, Strachan suffering just six killed and eleven wounded, but the action had occurred in peacetime; as no contraband could be found, Strachan had to tow the prize to Mahé and release her.[9]

Stern gallery of the *Formidable* on display at the
National Maritime Museum, Greenwich. (Author's photograph)

In 1793 Strachan returned to England and was appointed to the frigate *Concorde* (32). In the following spring he joined a squadron patrolling off Brest under the command of Sir John Borlase Warren. The squadron engaged a rival squadron of four French frigates on 23 April 1794 and succeeded in capturing three of them, Strachan in *Concorde* forcing the surrender of the frigate *Engageante* (38).[10] He was then appointed to *Melampus* (42), which was attached in the summer to the main British fleet. In the following spring, Strachan commanded a squadron of five frigates cruising off the Normandy and Brittany coasts, successfully capturing or destroying a number of French coastal craft, many laden with military stores and conveyed by armed French warships.

In 1796 Strachan was moved to *Diamond* (38), after her captain Sir Sidney Smith had been captured on a cutting-out expedition, and remained there until 1799 when he was appointed to *Captain* (74) and employed off the west coast of France, either alone or in command of a detached squadron. In 1802 he was appointed to *Donegal* (74) and during 1803/4 he was the senior officer at Gibraltar, charged with the watch of Cadiz under the orders of Nelson. In November 1804 the *Donegal* captured the Spanish frigate *Amfitrite* (42), carrying dispatches from Cadiz to Tenerife and Havana, and another Spanish vessel carrying a cargo reputedly worth over £200,000. On 23 March 1804 he was made a colonel of marines.[11] In March 1805 he returned to England, but was almost immediately appointed to *Caesar* (80), in which he commanded a detached squadron of four other line-of-battle ships[12] and two frigates[13] in the Bay of Biscay.

Strachan was promoted to the rank of rear-admiral of the blue on 9 November 1805.[14] On 28 January 1806, when the thanks of both Houses of Parliament were voted to those who had fought at Trafalgar, Strachan and his command were specially included. He was also, by private Act of Parliament, rewarded with a pension of £1,000 a year.[15] On 29 January he was created KCB[16] and the City of London voted him its freedom and awarded him a sword of honour.

Strachan was soon back in service, being dispatched early in 1806 to search for a French squadron reported to have sailed for America. After searching for some time, he failed to locate it and instead returned to watch the port of Rochefort. Thick fog and poor weather covered the port in January 1808, allowing the French to sail out undetected and escape to the Mediterranean. Strachan gave chase, joining Admiral Collingwood's forces, but the French were able to gain the safety of Toulon. Strachan was ordered to return home and was given command of a squadron watching the Dutch coast. On 9 June 1809 he was appointed naval commander of the immense expedition against the island of Walcheren and for the destruction of the French arsenals in the Scheldt; however:[17]

> Strachan was ill qualified either by experience or temperament for the joint command of such a large and complex combined operation. Attentive to the delays to his own service from bad weather, intricate channels, and a shortage of pilots, he was insufficiently appreciative of the problems of the army, and long before the expedition was abandoned his relations with the army commander, Chatham, had degenerated into acrimony. Nothing was achieved beyond the capture of Flushing, and the force's return home was the signal for an outbreak of angry recriminations.

Chatham presented a narrative to the King in 1810, blaming Strachan for the expedition's failure. Strachan defended himself, declaring that the ships had done all that had been required of them. He nevertheless became the scapegoat for the failure and was not given any more assignments. The fiasco led to the celebrated doggerel:

> Great Chatham, with his sabre drawn,
> Stood waiting for Sir Richard Strachan;
> Sir Richard, longing to be at 'em,
> Stood waiting for the Earl of Chatham.

After the defeat of Bonaparte and his temporary incarceration aboard *Bellerophon* (74) in 1815, Strachan set out to see the man he had spent most of his career fighting to defeat. Napoleon himself was apparently aware of Strachan's deeds:[18]

> On Thursday he (Napoleon Bonaparte) gratified the spectators with his appearance frequently on the poop and gangway, on which occasions the British, as well as the French officers, stood uncovered and apart! One of his officers intimating to him, that Sir Richard Strachan was in a barge alongside, Bonaparte instantly took off his hat, and bowed to him with a smile.

He was made a rear-admiral of the white on 28 April 1808, rear-admiral of the red on 25 October 1809,[19] vice-admiral of the blue on 31 July 1810,[20] vice-admiral of the white on 12 August 1812,[21] vice-admiral of the red on 4 June 1814,[22] and admiral of the white on 19 July 1821,[23] dying at his home in Bryanston Square on 3 February 1828.

Strachan's ungovernable temper and violent cursing earned him the nickname 'Mad Dick' among his men, but he was a popular and sought-after commander, known affectionately to others under his command as 'Sir Dicky'. Captain Graham Moore, the brother of Sir John Moore, described him on the eve of the Walcheren expedition as: 'One of those in our service whom I estimate the highest. I do not believe he has his fellow among the Admirals, unless it be Pellew, for ability, and it is not possible to have more zeal and gallantry.'[24] Despite the failure of the venture, he was later to declare that:[25]

> It is my wish to serve with Strachan, as I know him to be extremely brave and full of zeal and ardour, at the same time that he is an excellent

seaman, and, tho' an irregular, impetuous fellow, possessing very quick parts and an uncommon share of sagacity and strong sense.

Yet, for all his martial bravery, zeal and ardour, his domestic life was entirely different and the brazen conduct of his wife one of the scandals of the age.

The admiral's wife, her family and her daughters
In April 1812 he married Louisa Dillon (1783–1868). There was some question over her birth, as the writer Maria Edgeworth wrote to her correspondent Mary Sneyd on 21 November 1811:[26]

> Do you remember our telling you a story we heard from Mrs Moutray of a fair Incognita whom she met many years ago abroad, whose daughter is now living with [long deliberate blank]? The mystery of her birth has never been cleared up; but nevertheless she has conquered the heart of one of our conquering heroes, and is soon to be the bride of Sir Richd Strachan. Mrs M says she is not a woman of talents or beauty; but well brought up & pleasing. So ends that romance most happily for the heroine, but not satisfactorily for the curious.

There are, however, some suggestions, not yet proven, that she was the daughter of Count Arthur Dillon and his second wife, Marie-Françoise Laure de Girardin de Montgerald.[27]

If the link between Arthur Dillon and Louisa Dillon can be substantiated, it would mean that Sir Richard had a series of remarkable family connections to Revolutionary and Napoleonic France. Arthur Dillon (1750–1794) was an Englishman of Irish extraction born in Berkshire, the second son of Henry Dillon, 11th Viscount Dillon (1705–1787), also an army officer in French service. Arthur Dillon became a general in the French army, but fell into disfavour because of his ambivalent attitude to the overthrow of the monarchy and his association with Camille Desmoulins, and died on the guillotine on 14 April 1794, crying 'Vive le roi!'[28] That would make Sir Richard Strachan the only British admiral of the Revolutionary and Napoleonic Wars whose father-in-law is commemorated on the Arc de Triomphe.[29]

Arthur Dillon's second wife, Marie-Françoise Laure de Girardin de Montgerald, Comtesse de la Touche (1764–1817), was the second cousin of the Empress Josephine[30] (and had herself been the mistress of Alexandre de Beauharnais, Josephine's first husband, by whom she had had an illegitimate son).[31]

Moreover, Louisa Dillon's younger sister, Fanny (Françoise-Elizabeth Dillon) (1785–1836), was married to General Henri Bertrand (1773–1844), governor of Illyria and Grand Marshal of the Palace to none other than Napoleon Bonaparte. The Bertrands went with the former emperor to St Helena (after Fanny had tried to commit suicide by throwing herself out of the cabin windows of HMS *Bellerophon* when she found out where they were going),[32] and were by his bed when he died.

Together Sir Richard and Lady Louisa Strachan had three daughters, Matilda Frances (1813–1899), Charlotte Leopoldina (1815–1851) and Sarah Louise (1818–1881), who was born in Genoa and died there. But the marriage was not a success (on any footing), and Lady Strachan soon forsook her husband's bed and cuckolded him with, first, Sarah Elizabeth Greville, the 3rd Countess of Warwick (1786–1851), and then (or perhaps simultaneously) with Francis Seymour-Conway, Earl of Yarmouth and, from 1822, 3rd Marquess of Hertford (1777–1842),[33] as appears from a series of contemporary cartoons which leave absolutely nothing to the imagination. Given the circumstances, it is hardly surprising that the three girls were widely said to be the offspring of the earl (and later marquess) and Lady Strachan rather than the legitimate progeny of the admiral and his wife. Thus, according to Lady Charlotte Schreiber, speaking of the eldest daughter Matilda in later life, when she was Countess Berchtold, 'She is a natural daughter of old Lord Hertford's by Lady Strachan'.[34]

The Strachan cartoons

The first cartoon is titled *Amorous Ladys, or tete-a-tete ex Strachnary*, an uncoloured etching, possibly by William Heath, dated 9 June 1820.[35] Two ladies embrace, seated on a sofa, not noticing the entry of their husbands. One, Lady Strachan, says: 'You know my dear Sarah I love you very well yet I must reserve a few Kisses for the worthy old Ad-l.' Lady Warwick replies: 'Oh never mind him, my Sweet Louisa he's undeserving your embrace's and only fit for walking the Quarter Deck.' In the doorway is Sir Richard Strachan, in admiral's uniform, followed by Lord Warwick, indicated by a paper or pamphlet: 'Warwick Gude' [*sic*].

The second is entitled *Love- a- la- mode, or two dear friends*, a hand-coloured etching, unattributed, but also dated 1820.[36] In this image Lady Strachan and Lady Warwick embrace on a garden seat, in a park-like landscape; one says: 'Little does he imagine that he has a female rival.' The heads and shoulders of their husbands appear above bushes on the right. Strachan, in admiral's uniform, asks: 'What is to be done to put a stop to this disgraceful Business?'; Lord Warwick answers: 'Take her from Warwick'.

The third and last of this remarkable and explicit troika is called *Paul Pry's Extrachan-ary Peep into Piccadillo* ('Strachan' was pronounced 'Strawn'), another hand-coloured etching by Henry Heath, dated 29 May 1826.[37] Lord Hertford (Yarmouth) and Lady Strachan, holding Ovid's *Art of Love*, sit together on a sofa behind an ornate table, looking at Paul Pry (left), who stands holding hat and umbrella in his characteristic attitude. Hertford exclaims 'Cursed intruder!!' Paul Pry replies:

Beg pardon hope I don't intrude, merely drop't in to see who & who's together, snug Tete a Tete! eh? do as you'd be done by, that's the time of day, quite correct, a great change in affairs, fresh Election new Members—don't like Female Vote-ries prefer Hertford to Warwick eh? better prospects, move in Style now eh? plenty of Corn there, boxing the Compass, mind a Lee shore, dont sink the Admiral, fare Well, call again shortly don't mean to intrude no. no.—

On the wall are two pictures. On the left is a bust portrait of a naval officer, who is clearly meant to be Sir Richard Strachan, with Hertford's hat hung from the frame to hide his head. On the right is *The Death Blow to Augustus*: Hertford as Hercules with a huge club stands over a puny and dandified military officer whose sword he has snatched; the latter, falling back, exclaims: 'Merciless Wretch to use such power to crush a Worm.' On the table are two books: *All For Love* and *The Ruling Passion*. On the floor is an *Essay on Gambling Bed to the—[? King] D. York D. Devon &c &c.*

Lady Strachan and her daughters' marriages

Lady Strachan became the constant companion of the marquess during her husband's lifetime:[38]

For some time past, Lady Strachan, a forcible creature many years her husband's junior, had been the Marquis's principal mistress, figuring prominently in the house-parties at Sudbourne Hall, the Hertford mansion situated near the Suffolk coast. Being the most presentable person in the nobleman's constantly replenished harem, she was invariably numbered among his guests; whereas the other inmates, ranging from promoted maidservants to avowed harlots recruited from the continent, remained discreetly in the background. Sir Richard Strachan either noticed nothing in his wife's conduct to arouse his suspicions, or, which is much more probable, was that odious character, the complaisant husband. Most decent-minded people took him to be such, and avoided him on every possible occasion. That, in the winter of 1824, he should suddenly turn up for dinner at Sudbourne made Peel, who was one of the guests, feel decidedly uncomfortable. Apologising to Mrs Peel for having to ensure such 'disgusting' company, he remarked that it was now clear to him why Lord Hertford had not included her in the invitation.

On 23 July 1824 Hertford wrote to Sir Robert Peel that he had made a codicil to his will leaving him £50,000 absolutely, but on his honour to be applied and laid out as Lady Strachan of 21 Bryanston Square might wish, for her own separate benefit.

Bizarrely (but not entirely surprisingly if the girls were Hertford's children rather than his own), on his deathbed, Strachan named Hertford the guardian of his three daughters:[39]

His wife's future fully assured, Sir Richard Strachan, as we may well believe, died happy. His widow was not one to waste time in hypocritical mourning. Having seen her accommodating husband safely buried, she accompanied the Marquis on his travel abroad, and helped by her three daughters, Matilda, Charlotte and Louisa, to a large extent supervised his household ... That Lady Strachan and her three beautiful daughters should be properly dressed, he placed large sums of money to their credit, increasing the amounts when jewellery was required.

With the girls growing into women, and the Marquis's character progressively degenerating, it was obvious that the arrangement of all being under the one roof could not be indefinitely prolonged, even granted that the mother's presence was an insurance policy against unpleasant complications. First to break away was Matilda, the eldest daughter. She married Count Berchto'd, and more or less went out of her guardian's life.[40] Lady Strachan sighed for a real husband, and having bought an Italian title, that of the Marquess Salza, allowed herself to be wooed and won by a persistent suitor with the musical name of Pisolilli, whom the angry and abandoned Marquis chose to represent as a pure adventurer.

By 1830 Hertford had revoked all his bequests to Peel, but instead directed that his former mistress should receive the income produced by a trust fund of £60,000, but no more, explaining:[41]

Aware of the infamy of my successor's character, I wish her to be as little as possible in his power. Tho' he will, of course, rob her each quarter, yet, when she may quit him, she will be independent, and he will have no temptation to shorten her days.

Louisa, the youngest of the Strachan girls, thought it prudent to join her mother, but made the most glittering marriage, being married off to the Prince Antimo Ruffo and thus becoming an Italian princess.[42] Of the quartette, only Charlotte, in her eighteenth year, remained with Hertford, yet well able to look after herself. To her mother's business-like instinct, she added acumen of her own: for the companionship which she afforded Hertford, he was required to pay on a scale proportionate to his vast means. As the months went by, she wheedled out of him jewellery to the value of many thousands of pounds, besides large pecuniary gifts euphemistically described as 'pin money'. In all, not including the later benefactions which she would receive under his multifarious testamentary dispositions, 'this sharp-witted woman, luckiest of the wards', drew on Hertford's largesse to the extent of £70,000.

As an immensely rich young woman, she soon had innumerable suitors buzzing around her, amongst whom was Count Emanuel Zichy-Ferraris,[43] chamberlain to the Austrian emperor, who persuaded his sister, Princess Metternich, to take up his cause. The marquess consented to the marriage and they were duly married on 3 April 1837, conspicuous among the wedding gifts being a cheque for £20,000 from the bride's open-handed guardian, drawn on Coutts Bank. To minimise the inconvenience which her marriage had caused to the marquess, Charlotte agreed to stay with him for long periods of time, and her obliging husband was only too keen to agree. One morning the count found a cheque for £20,000 under his plate; on another, his wife was given £4,000 for the purchase of 'the finest pearl necklace and bracelet in London'. The countess reckoned it a poor day's spoils if all she managed to extort out of her pliant guardian was the price of a phaeton and four ponies.

The largesse continued in death. The marquess's convoluted testamentary dispositions were extraordinary. His last will, accompanied by no less than twenty-nine codicils, was made in Milan on 9 November 1839, and was largely an instrument of defamation, but under it the countess and her sisters stood to benefit by some £300,000. Disraeli offers the tantalising vignette that the countess stood to benefit so handsomely because she had saved the marquess from being poisoned by her mother.[44] The litigation which entailed embroiled the countess and both of her sisters and lasted a whole generation, being complicated by the childless Countess Charlotte's early death in 1851.[45] The fourth marquess never forgave Countess Charlotte for her depredations of the ancestral estate:[46]

> At some public entertainment he inadvertently ran up against the Countess Zichy, who was flaunting the second Marchioness's pearls which she had wheedled out of his father. It so happened that Lord Hertford himself was wearing 'pearl' studs which could not have cost more than a shilling the set. On this account the lady started to quizz him. After hearing what she had to say, he made a low bow, following it up with the crushing retort: 'Yes, Ma'am. The difference between us is that I wear mother-of-pearl, and you wear grandmother's pearls!'

The marquess's death in 1842 provided a vehicle for Victorian moralising on a grand scale:[47]

> March 19th.—This day Lord Hertford is buried at Ragley, a man whose death excited much greater interest than anything he ever did in his life, because the world was curious to learn the amount of his wealth, and how he had disposed of it. A pompous funeral left Dorchester House three days ago, followed by innumerable carriages of private individuals, pretending to show a respect which not one of them felt for the deceased; on the contrary, no man ever lived more despised or died less regretted. His life and his death were equally disgusting and revolting to every good and moral feeling. As Lord Yarmouth he was known as a sharp, cunning, luxurious, avaricious man of the world, with some talent, the favourite of George IV (the worst of kings) when Lady Hertford, his mother, was that Prince's mistress. He was celebrated for his success at play, by which he supplied himself with the large sums of money required for his pleasures, and which his father had no inclination to give him, and the son had none to ask of him. He won largely, not by any cheating or unfairness, but by coolness, calculation, always backing the best players, and getting the odds on his side. He was a bon vivant, and when young and gay his parties were agreeable, and he contributed his share to their hilarity. But after he became Lord Hertford and the possessor of an enormous property he was puffed up with vulgar pride, very unlike the real scion of a noble race; he loved nothing but dull pomp and ceremony, and could only endure people who paid him court and homage. After a great deal of coarse and vulgar gallantry, generally purchased at a high rate, he formed a connexion with Lady Strachan, which thenceforward determined all the habits of his life. She was a very infamous and

shameless woman, and his love after some years was changed to hatred; and she, after getting very large sums out of him, married a Sicilian. But her children, three daughters, he in a manner adopted; though eventually all his partiality centred upon one, Charlotte by name, who married Count Zichy-Ferraris, a Hungarian nobleman. She continued to live with Hertford on and off, here and abroad, until his habits became in his last years so ostentatiously crapulous that her residence in his house, in England at least, ceased to be compatible with common decency. She was, however, here till within a week or ten days of his death, and her departure appears curiously enough to have led to the circumstances which immediately occasioned it.

For some months or weeks past he lived at Dorchester House, and the Zichys with him; but every day at a certain hour his women, who were quartered elsewhere, arrived, passed the greater part of the day, and one or other of them all the night in his room. He found the presence of the Countess Zichy troublesome and embarrassing to his pleasures, and he made her comprehend that her absence would not be disagreeable to him, and accordingly she went away. He had then been ill in bed for many days, but as soon as she was gone, as if to celebrate his liberation by a jubilee, he got up and posted with his seraglio down to Richmond ...

By that stage Lady Strachan was long gone. She married her Sicilian amour Pisolilli, purchased the title of Marchesa di Salsa from the King of Sardinia in 1835, separated from her second husband and retired in 1842 to the Villa Matilde, named after her eldest daughter, on the Bay of Naples[48] and died in 1868. All a far cry from her husband's gilding of the gingerbread of Trafalgar by his capture of Dumanoir's squadron over six decades before.

'Paul Pry's Extrachan-ary peep into Piccadillo', see colour plate 13

Samuel Brokensha, Master RN[1]

Nigel Hughes

Introduction

This essay aims to explore the life and naval career of Samuel Brokensha, Master RN, and is mainly derived from multifarious surviving Admiralty records with their wealth of detail. In tracing Samuel's career, some idea may be gained of the uncertainty, irregularity and often dangerous nature of a naval warrant officer's employment during the French Revolutionary and Napoleonic War period, but also of the excitement and occasional welcome financial windfalls of prize money. By comparison, very few records of Samuel's private civilian life exist, either from before or after his naval service. Samuel was the elder brother of Luke Brokenshaw, Master RN, whose story has been explored in previous *Trafalgar Chronicle*s and it is undoubtedly due to Samuel's position as master of *Fortunee* in 1801 that his younger brother Luke began his meteoric rise in the service, natural talent notwithstanding.[2]

Samuel has a significant story to relate, his naval career commencing in 1795 following a dramatic, nationally-reported escapade that arguably may have contributed to, or even shaped, the course of future political and military events, the ripples from which continue to influence our lives in the guise of today's Europe.

Samuel Brokensha (1771–1839)

Samuel was the second of eleven children born to Samuel Brokensha, mason, and Elizabeth (Gill) in Mevagissey, Cornwall, illustrated by the extract from the Brokensha family tree. The parish baptism register shows that young Samuel was baptised on 17 March 1771,[3] but nothing further is known about his early life until the Mevagissey parish marriage register records his marriage to Mary Thomas, also of Mevagissey, on 28 October 1794, his occupation shown as 'mariner'.[4] The next few months of Samuel's life would prove to be of the utmost significance for him and, ultimately, for the future of his younger brother Luke.

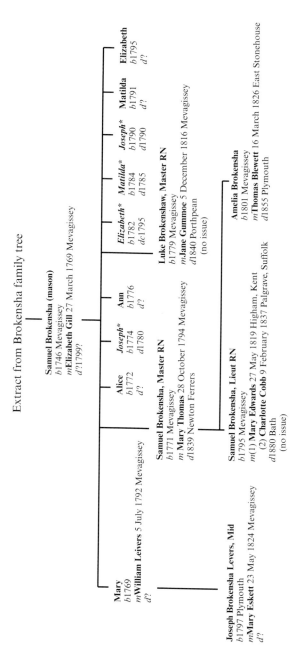

Extract from Brokensha family tree

Samuel Brokensha (mason)
*b*1746 Mevagissey
*m***Elizabeth Gill** 27 March 1769 Mevagissey
*d?*1799?

Mary
*b*1769
*m***William Leivers** 5 July 1792 Mevagissey
d?

Alice
*b*1772
d?

*Joseph**
*b*1774
*d*1780

Ann
*b*1776
d?

*Elizabeth**
*b*1782
*dc*1795

*Matilda**
*b*1784
*d*1785

*Joseph**
*b*1790
*d*1790

Matilda
*b*1791
d?

Elizabeth
*b*1795
d?

Samuel Brokensha, Master RN
*b*1771 Mevagissey
m **Mary Thomas** 28 October 1794 Mevagissey
*d*1839 Newton Ferrers

Luke Brokenshaw, Master RN
*b*1779 Mevagissey
*m.***Jane Gummoe** 5 December 1816 Mevagissey
*d*1840 Porthpean
(no issue)

Samuel Brokensha, Lieut RN
*b*1795 Mevagissey
m(1) **Mary Edwards** 27 May 1819 Higham, Kent
(2) **Charlotte Cobb** 9 February 1837 Palgrave, Suffolk
*d*1880 Bath
(no issue)

Amelia Brokensha
*b*1801 Mevagissey
*m***Thomas Blewett** 16 March 1826 East Stonehouse
*d*1855 Plymouth

Joseph Brokensha Levers, Mid
*b*1797 Plymouth
*m***Mary Eskett** 23 May 1824 Mevagissey
d?

Notes:

1. *Italicised names indicate death in infancy. Note subsequent reuse of names.
2. The tree demonstrates that Joseph Brokensha Levers was a nephew of Samuel *b*1771 and Luke *b*1779, and first cousin to Samuel *b*1795.
3. Brothers Samuel and Luke always used a different spelling of their surname in their personal signatures. Conjecturally, this may have been a ploy to avoid confusion of identities in RN records.
4. The author is second cousin (five times removed) to Samuel *b*1771 and Luke *b*1779.

197

Capture and escape from France

It must first be stated that in the interests of historical verisimilitude, a modicum of caution should be observed, in that to date it has not been possible to uncover official documentation that would indisputably substantiate Samuel's claim to be the hero of the hour in the following story. However, subsequent events, the absence of any other candidate who could be identified after many years' research, and the overwhelming balance of probability make him firm favourite. The following supporting evidence is offered.

Ship registers for the Cornish port of Fowey show that on 16 October 1794 Samuel Brokensha was appointed master of the square-sterned brigantine *Sophia* of 91½ tons, her registration details stating that she had been 'captured from the French' in 1793.[5] The register also states that *Sophia* was 'subsequently taken back by the French', but unfortunately the date is not recorded. However, the ship news section of *The Times* newspaper dated 22 November 1794 includes a report made by the captain of an American ship recently sailed from Lorient of the capture of *Alexander* (74), Captain Richard Rodney Bligh (*The Times* article named him as Admiral Bligh, he having been promoted whilst at sea), and significantly passed on 'express news' from Brest of the capture of a convoy of forty sail of ships and vessels.

On 11 December 1794 *The Times* carried several short paragraphs describing the situation and treatment of a group of English 'confined in that country' near Brest. The article describes in some detail the situation of a Lady Ann Fitzroy, held on parole, and reported that an attempt by a group of prisoners to hire boats to effect an escape had been foiled, resulting in loss of privileges, confiscation of personal money, and a forced march to Brest in company with other British prisoners. There, an attempted mass escape by a reported five hundred prisoners largely failed, about fifty managing to get to Guernsey, the rest being recaptured.

Events then took a particular turn, as described in an article published in the *Gentleman's Magazine*:[6]

Plymouth January 10th 1795. This day Captains Clarke and Wells of two Riga Ships, who were captured September 11th in the Bay and carried to Brest by Admiral Nielly's division of six Sail of the Line and Frigates arrived here from Brest last from Mevagissey. They bring the following accounts:

December 25th. The Republicain of 110 guns in a gale of wind drove from her anchor in Brest Water and went on shore and on the 10th instant was gone to pieces. The Hon. Mr. Wesley, brother of Lord Mornington, who was at Quimper with Lady Anne Fitzroy and several other ladies came to Brest and passing for an American with the above named Captains and Captain Brokenshire of Mevagissey concerted a plan for an escape and purchased a boat of a Swedish Captain of 22 feet long for the moderate sum of 80 guineas.

On the 10th in number 14, they committed themselves to the waves and at 8 o'clock at night sailed from Brest with a tolerably fair wind; when about half-channel over, three of the crew from intense and severe weather died, and one, whose limbs were frozen, attempting to hand the spritsail, fell overboard and was drowned, the sea then running very high. Fortunately about five o'clock on Sunday 11th they made the Deadman [Dodman Point]. Capt. Brokenshire knew the appearance of the land and requested to steer the boat for Mevagissey.

By this time, Lord Mornington's brother and the whole were so benumbed with cold they could scarcely row; but the sight of their native land gave them heart and they, with a cheerful 'Ahoy lads for Old England' pulled hard and got into Mevagissey Bay, providentially at 11 o'clock at night, but so much exhausted that the people of Mevagissey were obliged to help them out of the boat to a neighbouring inn where every accommodation was afforded them that could be procured.

The living, ten in number, were all put in warm beds and the unfortunate victims to the severity of the weather were placed in a room till Monday morning when they were, on the evening of that day, decently interred in Mevagissey Churchyard, attended by Lieut. Reed, the Privates of the Royal Cornwall Militia quartered there, the Clergymen of the town and nearly all the inhabitants. A more melancholy funeral was perhaps never witnessed as unfortunately the names of the deceased could not be procured having jumped into the boat at the moment of getting under way. The kindness and attention shewn by all ranks of people in and near Mevagissey reveals the highest honour on their feelings as Englishmen. Six of the Masters were left at Mevagissey to recover; two came here; Lord Mornington's brother set off for London express with a large sealed pacquet for the Cabinet. Capt. Clarke says that the French fleet did not sail till the 31st December, and were 33 of the Line, 20 Frigates and 16 Corvettes. Their destination unknown but supposed to be for the protection of 60 sail of prizes taken in the North Sea and laden with naval stores coming North about. There had been for some months past an absolute embargo on all vessels of every description and it was to continue until the French Fleet returned.

Previous to their leaving Brest, a Decree of the Convention had arrived to release and send home in neutral vessels all English female prisoners in consequence of which Lady Anne Fitzroy and nine English prisoners were marched in this inclement season from Quimper to Brest where they embarked on an American vessel which will sail as soon as the embargo is taken off.

The treatment of our prisoners at Brest is to a degree unworthy of any nation. If complaints are made to the Commissary the answer is nothing is too bad for the English prisoners and to make it still worse the Commissary will not allow the English prisoners to lay out their money to purchase any little comforts or conveniences. The gallant Admiral Bligh, officers, seamen and marines of the Alexander are all confined in the prison ship.

Collating and summarising the evidence from these sources, we thus have the Mevagissey mariner Samuel Brokensha, married in Mevagissey in late October 1794 and not long appointed master of the ex-French vessel *Sophia* subsequently recaptured by the French. In November 1794 many vessels were reported captured and carried into Brest, where a number of English prisoners including Lord Mornington's brother the Hon Mr Wesley [*sic*] and Lady Anne Fitzroy were being detained. Other sources show that the Hon Henry Wellesley, a diplomat, had been captured by the French in 1794 en route home from Lisbon in company with his sister, Lady Anne Fitzroy.[7] An escape plot was hatched by a group of the prisoners, and a small boat containing fourteen people including the Hon 'Mr Wesley' made a successful dash across the Channel, navigated into Mevagissey by 'Captain Brokenshire' who knew the coast.

It is undoubtedly of significance that Henry Wellesley was the younger brother of Arthur Wellesley, Duke of Wellington, and that in facilitating the safe return of Henry, who was carrying diplomatic papers, Samuel Brokensha aka 'Captain Brokenshire' made a very favourable impression. Speculatively, Samuel was recognised for his actions by a recommendation to the Navy Board, since four months later on 30 April 1795 at Trinity House, London, Samuel was examined and gained a master's ticket for sloops and cutters,[8] and on 29 July was appointed acting master of the fifth-rate frigate *Dryad*, Captain the Hon Robert Forbes.

Dryad (36)

The brand new frigate *Dryad* began victualling for sea at King's Moorings, Deptford, on 28 June 1795, on which day Captain Forbes made his appearance onboard.[9] Samuel Brokensha was appointed acting master by warrant on 29 July, and duly commenced the master's log that day.[10] The muster book records that of the final complement of crew of 264, every home nation was represented, plus people from the Channel Islands, Jamaica, Philadelphia, Amsterdam and Stockholm.[11]

During September, *Dryad* completed victualling at the Nore and on 1 October arrived at Yarmouth Roads to join a squadron bound for the Baltic. Sailing again the same day, her active and eventful sea service soon began with the chase of several 'strange sail', and within days a Danish schooner and a Norwegian brig had been boarded and inspected.

High drama followed on 8 October when, as recorded in the captain's log by First Lieutenant Adam Mackenzie, in strong gales and a heavy sea off the Naze of Norway, Captain Forbes fell overboard and drowned. Samuel Brokensha's master's log expands on events, stating that a ship's boat was launched over the stern in an attempt to rescue Forbes, but was immediately stove and sank with all its gear. A man-overboard signal was made to *Kite*, astern of *Dryad*, and one of her boats picked up the body. 'Every animation' was made to restore Forbes to life but in vain, and his corpse was returned to *Dryad* some hours later. The next day *Dryad* entered Flackeroe (Kristiansand) harbour, touching ground in shallows, but was successfully hauled off by her own boats. *Dryad*'s barge bore Forbes's body into 'Christian Sands' for burial, accompanied by the ship's officers and others from the squadron. Thirty minute-guns were fired in Forbes's honour. Seniority dictated that Captain Micajah Malbon of *Kite* take command of *Dryad,* exchanging places with Lieutenant Mackenzie, who assumed command of *Kite*.[12]

Despite the calamity, it was business as usual and *Dryad*, in company with *Kite*, continued to chase and inspect 'strange sail' in the North Sea, but the crew may have begun to wonder if *Dryad* was jinxed when on 8 November John McCracken fell from the mizzen topsail yard and was 'killed on the spot'. *Dryad* arrived back in the Downs on 13 November, and on 20 November Captain the Rt Hon Lord Amelius Beauclerk made his appearance to supersede Malbon. Thus began a long and successful professional relationship between Beauclerk and Samuel.

Back at sea on 30 November, James Doyle was lost overboard on 2 December, but *Dryad* continued to be very active, in spite of losing small sails, topmasts, yards and rigging in a bout of stormy weather. Christmas 1795 saw her back in Yarmouth Roads before moving round to the Nore and Gravesend, and on 5 February 1796 *Dryad* was in Cuxhaven on a special mission. The master's log tells that on 10 February 'came on board

His Royal Highness Prince Ernest Augustus. Saluted him with 21 guns'. Prince Ernest Augustus, fifth son of King George III, was landed back at Gravesend on 16 February.[13] Then 28 February heralded a rather more serious entry, when 'came on board three Captains to examing into a complaint sed to be made by the ship's company' [*sic*]. The nature of the complaint was not stated, but it could hardly relate to excessive flogging, since *Dryad*'s logs rarely noted such punishments, and even more rarely for more than twelve lashes.

Between March 1796 and December 1800, when Samuel Brokensha removed to his next ship, *Dryad* sailed mainly out of Cork, shepherding inbound and outbound convoys through the waters off southern Ireland and patrolling for privateers off Cape Clear. On 2 May 1796, a busy day, a Guernsey smuggler bound for Cornwall with a cargo of brandy and gin was brought-to after firing 'a great number of shot', and later the French cutter *Abeille* of twelve guns was captured after firing two guns at her.

On 13 June *Dryad* achieved a stunning success by capturing the French frigate *Proserpine* of forty-four guns and 348 men, after a thirteen-hour pursuit during which the French vessel inflicted relatively minor damage to *Dryad*'s sails and rigging with her stern chasers. Ranging up alongside *Proserpine*, within forty-five minutes *Dryad*'s broadside inflicted sufficient carnage to cause the French frigate to strike her colours, with the loss of thirty killed and forty-five wounded to *Dryad*'s losses of two killed and seven wounded.[14]

On 17 October 1796 the French privateer brig *Vautour* of eight guns and seventy-eight men was brought-to and captured after *Dryad* fired three guns. Back in Cork harbour on 19 October, *Dryad*'s main mast was surveyed and repaired – a portentous event.

The captain's log records that on 28 December, during strong gales and heavy squalls, the main topsail was handed down, 'the ship lurching a good deal and the main mast complaining'.[15] The mainmast soon went over the side close to the deck, breaking into two pieces and in its fall carrying away the fore topsail yard, mizzen topmast and topgallant mast and yard, along with sundry sails and rigging. Clearing away the wreck, the staysail was set and the lashings for all guns doubly checked. The gales moderating but with a heavy swell running, a spare fore topsail yard and main topgallant mast and yard were jury-rigged for a mizzen topmast and yard.

Fortunate to survive such potential disaster, and as if this were not sufficient travail, the next day two strange sail were observed bearing down, identified as men of war. *Dryad* cleared for action and made the private signal, which was unanswered. At noon the enemy vessels approached within three or four miles, but luckily for the crippled *Dryad* they then hauled to the wind and hoisted Spanish colours, oddly declining battle despite superiority of numbers. Despite losing more sails in continuing squalls and heavy seas, *Dryad* limped into Cork harbour on 2 January 1797, with the assistance of boats of the fleet. Cannibalising the mainmast from another vessel, by 24 January *Dryad* was repaired and assisting a convoy of forty merchantmen into Plymouth, where over the next five weeks she underwent a refit to replace the jury mainmast. On 19 February the agent came aboard and paid the prize money for *Proserpine,* and 7 March saw the crew served grog before next day receiving wages from the commissioners.

Later in the year, 20 August saw the capture of the privateer *Eclair* of fourteen guns and 108 men, followed on 9 September by the chase of a strange sail that required several shots to bring her to. On coming alongside, it was found that *Dryad*'s gunnery had been rather too effective and the French privateer *Cornelie* of twelve guns and ninety men was in a sinking condition. *Dryad* lowered boats, but it was blowing hard, with high seas, and only seventeen were saved.[16]

On 2 October *Dryad* stopped an unnamed vessel and hove-to, but attempting an escape manoeuvre the stranger moved across *Dryad*'s stern so closely that she carried away the spanker boom and gaff and got away. In company with *Doris* (36), on 11 October *Dryad* brought-to the French privateer *Brune* of sixteen guns and 180 men, nine weeks out from Bordeaux and having captured two English brigs, but whilst transferring prisoners, *Dryad*'s launch filled and broke adrift.

Not best known for his spelling prowess, on 2 November Samuel Brokensha noted in the master's log that J Garman had been punished with twelve lashes for 'indeavouring to make disturbances'.

Setting sail on 13 January 1798 in company with *Magnamine* (44), escorting a convoy bound for Madeira, the year began inauspiciously when on 17 January Bosun's Mate James Whiteside died suddenly and was committed to the deep the next day. On 4 February *Dryad* was in chase of a strange sail, having fired a shot at her. An hour later the quarry began firing her stern chasers at *Dryad*, who returned 'a great number of shot' before the enemy hove-to. She was found to be the French privateer *Mars* out of Nantes mounting twelve 12pdrs and two 18pdrs, and 222 men. The convoy by now safely on its way, *Dryad* entered Cork harbour on 9 February with her prize in company.

Leaving Cork on 17 February to assist with escorting a merchant convoy bound for Plymouth, *Dryad* entered the Hamoaze for survey and refit. On

19 March the signal to attend an execution onboard *Amelia* (38) was answered, and 'at 11 was executed Denis Brougham and William Larking' for unspecified offences.

Back to sea towards the end of April, the next fifteen months were quiet by comparison, comprising regular convoy duties with no enemy engagements. The winter of 1798/99 was spent in Cork harbour, *Dryad* returning to Portsmouth in February 1799, where Beauclerk was superseded by Captain Charles John Moore Mansfield, a move that was to have an interesting sequel for Samuel.[17]

Under her latest captain, *Dryad* continued her active service, often in the company of the fifth-rate frigates *Diamond* and *Revolutionaire*, sharing in the capture of the letters of marque *Hippolyte* (29 May), *Determiné* (7 July), and *Cères* (19 September), the latter shared only with the British *Revolutionaire*.

The year 1800 saw *Dryad* almost wrecked after a severe April Atlantic storm in which she lost her fore yard and sundry rigging. Happening across *Revolutionaire*, who had lost her rudder in the same gales, the two frigates assisted each other to make for Cork, but yet more gales rendered this port unattainable and the pair tried to steer for Plymouth. Failing to weather the Scillies and still unable to make Cork, the two vessels were blown helplessly towards the coast of Ireland, where *Dryad* attempted to take *Revolutionaire* in tow to prevent her being wrecked on the rocky Waterford shore. The tow parting, a change of wind fortunately precluded a disaster and on 19 April both ships made 'Milford Heaven [*sic*] in a most distressed state'.[18] Emergency repairs shortly enabled both frigates to escort a small convoy of seven merchantmen into Falmouth, after which they sailed for Plymouth for dockyard repairs. On 8 July *Dryad* was back in Cork, and on 30 July two strange sail were chased, stopping and boarding one, a brig, after firing several shot.[19] She was found to be the English ship *Albion*, captured two days previously by a French privateer of twenty-two guns. After leaving her to chase, stop and examine yet another strange sail, *Dryad* returned to take *Albion* in tow, she being a slow sailer.

The remainder of 1800 was uneventful, comprising routine patrols out of Cork, but on 6 September 'departed this life Mr William Parfrey, Carpenter', whose body was committed to the deep next day.

Beauclerk obviously held Samuel Brokensha in high regard, for contained in Samuel's service record is a letter to the Comptroller of the Navy Sir Andrew Snape Hamond, dated 8 April 1800, in which Beauclerk makes a very polite but forceful case for Sir Andrew's personal intervention in a dispute over Samuel's services:

Lord Beauclerk presents his comp^{ts} to Sir Andrew Hammond, as he has not yet received an answer from Capt. Mansfield, hopes the vacancy for Mr. Brokensa will not be filled up. L$^{d.}$ B. is very certain Capt. M. will have no objections to part with Mr. B. as at the time of superseeding each other it was a settled point between them. L$^{d.}$B. will put up with the inconvenience of fitting the ship without the Master. Hoping Sir Andrew will take those steps which will cause Mr. B. to join as soon as possible. L$^{d.}$ B. troubles Sir Andrew with this note fearing it might escape his memory.

In a letter of reply to the Navy Office, London, dated 21 December 1800, Samuel acknowledged receipt of his appointment to the frigate *Fortunee* (36), Captain the Rt Hon Lord Amelius Beauclerk. Samuel's last entry in the master's log dated 30 December 1800 includes the statement 'came on board Mr Verling', to supersede him as master.

Fortunee (36)

Fortunee's muster book records Samuel as joining the brand new 36-gun fifth rate on 26 January 1801 at Gravesend, by which time provisioning for sea and crewing had already commenced, and by 2 February, now at the Nore, more men had been received from *Zealand*.[20] Under Beauclerk, *Fortunee* sailed from Spithead in early March, and on 6 April in the Channel boarded a Guernsey privateer before returning to Spithead. For the next three months, *Fortunee* cruised in the Channel, and on 20 April, near Guernsey, the French privateer *Namard* was stopped and boarded.

In Portsmouth, on 13 June the muster book records that Samuel's brother Luke Brokenshaw joined the crew as 'Volunteer AB', but after a month was rated master's mate. Luke was discharged 'for Admiralty orders' on 15 July 1802.[21]

Expectations of more and bigger prizes were put on hold when on 28 June 1801 *Fortunee* was despatched to Lymington to become part of a small squadron of guard ships to His Majesty George III, whilst he holidayed in Weymouth and onboard the Royal Yacht *Royal Charlotte*. Between 4 July and 22 September, *Fortunee* fired 21-gun salutes whenever the King embarked and disembarked, which was sometimes daily, the master's log recording every salute with an ever-increasing air of boredom.

Released from this prestigious but tedious service at the end of September, *Fortunee* arrived at Cork Harbour on 11 October to escort a convoy of twenty-five merchantmen to Madeira, an uneventful sortie that saw her back in Cork on 16 November, where she was to remain employing the crew on routine maintenance until 15 February 1802, when she sailed for a new base at Tarbert on the River Shannon.

On 2 April 1802 Beauclerk was superseded by Captain John Clements but, hindered by frequent gales, *Fortunee* made only a few tentative sorties out of the Shannon and saw no action, remaining moored at Tarbert until 7 July, on which day she sailed for Plymouth, arriving 10 July.[22] On 24 July in Plymouth, Clements was in turn superseded by Captain John Ferrier, a move which may have been the trigger for Samuel Brokensha to write to the Navy Office, acknowledged on 13 August 1802, requesting that he be superseded as master of *Fortunee*. Samuel's original letter is not present in his service records and no reason was recorded. Speculatively, there may have been several – the tedious guard duty in Weymouth Bay; long periods of relative inactivity in Tarbert far from home and family (Samuel's wife Mary had given birth to their daughter Amelia in the spring); the departure of his patron Beauclerk – or maybe Samuel did not get along with Ferrier? Whatever his reasons, Samuel was to have his wish granted sooner than expected and under circumstances he could not have envisaged.

In early September *Fortunee* sailed for the Texel, to transport for repatriation a number of Dutch troops who had been in British service. As the captain's log for 11 September graphically records, whilst bearing up for the Texel in fresh gales and squally rain under the direction of a Dover pilot, in passing the outer buoy to make for the outer channel, the ship struck on a sandbank, despite the pilot having earlier frequently declared that he had surveyed the channel and was well acquainted with it.[23] 'Setting' the foresail forced her off the bank, Ferrier 'observing' to the pilot that they could not be in the correct channel, but the pilot persisted that they were and stated that they would soon have more water. However, whilst letting go the small bower and clewing up the sails the ship struck again. Making the signal of distress and signalling the following *Diamond* to anchor, *Fortunee* struck her yards, topgallant and topmasts, and in moderate gales carried out the stream anchor, firing several guns of distress, and sending an officer on shore to obtain schootes to take off the Dutch troops.[24] The ship began to make 2ft of water and despite the precautions, in rising gales struck the bank again very hard. Cutting away the masts, the foremast carried away the bowsprit, and the ship's cutter and launch were also lost. Letting go the best bower, the ship settled over the sandbank and an 18pdr was thrown overboard in an effort to reduce the strain, but by this time a strong tide was causing seas to break over the deck. The rudder broke off and the ship began to make over 3ft of water per hour. Next day, a large schoote managed to get alongside, but with no prospect of any more arriving overnight and the ship considered 'much fatigued' and likely to be under less strain if allowed to fill, the decision was taken to get the crew and their belongings to safety aboard *Alcmene* (32). A boat was later sent back to check the situation and found the water to be 2ft above the orlop deck.

On 13 September the ship's company returned to *Fortunee* to find the water 'over the between decks', and began to pump and bale the ship, gaining 2ft of water by noon, but finding the bread, powder and some part of the provisions to be entirely ruined. Next day, more pumping and baling got the water level down to 3ft in the hold and preparations to get the guns out began, forty men from *Alcmene* and twenty from *Autumn* being received to help pumping, with the ship now making over 5ft of water per hour. During the next three days, a further sixty men from *Magicienne* and forty from *Alcmene* assisted in clearing the ship, getting the guns, stores and shingle ballast out, and casks were lashed fore and aft to improve buoyancy. On 18 September preparations to get the ship off the sandbank commenced with carrying out a bower anchor and cables, and assisted by *Alcmene, Magicienne* and *Autumn*, a purchase was taken on the cables, *Fortunee* coming half out of her 'dock', but still making over 5ft of water. Sixty men from *Diamond* were employed to continue pumping overnight to relieve the exhausted ship's company. Work to lighten ship and pumping continued until on Sunday, 19 September, another anchor was carried out and by heaving on the cables, the ship was got over the bank and into the Texel, where boats towed her into the New Deep and she was beached.

Over the next six days, the iron ballast was replaced along with some gun carriages, jury masts and yards were rigged, a temporary rudder fitted and sails bent. Water and provisions were put aboard, and on 26 September *Fortunee* was warped out into Texel Roads. At 5.30am on 27 September, in company with *Magicienne* and *Autumn*, *Fortunee* weighed anchor and sailed for home, 'steering very bad with the temporary rudder', but a few hours later this broke and *Magicienne* took *Fortunee* in tow with a stream cable trailed over her stern to help keep her steady. This measure was deemed inadequate, as the English coast was sighted at Orford Ness, and the ship making up to 7ft of water per hour, she was hove-to for rudder repairs and to pump out. Limping into the Nore on 30 September, the tow towards Sheerness was taken up by boats; Chatham was reached at 3pm on 1 October where *Fortunee* was lashed alongside the hulk *Alcmaar*, in preparation for docking. Warped into dock to get out the jury masts, return stores and clear the ship, on 3 October the crew was mustered by the clerk of the cheque; 8 October saw the guns got out with the assistance of men from *Prince of Orange*, and on Sunday, 10 October, the commissioners came onboard and paid off the crew, including Samuel Brokensha, who must have been relieved that the events of the previous month and his blameless part in them had concluded safely.

Samuel's service record contains no information on his employment from this date until mid-1806.

Recall to sea service

On 18 June 1806 Samuel replied to Mr R Nelson at the Navy Office:

Ordnance Office Dover

Sir,

In answer to your letter of the 2nd.Ult. informing me that the Commissioners could not allow me an extension of leave for the purpose of my employment in the Ordnance Service.

I beg you will inform them that I am ready to serve immediately and understanding that the Princess of Orange is fitting at Chatham would be very thankful for an appointment to that ship.

The letter was annotated:

Mr. Smith

Acqt. him his name is down for an appointment the first opportunity that offers, and he will be apprised of it.

HMS *Trincomalee*, preserved at Hartlepool, a 38-gun frigate similar to the *Shannon*, in which Samuel Brokensha served 1806/7. (Max Mudie)

Shannon (38)

Samuel was disappointed in his wish for the third-rate *Princess of Orange* (74) (actually the *Prince of Orange*), nevertheless landing a plum appointment to the brand new 38-gun frigate *Shannon*, Captain Philip Bowes Vere Broke, who was later to achieve fame in the epic action of 1 June 1813 against the American heavy frigate USS *Chesapeake*. The *Shannon* began wages and sea victualling at Chatham on 20 June 1806; Samuel was appointed master on 12 July and made his appearance 22 July.[25] Broke did not make his appearance until 16 September, the ship meanwhile under the command of a lieutenant. Her complement was intended to be three hundred men, but the muster book states that this was reduced to 284 'by Admiralty Order'.

The first master's log for *Shannon* is unfortunately in a very poor state of preservation,[26] with missing pages and many that are barely legible, hence the activities of the ship in her first few months at sea have mainly been gleaned from the captain's log.[27] From the frequent recordings of severe punishments, the impression formed of Broke is that he was a disciplinarian and a 'flogger', the very first entry in his log noting two dozen lashes handed out to a marine for striking a superior officer (obviously a serious offence), and a similar punishment to a second for contempt. Few weeks went by without a record of punishment, thirty-six lashes being given for cases of neglect of duty, and a notable four dozen to a Thomas King for contempt. Perhaps *Shannon* had a particularly unruly crew.

At sea, *Shannon* spent the first six months of her career routinely patrolling the Channel between the Downs and the Isle of Wight, regularly stopping and searching 'strange sail', but saw no action against the enemy. Broke was noted for being a keen gunnery exponent but, apart from exercises, the most notable entry in the log was on 5 November 1806 at Dover, when twenty-one guns were fired to celebrate the anniversary of the Gunpowder Plot. On 27 December a revenue cutter hastened to report four French privateers in the offing, but nothing came of the incident. On 18 February 1807 off Dungeness there were 'hard gales and heavy squalls', and *Shannon* lost topgallant masts, sails and rigging, along with other minor damage.

On 11 April a pilot came aboard to take the ship to Yarmouth, where on 14 April Broke noted that he 'sent Mr. Samuel Brokensha, 1 Seaman and 1 Boy to Sick Quarters'.

The muster book for sick quarters at Great Yarmouth shows that on 17 April 'Samuel Brokensha, Master of the *Shannon*' was admitted suffering from rheumatism and remained until 9 May, when he was discharged into the converted ex-fifth-rate hospital ship *Roebuck* to complete his convalescence whilst awaiting another warrant.[28] *Shannon* was on her way to Arctic waters, the captain's log showing that she was to exceed latitude 80° N, and it must remain a matter of speculation as to whether Samuel, suffering from rheumatism, was effectively excused from this arduous duty by his captain's sympathetic use of a ploy that would not adversely affect Samuel's record.

Emerald (36) and the Battle of Vivero

Appointed master on 22 July, the muster book for the 36-gun frigate *Emerald*, Captain Frederick Lewis Maitland, shows that Samuel Brokensha made his appearance on 7 August 1807,[29] the very day of sailing from Plymouth. Joining the fleet off Start Point, a fair wind saw *Emerald* and her consorts link up two days later with *Defiance* and another squadron in the vicinity of the Île de Groix off Lorient, establishing a powerful force to blockade the important French bases from Brest to Bordeaux. In this service, over the eleven months of Samuel's time in her, *Emerald*'s activities were determined by the machinations of what evolved into the Peninsular War, fought for control of Spain, which dragged on until 1814.

August and September 1807 found her patrolling off Île d'Oléron in company with *Eurydice,* assisting with the blockade of La Rochelle and Rochefort, maintaining a watch on the French fleets in port, and frequently stopping and boarding suspected blockade-runners. American, Dutch and Danish vessels appeared to form the majority of those apprehended.[30] On 19 October at 9am, the winds being favourable to the enemy, a French squadron made a token gesture of defiance by standing out with all sail set in chase of *Emerald*, but she bore up and out-sailed them and, honour notionally satisfied, by 10am the French had given up the chase and stood in again.[31]

Blockade duty was noted for being both hard work and frequently of a boring repetitive nature. Maitland appeared to be well aware of the need to maintain both morale and discipline, but the two did not always sit easily together. The captain's log records the dates of opening of casks of rum, no doubt morale-raising events, but it is noticeable that incidents of punishments for drunkenness and insolence invariably soon followed, as some men almost certainly illegally hoarded their rations for binges, with the inevitable consequences.

On 1 November *Emerald* was to be found at anchor in Basque Roads along with the squadron, and on 16 November a four-hour chase resulted in the capture of a French lugger, which was taken in tow: not a huge prize but certainly a boost to morale. On 18 December two boats were sent after a brig which, by keeping close inshore, evaded capture.

The year 1808 began on a high note, with the capture on 7 January of the French chasse-marée *Victoire*, which was taken in tow. By 10 January *Emerald* was heading back to Plymouth for revictualling and general maintenance, arriving on 19 January and remaining until 14 February.

Passing Île d'Oléron on 22 February, *Emerald* sailed on southwards towards Cap Feret and Bayonne, before turning westwards to patrol the northern coast of Spain.

Late afternoon on Sunday, 13 March 1808, in chase of a strange sail near Cape Veras, *Emerald* sighted a large schooner in Vivero Bay and cleared for action.[32] Coming to anchor, the two shore batteries were engaged and two boats sent to storm the batteries and spike the guns, which objective was soon achieved. Two further boats were launched to take possession of the French schooner *Apropos,* which mounted eight 12pdr carronades with a crew of seventy, but despite the batteries being silenced, the initially successful boarding party had to be evacuated under a heavy musketry fire from the shore, as the schooner, having run onto the rocky shore, proved impossible to float off on the ebbing tide. Two boats later returned and set fire to *Apropos* which soon blew up, *Emerald* weighing in light airs and standing off.

Next day, *Emerald* came under heavy fire from one of the batteries whose guns had by now been unspiked, losing her large cutter and all its gear. Later, at anchor, *Emerald* observed six gunboats (galleys) in chase of a brig and gave chase in turn until a flat calm descended, anchoring again with a spring on the cable in order to bring her guns to bear. Giving up on the brig, the gunboats turned their attention to *Emerald* and opened fire to no great effect, receiving grape- and roundshot in return. After several hits were observed on the gunboats, they withdrew to Veras Bay. *Emerald* suffered only relatively minor damage during the entire conflict, but lost nine men killed and sixteen wounded, a source of great regret to Maitland, whose comprehensive battle report appeared in the *London Gazette.*[33] Maitland was at pains to extend his warmest thanks to those officers and crew who remained onboard during the engagement, and amongst several officers singled out for individual praise was the master, 'Mr Brokensher'.

The engagement was eventually awarded a clasp to the Naval General Service Medal, but Samuel did not live to make a claim. In the *Trafalgar Roll*, Mackenzie erroneously credits Samuel's younger brother Luke Brokenshaw with being master of *Emerald* at what had become known as the Battle of Vivero, but this is clearly a case of mistaken identity, since

Luke died in 1840 before the NGSM was introduced and, in any case, in March 1808 his ship, *Ganges*, was in Lisbon.[34]

From Vivero, *Emerald* sailed northwards and on 23 March exchanged numbers with Samuel's previous ship *Shannon*, forty-six leagues off Ushant, but by 16 April was once more off Bayonne. The American schooner *Friendship* from Santander bound for Marblehead was boarded 22 April and sent to England in charge of two of *Emerald*'s officers. Then 15 May found *Emerald* back home in England at anchor in 'Barnpool' where 'Gunner's decayed stores' were sent ashore, along with condemned sails and rigging.

Emerald's muster book for April/May 1808 declared the master as 'on Admiralty leave',[35] an entry in the leave book dated 20 May explaining that Samuel had been granted 'Time to come to Plymouth town to pass for a higher rate'.[36] Samuel passed his examination by the board of Trinity House, London, obtaining a third-rate ticket dated 14 July 1808. Already discharged from *Emerald* on 13 July, within a week Samuel was duly appointed to a third rate.

An intriguing entry discovered in *Emerald*'s muster book was for Boy 2nd Class Joseph Brokensha aged eleven years, born in Plymouth, who appeared onboard 14 February 1808 and was discharged 31 May 'for Order'. Seemingly a protégé of Samuel's, but not immediately identified as a relative, young Brokensha went on to make further appearances, following his namesake from ship to ship.

Ruby (64)

Although appointed to *Ruby* on 21 July 1808, the muster book shows that Samuel did not appear onboard until 2 September, joining ship in Lisbon harbour to supersede John Lamb 'Master and North Sea Pilot'.[37] In a quirk of fate, Samuel's brother Luke had rejoined *Ganges* in Lisbon on 22 August following his period of sick leave, so it is possible that the brothers were able to meet before sailing again in convoy.

The master's log records that the next week was spent painting ship, repairing cables and getting ready for sea, and on 11 September *Ruby* sailed for England in company with *Barfleur, Conqueror, Donegal, Hercule, Alfred, Ganges, Elizabeth* and two captured, the Russian frigate *Katrizan* and a store ship.[38] Initially beating out due west into the Atlantic, the squadron turned due north then northeast to run up the Channel into Spithead, arriving 6 October when, perhaps unusually, *Ruby*'s gunner was sent into the Russian frigate to pilot her into St Helens.

On 10 October the clerk of the cheque mustered the ship's company of

491 people, and Joseph Brokensha, now shown as aged thirteen years and a midshipman, joined *Ruby* on 15 October.

His Royal Highness the Duke of Clarence came to review the fleet on 20 October, twenty-one guns were fired in his honour, and the yards manned, as His Royal Highness went onboard and left the different ships. Another event of note occurred on 1 November when 'came on board Mr. Moses and paid 14/6d. per man prize money for the Russian frigate and store ship', and 5 November once more heard twenty-one guns fired 'to commemorate the discovery of the Powder Plot'.

The captain's log records that on 19 November Captain Robert Hall came onboard to be acting captain whilst Captain John Draper was on leave.[39] A pilot took the ship into harbour on 23 November, when a master attendant came onboard. Next day the pilot transported *Ruby* further up the harbour, she was lashed alongside *Marengo*, and over the next fortnight the sails were sent ashore to the sail loft and the guns got out by use of the main yard. By 6 December the lower deck guns had been sent away and the masts were being stripped out, as *Ruby* was prepared for major overhaul, including having her hull scraped. An unfortunate accident took place on 7 December when seaman Christopher Harper was killed 'by the giving way of the main runner block strop which fell and struck him on the head and occasioned his instant death'. Three days later, *Ruby* was moved down harbour in charge of riggers and lashed to the hulk *Roebuck* for the ballast to be taken out. The remains of the ship's company were paid their prize money on 12 December and the captain's log records that on 15 December 1808 Mr Samuel Brokensha, Master, Mr Pollock, Assistant Surgeon, and Mr Joseph Brokensha, Midshipman, were discharged into *Norge.* The muster book provided the additional information that these appointments 'to act on board HMS *Norge*' were made 'per order of Admiral Montagu', Commander-in-Chief Portsmouth.

Norge (74) and the Battle of Corunna
Transferring immediately from *Ruby* into *Norge*, Captain Boger, a Danish ship taken into the navy following the Second Battle of Copenhagen, the muster book records the appearances of Samuel Brokensha, Master, and Joseph Brokensha, Midshipman, on 16 December 1808.[40] By 26 December *Norge* was off Vigo in company with first rates *Ville de Paris* and *Victory,* third rates *Barfleur, Zealous, Ganges, Alfred* and *Elizabeth*, and fifth rates *Venus* and *Diana.* Under Admiral Birch, the fleet sailed from Vigo 12 January 1809 with a convoy of transports, arriving at Corunna 15 January to find *Tonnant* (80), *Unicorn* (36) and some transports already there, to

213

take part in the Herculean task of evacuating Lieutenant-General Sir John Moore's retreating Peninsular Army. Anchoring in the bay, the master's log records that the reports of muskets could be heard from the heights above the town, and all boats were hoisted out and sent ashore to embark troops.[41] The next day, 16 January, the log reported 'This day a severe action commenced between our Army and the French', to become known as the Battle of Corunna, during which Sir John Moore was struck by a cannonball and mortally wounded, dying several hours later. Troop evacuation continued all through the night and the next day, the log observing that the French were firing (cannon) at three transports 'on shore'. Under fire, several transport ships had run aground whilst attempting evasive action during the somewhat panicky evacuation, and were burnt once their passengers and crews were rescued. Later that afternoon, *Norge*'s pinnace was found swamped, furniture, grapnels and grapnel ropes missing and no sign of 'the people'. Shifting her berth further out in the bay to avoid the French artillery fire, *Norge* continued to receive troops belonging to different regiments throughout the night until weighing anchor at 7.30 on the morning of Wednesday, 18 January, first making then shortening sail to send the launch ashore to take off the very last remaining troops that had made it to the beach-head. Receiving them onboard at 11.30am, the launch was hoisted in and *Norge* made all sail to join the rest of the fleet.

In an operation that presaged Dunkirk, in all some twenty-seven thousand troops were successfully evacuated from Vigo and Corunna to fight another day, although a huge quantity of equipment was lost, and some eight thousand soldiers had died during the retreat across northern Spain during the harsh Spanish winter. From her logs, it appears that *Norge* was the last ship to leave the Corunna shore, and by 23 January was at anchor in Cawsand Bay, where on 25 January thirteen sick men and wounded soldiers were sent on shore to hospital.

Sailing from Cawsand on 7 February, bound for Spanish waters, the log records that on 12 February Lieutenant William Lawrence died. Although Spain was once again an ally, on 22 February a Spanish brig from 'Gallesa' (probably Galicia) bound for Cadiz was stopped and a petty officer and eight men sent aboard to take possession, eight of the Spanish crew being taken into *Norge* in exchange.

Then on 6 March *Norge* was to be found at anchor in company with *Royal George* (100) and a fleet, Admiral Sir John Duckworth, some five or six leagues off Cape Trafalgar, and on 14 March at anchor in Cadiz with six other ships of the line. Over the next four months, *Norge* escorted Spanish convoys through the Straits of Gibraltar into the Mediterranean, and back. During this period ship's discipline was strict, the log recording instances of floggings of up to thirty-six lashes for disobedience of orders, neglect of duty and attempted desertion, as *Norge* proceeded between Gibraltar, Malaga, Majorca and Almeria. Unruly Spanish merchant vessels were reminded of the requirement to keep in convoy by firing guns, often shotted to emphasise the message. The guns were given further exercise as salutes were exchanged between ship and shore batteries on entering certain ports, and for matters of etiquette such as commemorating, whilst at anchor in Gibraltar, the restoration of 'King Charls' [*sic*] on 29 May, and the birthday of His Majesty King George III on 4 June, both royals receiving twenty-one guns.

By 18 June 1809 *Norge* was at anchor in the River Tagus, where on 3 July a punishment boat containing two men came alongside, one of the unfortunates receiving fifty lashes as part punishment, and Jeremiah Yates was given thirty lashes for 'mutinous expressions'. On 23 July Boger was superseded by Captain Rainier, and a week later *Norge* dropped down the Tagus to head for Ferrol and replenishment, returning to the Tagus via Corunna on 18 September, where over the next week Rainier attended four courts martial.[42]

Civilities and ceremony continued, when on 6 November the yards were manned as the Hon J C Villiers, HM Ambassador at Lisbon, came onboard to a 19-gun salute. On 17 December 1809 twenty-one guns were fired to salute the Queen of Portugal's birthday, but our own Queen Charlotte only merited nineteen guns for her birthday on 18 January 1810.

Norge unmoored 16 February 1810 and sailed for Spithead, arriving 27 February. Here Rainier was superseded on 11 March by Captain Waller, and on 15 March Samuel Brokensha was also superseded. Samuel's protégé, Midshipman Joseph Brokensha, remained in *Norge* until he was discharged on an unspecified date sometime before March 1811, but according to the pay book was not paid his due wages until 23 October of that year.[43]

Bedford (74)

Samuel Brokensha's service record shows that his next appointment was to *Bedford*, Captain James Walker, and the muster book for July–December 1810 showing that Samuel joined as master on 6 September in the Hamoaze, Plymouth.[44] Sadly, it appears that no master's, captain's or ship's logs survive for *Bedford*, rendering first-hand accounts of the ship's activities during Samuel's tenure impossible to relate. Happily however, relevant muster books and pay books have survived, and some idea of *Bedford*'s whereabouts can be gleaned from information contained within.[45]

Sailing from Plymouth in October 1810, *Bedford* probably arrived in the Downs in early November, remaining there until March 1811. Between March and October, *Bedford* made four sailings from the Downs of between one and two months' duration, before returning to Sheerness, shifting her anchorage to the Nore in mid-November, then to 'Hosely Bay' [*sic*], (probably Hollesley Bay on the Suffolk coast). The remaining operations of 1811 comprised several sailings from 'Hosely Bay' and the Downs, with voyage durations of typically up to two months; however, the muster book shows that whilst in the Downs on 28 January 1812, Samuel Brokensha was superseded. Given her east-coast deployment, *Bedford* probably patrolled the Dutch coast as part of the North Sea fleet operations, and it is possible that Samuel's old rheumatic ailment may have flared up as a result of cold North Sea conditions, since the master's personal signature at the end of that muster period is absent, replaced by 'Sick'.

An interesting discovery in *Bedford*'s muster book was the appearance on 7 October 1810 from *Mars* of Midshipman Samuel Brokensha, stated to be aged eighteen but actually just over fifteen years old. This was Samuel's son, who had entered the navy in February 1806 as a Volunteer 1st Class, stated to be fourteen years old. However, young Samuel was born/baptised in August 1795, so was then actually less than eleven years old. *Mars* was young Samuel's first ship, whose master at the time of his joining was his uncle, Luke Brokenshaw. The deliberate misrepresentation of Midshipman Brokensha's true age was endorsed by the Reverend Charles Lyne, vicar of Mevagissey, who later provided a signed statement in support of Samuel's examination for lieutenant that declared his year of baptism to be 1794, whereas the Mevagissey parish register plainly records the event in 1795. Young Samuel was examined and passed for lieutenant on 3 November 1813 onboard *Raisonnable* at Sheerness, then aged just over eighteen years – below the age of nineteen years as declared on his passing certificate, but nevertheless having served three days short of seven years' sea time.[46]

Bedford's muster books also showed that Midshipman Joseph Brokensha soon followed his namesakes into her, appearing on 5 March 1811 and remaining onboard until 26 February 1814, when he was discharged into the receiving ship *Raisonnable*.

Raisonnable (receiving ship)

After Samuel Brokensha quitted the *Bedford* 'sick' in January 1812, it was to be a full year before he received his next (and last) warrant to be master of *Raisonnable* at Sheerness, Captain Edward Sneyd Clay. The muster book shows that Samuel was appointed 14 January 1813, but did not appear onboard until 4 February.[47]

As well as acting as floating accommodation for men awaiting allocation to their next ship, *Raisonnable* thus provided a ready labour force for general harbour duties, keeping the people occupied and maintaining their skills. By the nature of *Raisonnable*'s employment, the captain's log reports predominantly mundane routine activities: cleaning and painting ship, sending working parties to assist with maintenance of vessels in harbour, holding courts martial. Prisoners of war were also processed into prison ships.[48] Discipline was an ongoing problem amongst what must inevitably have been an often bored and restless motley collection of men, and the log records floggings typically of twenty-four lashes for drunkenness and absence from duty, and thirty-six lashes given for theft.

Over the period of Samuel's tenure as master, few truly notable events took place, as would be expected in a ship employed in harbour duties. No master's log appears to have survived, but the captain's log provides the following much-edited record of happenings in Sheerness harbour as well as onboard.

On 1 March 1813 an unspecified number of prisoners of war were discharged to prison ships before a period of stormy weather necessitated the decks to be cleared of snow on 11 March. No less than 20 tons of beer was received onboard on 20 March and, inevitably, on 22 March landsman W Green was punished with twenty-four lashes for repeated acts of drunkenness. A fire broke out in the dockyard on 23 March, *Raisonnable* sending boatloads of men and an 'engine' (a pump) to assist with fighting the blaze.

Six gunboats went out of harbour on 27 July but, 'through force of the tide', the last got foul of the prison ship *Devonshire* and sank with the loss of two men drowned, provisions for six men for a fortnight, and all furniture and stores. A working party was sent to assist in raising the gunboat on 5 August, on which day a 21-gun salute to the Duke of Clarence was fired. The gunboat was eventually raised on 14 August, and on 9 September a working party was sent to help refit her.

On 21 September a fire was observed onboard the convict hulk *Zealand*. *Raisonnable* fired a gun and made the alarm, and once more sent boats and a pump. The fire was got under control, but '6 leather buckets and 4 iron hooped ditto' were lost. *Raisonnable* herself was not immune to accident, as during October she was twice rammed by victualling vessels, but on each occasion sustained only minor damage.

More ceremony was observed when on 7 December a 21-gun salute was fired for the Dukes of Clarence and Cambridge as they embarked in the admiral's barge bound for the Nore, and when, on 24 December, a Russian 74 came in to harbour, *Raisonnable* dressed ship, 'it being the birthday of

217

the Emperor of Russia'.

On 16 January 1814 a French prisoner fell from the deck into the hold but, despite being quickly transferred to the hospital ship *Sussex*, soon died; 27 February saw the appearance of Midshipman Joseph Brokensha, who remained onboard until 26 April, when he was discharged into *Tigris* (36).[49]

Raisonnable sailed for the Nore on 12 March to begin the process of decommissioning and paying off. A somewhat comical incident was recorded in the log when on 18 March Jno Thomas Taylor was punished with thirty-six lashes 'for attempting to desert in women's clothes'. It was not uncommon for a number of women to be onboard, hence not too difficult to obtain such garments.

The proper officers from the dockyard came aboard on 20 May and 'transported' the ship, to begin the process of stripping her over the next several weeks. The muster book records that on 1 June 1814 Samuel Brokensha was discharged, to end his sea service. A final examination of *Raisonnable* was made on 5 June, when the residual ship's company were sent on shore to be paid. The poignant final entry by Captain Clay reads, 'at sunset hauled down the pendant, the ship being paid off'. *Raisonnable* was broken up in 1815.

Chatham

Samuel's service record indicates that on 15 February 1816 he was appointed superintending master at Chatham. In this role, he would have had charge of a number of ships 'in ordinary' or repair and refit, and remained qualified to navigate and sail them between ports as required. Reporting to the yard's superior officers, the master(s) attendant, superintending masters retained their senior warrant officer status, but as a condition of their responsibilities and status were required to provide bonds to the value £500 (approximating to £35,000 in today's earnings) as a guarantee of their integrity.

According to the Chatham Royal Dockyard Library, no records of superintending masters or their activities survive, hence it has thus far not proved possible to investigate this chapter of Samuel's career or establish the term of his employment there. A possible indicator of residence in Chatham may be provided by the marriage on 27 May 1819 of Samuel's son Samuel to Mary Edwards in Higham, Kent, located the other side of the River Medway, about three miles from Chatham as the seagull flies.

Plymouth

Samuel signed his will on 30 September 1823, in which he described himself as 'a Master in the Royal Navy now residing at Stonehouse by Plymouth, Devon',[50] declared in the presence of witnesses including R M Oliver, Navy Agent Plymouth Dock, implying that Samuel remained employed by the Royal Navy. Further evidence of the Brokensha family's residence in Stonehouse may be inferred from the record of marriage of Samuel's daughter Amelia to Thomas Blewett, an officer in the African Colonial Corps, registered in East Stonehouse on 16 March 1826.

The Royal William Dockyard complex under architect Sir John Rennie began construction in 1825, completing in 1831, so it is probable that preparations involving existing yards and moorings in the Hamoaze required additional expertise, and Samuel's experience at Chatham would have been of great value. However, Samuel's surviving service record gives neither indication of cessation of employment at Chatham, nor mention of transfer to Plymouth Dock in any capacity. At the time of writing, no other records have been discovered that shed any light on the matter of Samuel's putative employment at Plymouth, so this remains conjectural.

Life in retirement

At some undetermined date, and probably subsequent to his final retirement from (assumed) employment in the Plymouth dockyards, Samuel became a resident of the nearby small picturesque Devon coastal village of Newton Ferrers. The Churchwardens and Overseers Parish Register for Newton Ferrers shows that in April 1829 'Mr. Brokensha' paid 2½d (approximately £10 in today's earnings) into the parish poor relief fund, a rate based on property levied 'as often as need requires'.[51] Samuel's property was described as 'House and Orchard', and over the next eight years it appears that he moved house several times, the levy varying along with each named property. On his last entry in the Register in 1837 Samuel paid 5d (about £20) into the fund.

Samuel died of a seizure aged sixty-nine on 30 December 1839, and was buried on 7 January 1840 in the cemetery of Holy Cross church, Newton Ferrers.[52] The actual grave site is unknown, there being neither a surviving cemetery grave map, nor any extant grave marker.

Samuel's will of 1823 left everything to his wife Mary, or in the event of her death to be shared equally between their two children, Lieutenant Samuel Brokensha and daughter Amelia. Mr Joseph Woodhead of Lyon's Inn, London, was nominated as the sole executor and the will proved on 4 February 1840. The 1841 Census reveals that Samuel's widow Mary, of independent means, was living in Newton Ferrers with her son-in-law,

219

daughter Amelia and family. Following Mary's death on 22 November 1855, her son Lieutenant Samuel Brokensha applied to the accountant general's department of the Admiralty for monies owed by the navy; the sum of £6 13s 4d for arrears of widow's pension was subsequently authorised.[53]

Nothing more is known of the last years of Samuel's life, there being neither documents nor artefacts surviving within the author's family, nor even handed-down yarns. It will probably forever remain a matter of complete conjecture as to whether the 'old salt' accomplice mentioned in the Porthpean smuggling incident associated with Luke Brokenshaw, was Samuel. Who better to keep quiet about the operation?

Postscript

Ongoing research into the Brokensha family history finally uncovered the family relationship between Samuel and Joseph, close scrutiny of the original Mevagissey baptism register for the year 1797 revealing an indistinct entry for Joseph Brokensha, son of William and Mary Rabblen Levers. Mary was the (married) eldest sister of Samuel and Luke Brokensha/w, thus making her son Joseph their nephew.[54] At face value, this baptismal evidence conflicts with his stated place of birth (Plymouth) as recorded in muster books, not to mention his proper surname; however, it is entirely feasible that Joseph was born in Plymouth, but taken to Mevagissey for baptism in his mother's family parish church. What is less clear is why Joseph entered the navy under the name Brokensha rather than Leivers, the spelling used by his 'sojourner' (ie, a non-resident, possibly itinerant worker) father, or Levers, as written down in the baptism register. Conjecturally, it may have been considered that use of the Brokensha name would, by association with his illustrious uncles, facilitate his career path.

The young Joseph followed his namesake from ship to ship, using the not uncommon ruse of an exaggerated age on joining. Samuel's son benefited from similar patronage, first serving in the same ship as his uncle Luke Brokenshaw, before later appearing in his father's ship along with cousin Joseph.

Joseph continued as a midshipman, from June 1814 without the benefit of Samuel senior, in the position of a serving warrant officer, to provide interest. Samuel junior quitted *Bedford* and the navy on 1 September 1814, almost a year after passing for a lieutenant, to join the coastguard service. The war over, the navy was quickly run down and there was no further opportunity for promotion.

Contributors' Biographies

Captain Michael Barritt is a former Hydrographer of the Navy, whose sea-going career took him to all the world's oceans. In *Eyes of the Admiralty* (2008), illustrated with the water colours of John Thomas Serres, he described wartime hydrographic activity during blockade and patrol duties of the fleet off the French and Spanish coasts in 1799–1800. He has published numerous articles and reviews, and is working on an account of the emergence of the RN Surveying Service during the wars of 1793–1815. He is immediate past president of the Hakluyt Society, which publishes important historic accounts of travel.

Anthony Bruce took degrees at Lancaster University and the University of Manchester, and was formerly director of policy development and then director of research at Universities UK, and has also worked in a number of other national higher education bodies. More recently he has been a higher education consultant.

Rear-Admiral Joseph Callo, USN is the author of three books about Nelson and an award-winning biography of John Paul Jones. Joe also was co-author of *Who's Who in Naval History*. He is an award-winning television producer and writer and currently producer of the New York Council of the Navy League of the United States speaker series titled 'The New Ways of War and Why They are More Important than You Think'. His latest book is *The Sea Was Always There*.

Kathryn Campbell has a master's degree in American History and Museum Studies, and became interested in Thomas Buttersworth while working as a curator at South Street Seaport Museum in New York. Her interest increased when she became curator of the Penobscot Marine Museum in Maine, and this became an obsession when she moved to England and began research for N R Omell, a maritime art gallery in London.

John Allan Conover graduated from the California Institute of Technology with a BSc in Mechanical Engineering and joined the US Air Force in 1959, served with Strategic Air Command as a pilot, an astronaut and development engineer, served three tours of duty at Headquarters Air Force and at the Department of Defense, and retired as a colonel in 1983. He then spent twenty-five years in private industry as a senior project engineer on military space programmes. An avid modeller of airplanes and ships, he began serious research on HMS *Victory* in 1999.

Charles Alan Fremantle is the last of a continuous line of Fremantles who served in the RN since 1777, and family historian with access to the comprehensive family archive loaned by his cousin Lord Cottesloe to the Buckinghamshire County Council.

Tom Fremantle is also a great-great-great-grandson of Thomas Francis Fremantle, who served ten years in the RN, followed by spells in a firm of stockbrokers, an MBA, twenty-five years of sales and marketing in the engineering industry.

Caroline Girard graduated from the Université Laval in Quebec City, worked for various museums and heritage organisations, including the Musée de la civilisation in Quebec City, and is the archivist at the Naval Museum of Québec.

Peter Hore is a former naval officer, spent ten years in the film and TV industry, is author or editor of a dozen books, and an elected member of the Royal Historical Society, the Swedish Royal Society of Naval Sciences and of the Society for Nautical Research, and a freelance obituarist at the *Daily Telegraph*.

Nigel Hughes comes from a Cornish seafaring family, is a retired mechanical design engineer, and has four blood-relatives plus three by marriage who served in the RN during the French Revolutionary and Napoleonic Wars.

Byrne McLeod, after careers in the City and the classroom, took an MA in maritime history, followed by a PhD in naval history, and published *British Naval Captains of the Seven Years' War: The View from the Quarterdeck* in 2012. She is honorary secretary of the Society for Nautical Research.

Kate Milburn graduated from Boise State University, Boise, Idaho, has won numerous prestigious scholarships in the USA and currently teaches English language and American history; she is currently a part-time postgraduate student at the State University, Huntsville, Texas.

Charles Neimeyer enjoyed a twenty-year career in the USMC, including tours in all three active US Marine Divisions and service at the White House. He became a professor of National Security Affairs 1997–2002 and taught history at the US Naval Academy in the late 1980s, became Dean of Academics at the Naval War College and Forrest Sherman Chair of Public Diplomacy in Newport, Rhode Island, and then Vice President of Academic Affairs at Valley Forge Military Academy and College. He is currently the Director of Marine Corps History and the Gray Research Center at Marine Corps University, Quantico, Virginia. His most recent monograph published by the US Naval Institute Press in 2015 is titled *War in the Chesapeake: The British Campaigns to Control the Bay, 1813–1814.*

Chipp Reid is a veteran of the United States Marine Corps and lives in Annapolis, Maryland, and is a naval historian for the US Naval Institute, specialising in Navy and Marine Corps history. He was a newspaper reporter and editor for many years, winning awards for his coverage of baseball, soccer, anti-piracy operations off Somalia, and the wars in Iraq and Afghanistan. His first books, *Intrepid Sailors: The Legacy of Preble's Boys and the Tripoli Campaign*, and *Lion in the Bay: The British Invasion of the Chesapeake, 1813–1814*, have received critical acclaim.

Victor Suthren was born in Montreal, Quebec, and after studies at Bishop's University, McGill and Concordia, entered the Canadian Parks Service as an historian, serving in Louisbourg and Halifax. In 1975 he joined the staff of the Canadian War Museum and was director-general 1986–97. He has written thirteen books, including seven sea novels of the eighteenth century and a popular history of the War of 1812, and, most recently, *The Island of Canada,* a study of Canada's relationship with the sea.

Peter Turner had the ambition to be a cartoonist, but everyone laughed, he became a draughtsman, an engineer, and a freelance consultant, specialising in lighting and elevator design. Patrick O'Brian takes the blame for his interest in the Georgian navy, and his AB&OS led to his membership of The 1805 Club.

Samuel Venière is a historian with the Naval Museum of Québec specializing in eighteenth- and nineteenth-century Canadian and Quebec history. He has a degree in history from Université Laval and is a historical consultant to a number of cultural events and gives historical presentations for the National Battlefields Commission.

Mark West read law at Corpus Christi College, Cambridge, is a barrister specialising in real property and trust law, and a deputy judge. He has a longstanding interest in the military and naval aspects of the Napoleonic Wars and is the chairman of the Forlorn Hope, a group which organises tours of Peninsular War sites in Spain and Portugal.

Notes

Nicholas Biddle: America's Revolutionary War Nelson

1 Notre Dame letter, 9 March 1778, *Naval Documents of the American Revolution* (Washington: Government Printing Office, 2012), 11:562 (NDAR).

2 Nicholas Vincent to James Young, 17 March 1778, NDAR, 11:683–4.

3 Washington Irving, Nicholas Biddle, in John H Frost (ed), *American Naval Biography* (New York: John Low, 1821), p90 (ANB).

4 Ibid.

5 Ibid, p19.

6 Ibid, p20.

7 William Bell Clark, *Captain Dauntless: The Story of Captain Nicholas Biddle of the Continental Navy* (Baton Rouge, La: Louisiana State University Press, 1949), p32.

8 Ibid, p23.

9 Ibid.

10 Ibid, p26.

11 Ibid, pp27–8.

12 Description from Charles Wilson Peale portrait.

13 The National Archives, Kew (TNA) ADM 36/7678 Admiralty Ships' Musters, HMS *Seaford* 1771: Biddle probably already knew of Scotsman Stirling (1713–1786), from Faskine, Lanarkshire, who married in 1753 Dorothy Willing, daughter of Charles Willing of Philadelphia. See also Nicholas Biddle to James Biddle, 17 July 1771, Nicholas Biddle Papers, Manuscript Division, Library of Congress, Washington DC (NBP).

14 Clark, *Captain Dauntless*, pp46–50.

15 Nicholas Biddle to Lydia McFunn, 20 October 1772, NBP.

16 Edward Biddle Memoir, NBP.

17 TNA ADM 36/7567 Admiralty Ships' Musters, HMS *Carcass* 1773. Biddle's name is spelled 'Beddle' in the muster books. He was rated 'AB' and from 11 May as 'Coxswain'. He received his £3 bounty as a volunteer.

18 ANB, p93.

19 TNA ADM 36/7567.

20 Nicholas Biddle to Lydia McFunn, 23 October 1773, NBP.

21 ANB, pp94–5.

22 Constantine John Phipps, Baron Mulgrave, *A Voyage Towards the North Pole Undertaken by His Majesty's Command, 1773* (Dublin: Sleater, Williams, Wilson, Husband, Walker and Jenkin, 1775), p63.

23 Clark, *Captain Dauntless*, pp66–8.

24 Robert Southey, *The Life of Horatio Lord Nelson* (New York: Barnes and Noble, 1993), pp7–8; ANB, p95.

25 Nicholas Biddle to Lydia McFunn, 23 October 1773, NBP.

26 Clark, *Captain Dauntless*, p70.

27 Ibid, p73.

28 *Journals of the Continental Congress*, 1774–1789, ed Worthington C Ford et al (Washington: Government Printing Office, 1904–1937), Electronic Edition, 3:443.

29 *Dictionary of American Fighting Ships*, Electronic Edition, Naval History and Heritage Center.

30 *Journals of the Continental Congress*, 3:443.

31 Captain Matthew Squire to Lord Dunmore, 18 September 1775, NDAR, 2:275.

32 John Hewes to Robert Smith, 7 January 1776, NDAR, 3:675.

33 Journal of the *Andrea Doria*, 4 March 1776, NDAR, 4:171.

34 Report of Captain Samuel Nicholas, Continental Marines, 10 April 1776, NDAR, 4:748–52; Journal of the *Andrea Doria*, 14 April 1776, NDAR, 4:818.

35 Clark, *Captain Dauntless*, p148.

36 Ibid.

37 *Journals of the Continental Congress*, 5:412.

38 Charles Biddle, *Autobiography*, pp90–1.

39 Robert Morris to Commissioners in France, 15 February 1777, NDAR, 7:1229

40 Clark, *Captain Dauntless*, pp182–6.

41 Ibid, p189.

42 Ibid, p191.

43 Charles Biddle, *Autobiography*, pp100–102.

44 William Moultrie, *Memoirs of the American Revolution So Far as It Related to the States of North Carolina, South Carolina, and Georgia* (New York: David Longworth, 1802), 1:100.

45 Marine Committee to Nicholas Biddle, 29 April 1777, Journals of the Continental Congress, Letters of Delegates, 6:681. (Instructions on the orders prevented Biddle from opening them until 10 July.)

46 Moultrie, *Memoirs*, 1:102.

47 Nicholas Biddle to Robert Morris, 12 September 1777, NDAR, 9:919–20.

48 John Dorsius to Robert Morris, 12 September 1777, NDAR, 9:920–1.

49 Moultrie, Memoirs, 1:195.

50 Charles Biddle, *Autobiography*, p106.

51 Ibid, p107.

52 Ibid.

53 Notre Dame Letter, NDAR, 11:562.

54 Nicholas Vincent to James Young, NDAR, 11:684

55 Account of the battle from Clark, Captain Dauntless, 237–42; Biddle, *Autobiography*, pp107–9; ANB, pp 97–101; Notre Dame letter, NDAR, 11:562 and Vincent to Young, 11:684.

56 Nicholas Biddle to Charles Biddle, 16 June 1776, NBP.

The Earliest Known 'Stars and Stripes'

1 The author is grateful to Walter Lewis for his assistance in tracking down several references, and to K N Kellow of the website 'The American War of Independence at Sea' (http://www.awiatsea.com) for the resources which he has made available, and to Christie's for permission to reproduce the painting by Francis Holman. Thanks are also due to Professor John Hattendorf, Mark West QC, and Captain Richard Woodman for reviewing this essay.

2   Modern references give his name as 'Pickering', but Thomas always spelled and signed his name without the final 'g' and that practice is used in this article.

3   See *American National Biography*. John Langdon (1741–1819) was a revolutionary, shipbuilder and shipowner, financier, speaker of the New Hampshire house of representatives, later federal senator, and, in 1779, president of the New Hampshire Convention for Regulating the Currency and also Continental agent whose role was to sell the prizes which local privateers brought into port.

4   Six 9pdrs, fourteen 6pdrs and two 1pdrs.

5   Edgar Stanton Maclay, *A History of American Privateers* (New York: D Appleton & Co, 1899), p135. Maclay erroneously lists her commander as Salter, who commanded her later during the Penobscot Expedition.

6   *The Freeman's Journal, or, The New-Hampshire Gazette* [NHG], Tuesday, 9 June 1778.

7   NHG, Tuesday, 20 April 1779.

8   Nicholas Carlisle, *Topographical Dictionary of Ireland* (London: William Miller, Albemarle Street, 1810).

9   NHG, Tuesday, 20 April 1779.

10 India Office Records IOR/L/MAR/B/42G: 12 Nov 1776–26 Mar 1779, log of HEIC *Bridgewater*; see also Nicholas Carlisle, *Topographical Dictionary of Ireland* (London: William Miller, Albemarle Street, 1810).

11 James Fenimore Cooper, *The History of the Navy of the United States of America* (Paris: A & W Galignani, 1839), vol I of II, pp105–6.

12 Richard Elliott Winslow, *Wealth and Honour: Portsmouth During the Golden Age of Privateering* (Portsmouth, New Hampshire: Portsmouth Marine Society, 1988), pp44–9.

13 India Office Records R/15/1/4: 8 Jun 1778–28 Jan 1787. Minutes of the Court of Directors.

14 *The Gentleman's Magazine and Historical Chronicle*, 49 (June 1799) p324; *The Scots Magazine*, 41 (July 1779), pp394–5; William Schaw Lindsay, *History of Merchant Shipping and Ancient Commerce* (London: Sampson Low, Marston, Low, & Searle, 1874), p580.

15 Jane Turner, Sarah Reynolds, and Peter Hore, *Catalogue of Maritime Art, 21 November 2012* (South Kensington: Christies's, 2012).

16 For background reading see Sir Charles Fawcett, 'The Striped Flag of the East India Company, and its Connexion with the American "Stars and Stripes"', *Mariner's Mirror*, 23 (1937).

17 North American Vexillological Association (NAVA) News no. 167 (April–June 2000) with addenda NAVA NEWS nos 168 (July–September 2000), 178 (April–June 2003) and 188 (October–December 2005); Martucci, David, 'The 13 Stars and Stripes: a Survey of 18th Century Images', Vexman.net, 2005 <http://www.vexman.net/13stars/> [accessed 27 June 2016].

18 Dale W Burbank, Major US Army, 'Want of Proper Spirit and Energy: The Penobscot Expedition of 1779' (unpublished Master's thesis, US Army Command and General Staff College, 2011); Richard Elliott Winslow, *Wealth and Honour: Portsmouth during the Golden Age of Privateering* (Portsmouth, New Hampshire: Portsmouth Marine Society, 1988), p46; George E Buker, *The Penobscot Expedition: Commodore Saltonstall and the Massachusetts Conspiracy of 1779* (Camden, Maine: Down East Books, 2002), pp19, 29, 67, 73, 82, 95, 122, 157.

19 NHG, Tuesday, 27 April 1779.

20 NHG, Tuesday, 20 April 1779.

21 *American National Biography*.

22 William Laird Clowes, *The Royal Navy a History from the Earliest Times to the Present*,

vol IV (London: Sampson Low, Marston & Company, 1899), p29.
23 NHG, Tuesday, 11 May 1779.
24 NHG, Tuesday, 29 June 1779.

Nelson in Troubled Waters

1 This article is adapted from *Nelson in the Caribbean – The Hero Emerges 1784–1787* (Naval Institute Press, 2003).
2 *The Dispatches and Letters of Lord Nelson,* vol 1, edited by Sir Nicholas Harris Nicolas, republished by Chatham Publishing, London, p113.
3 Ibid, p191.
4 Ibid, p192.
5 Rawson (ed), *Nelson's Letters from the Leeward Islands and Other Original Documents in the Public Record Office and the British Museum* (Golden Cockerel Press, 1953), p27.
6 Ibid, p29.
7 Ibid, p33.
8 Ibid, p34.
9 Ibid, p34.
10 *The Dispatches and Letters of Lord Nelson, Vol I*, edited by Sir Nicholas Harris Nicolas (republished London: Chatham Publishing, 1997), p156.
11 Ibid, pp134, 135.
12 Ibid, p178.
13 Ibid, p167.
14 Ibid, p115.
15 *The Dispatches and Letters of Lord Nelson, Vol IV*, edited by Sir Nicholas Harris Nicolas (republished London: Chatham Publishing, 1997), pp297, 298.

The Chesapeake–Leopard Affair, 1807

1 John Ehrman, *The younger Pitt: the years of acclaim* (London: Constable, 1969), p160.
2 Spencer C Tucker and Frank T Reuter, *Injured honor. The Chesapeake–Leopold affair, June 22, 1807* (Annapolis: Naval Institute Press, 1996), p20.
3 Ibid, pp20–1.
4 Denver Brunsman, *The evil necessity: British naval impressment in the eighteenth-century Atlantic world* (Charlottesville: University of Virginia Press, 2013).
5 Richard D Burns, Joseph M Siracusa, Jason C Flanagan, *American foreign relations since independence*, Santa Barbara: Praeger, 2013), p30.
6 Recent general histories include: Donald R Hickey, *The War of 1812: a forgotten conflict*, revised edition (Urbana: University of Illinois, 2012); Andrew Lambert, *The challenge. America, Britain and the War of 1812* (London: Faber and Faber, 2012); Jon Latimer, *1812: War with America* (Cambridge, Mass: Belknap Press, 2007).
7 Admiral Sir George Cranfield Berkeley (1753–1818) was an experienced and popular naval officer who saw action at all three Battles of Ushant and on the Glorious First of June, and during the Peace of Amiens, as inspector of the Sea Fencibles, he had reorganised the defences of Britain against French invasion. He was also a politician and was involved in several scandals, including feuds with Charles James Fox and Hugh Palliser. In 1806–7 he was temporarily out of political favour and as the naval commander-in-chief on the North America Station had been effectively banished from London. After the *Chesapeake–Leopard* affair he was particularly successful in helping to sustain Wellington's armies in the field during the Peninsular War. See *DNB* and Christopher D Hall, *Wellington's Navy:*

Sea Power and the Peninsular War 1807–1814 (London: Chatham, 2004).

8 Quoted in C E S Dudley, 'The "Leopard" incident', *History Today*, 19:7 (1969), p469.

9 *The trial of John Wilson, alias Jenkin Ratford, for mutiny, desertion and contempt* (Boston: Snelling and Simons, 1807), p12.

10 Henry Adams, *History of the United States of America* (New York: Charles Scribner's Sons, 1890), IV, p12.

11 *The naval war of 1812. A documentary history*, ed William S Dudley (Washington, DC: Naval Historical Center, 1985), I, p28.

12 *Proceedings of the general court martial convened for the trial of Commodore James Barron, Captain Charles Gordon, Mr William Hook, and Captain John Hall, of the United States' ship Chesapeake, in the month of January, 1808* (Washington, DC: Navy Department, 1822), p226.

13 Quoted in Spencer C Tucker and Frank T Reuter, op cit, p15.

14 Robert E Cray Jr, 'Remembering the USS *Chesapeake*: the politics of maritime death and impressment', *The Journal of the Early Republic*, 25:3 (2005), pp445–74.

15 *Memoirs, correspondence and private papers of Thomas Jefferson*, ed Thomas J Randolph (London: Henry Colburn and Richard Bentley, 1829), III, p100.

16 *The naval war of 1812. A documentary history*, op cit, p27.

17 Nick Mann, 'Sailors board me now: the *Chesapeake* affair', *Western Illinois Historical Review*, III (2011), p73.

18 Spencer C Tucker and Frank T Reuter, op cit, p127.

19 Robert E Cray, op cit, pp465–6.

20 Ibid, p471.

21 Alfred T Mahan, *Sea power in its relations to the war of 1812* (Boston, Mass: Little, Brown, and Company, 1905), I, p168.

22 Robert Ferrell, *American diplomacy: a history* (New York: W W Norton, 1959), p130.

23 Reginald Horsman, *The causes of the War of 1812* (Philadelphia: University of Pennsylvania, 1962); Andrew Lambert, op cit; Jasper M Trautsch, 'The causes of the war of 1812: 200 years of debate', *Journal of Military History*, 77:1 (2013), pp273–93.

24 Donald R Hickey, op cit, p3.

Impressment: Politics and People

1 Keith Mercer, 'Northern Exposure: Resistance to Naval Impressment in British North America, 1775–1815', *Canadian Historical Review*, 91:2 (2010), p201.

2 Daniel Baugh, *British Naval Administration in the Age of Walpole* (Princeton, New Jersey: Princeton University Press, 2015), p224.

3 Nicholas Roger, 'Impressment and the Law in Eighteenth-Century Britain', in *Law, Crime, and English Society, 1660–1830*, ed Norma Landau (Cambridge, United Kingdom: Cambridge University Press, 2002), p207.

4 *Law Notes*, volume 20 (Long Island, New York: E Thompson Company, 1917), p177.

5 Mercer, p207.

6 Denver Brunsman, 'Subjects vs Citizens: Impressment and Identity in the Anglo-American Atlantic', *Journal of the Early Republic*, 30:4 (2010), p562.

7 Nicholas Roger, *The Press Gang: Naval Impressment and its opponents in Georgian Britain* (Great Britain: Continuum, 2007), p20.

8 Brunsman, p567.

9 Brunsman, p567.

10 J Ross Dancy, *The Myth of the Press Gang: Volunteers, Impressment and the Naval*

Manpower Problem in the Late Eighteenth Century (Suffolk, United Kingdom: Boydell & Brewer, 2015), p126.

11 Brunsman, p565.

12 Francis Cogliano, *Emperor of Liberty: Thomas Jefferson's Foreign Policy* (Massachusetts: Yale University Press, 2014), p81.

13 Thomas Jefferson, *The Papers of Thomas Jefferson, vol 18, 4 November 1790 – 24 January 1791*, ed Julian Boyd (Princeton: Princeton University Press, 1971), p288.

14 Cogliano, p81.

15 Brunsman, p569.

16 Roger, 'Impressment and the Law', p89.

17 Troy Bickham, *The Weight of Vengeance: The United States, The British Empire, and the War of 1812* (New York: Oxford University Press, 2012), p35.

18 Mercer, p202.

19 Dancy, p134.

20 Dancy, p144.

21 Brunsman, p574.

22 Donald Hickey, *Don't Give Up the Ship: Myths of the War of 1812* (Chicago: University of Illinois Press, 2006), p20.

23 Paul Gilje, *Free Trade and Sailors' Rights in the War of 1812* (United Kingdom: Cambridge University Press, 2013), p115.

24 J Murray, *The Right and Practice of Impressment, as Concerning Great Britain and America, Considered* (London: University of Michigan, 2013), p150.

25 Dancy, p150.

26 Dancy, p150. Dancy's research only covers 1793–1801, so it should be noted that since the British navy grew to 145,000 by 1811, these numbers also likely grew.

27 A L Burt, 'The Nature of the Maritime Issues', in *The Causes of the War of 1812: National Honor or National Interest*, ed Bradford Perkins (USA: Holt, Reinhart, and Winston, 1962), pp11–22 (p14).

28 James Zimmerman, *Impressment of American Seamen* (Port Washington, New York: Kennikat Press, 1966), p164.

29 Zimmerman, p164.

30 Donald Hickey, *The War of 1812: A Forgotten Conflict* (Chicago: University of Illinois Press, 2012), p21.

31 Zimmerman, p164.

32 Edgar Maclay, *A History of the United States Navy from 1775 to 1893*, vol 3 (New York: Appleton, 1901), p308.

33 Pam and Derek Ayshford, 'Ayshford Trafalgar Roll', *Age of Nelson* (2010) http://www.ageofnelson.org/TrafalgarRoll/index.html>. It should be noted that this is the best estimate currently available.

34 'Ayshford Trafalgar Roll'.

35 Alexander Gillespie, *A History of the Laws of War* (Oxford: Hart Publishing, 2011), p43.

36 Gillespie, p25.

37 See Cobden, *The White Slaves of England: Compiled from official documents*, especially Chapter 7.

38 Brunsman, p571.

39 'Desertion, identity, and the North American squadron 1784–1812', Maritime Museum of the Atlantic (2015) <https://maritimemuseum.novascotia.ca/desertion-identity-and-north-american-squadron-1784-1812> (para 14).

40 Bickham, p25.
41 Burt, p13.
42 James Monroe, 'Mr Monroe, Secretary of State, to Plenipotentiaries of the United States, for treating of Peace with Great Britain dated 15 April 1813', in *The Examiner: Containing Political Essays on the most Important Events of the Time; Public Laws and Official Documents*, vol 2, ed Barent Gardenier (New York: General Books, 2012), pp402–16 (p406).
43 Jon Latimer, *1812: War with America* (Cambridge, MA: Belknap of Harvard UP, 2007), p31.
44 Thomas Jefferson, 'Jefferson to Levi Lincoln, 16 September 1804, in *Writings of Jefferson vol 8*, ed Paul Ford (Silver Street Media, 2009), pp321–2.
45 Henry Adams, *History of the United States of America During the First Administration of Thomas Jefferson to the Second Administration of James Madison: The Second Administration of Thomas Jefferson, 1805–1809* (Virginia: University of Virginia, 1890), p2.
46 Adams, p2.
47 Adams, p20.
48 Robert Rutland, *The Presidency of James Madison* (Lawrence, Kansas: University Press of Kansas, 1990), p78. 1811 did see an agreeable closing to the *Chesapeake* Affair. Humphreys and Berkley, the men commanding the *Leopard* were recalled to England in the aftermath of the *Chesapeake* Affair, but neither man was publicly censured. For more see *Injured Honor: The Chesapeake–Leopard Affair* by Spencer Tucker and Frank Reuter.
49 Reginald Horsman, *The Causes of the War of 1812* (Great Britain: Oxford University Press, 1962), p85.
50 Cogliano, p225.
51 Rutland, p48.
52 Horsman, p85.
53 'A Century of Lawmaking for a New Nation: US Congressional Documents and Debates 1774–1875', *Annals of Congress, House of Representatives, 9th Congress, 1st Session*, Library of Congress, p537.
54 Horsman, p79.
55 Hugh Howard, *M and Mr Madison's War* (New York: Bloomsbury Press, 2012), p10.
56 Adams, p178.
57 Adams, p79–80.
58 Adams, p126.
59 Horsman, p140.
60 Later the Embargo Act was replaced with the Non-Intercourse Act that pitted France and Britain against each other. The Non-Intercourse Act suspended trade with both belligerents for three months but would reinstate trade with the nation that repealed their respective restrictions on the United States.
61 Stephen Heidler, *The War of 1812* (United States: Greenwood Press, 2002), p31.
62 Alexander Hamilton, 'Hamilton to Porter, 23 May 1809', *War of 1812 MSS*, Indiana University Library.
63 *Annals of Congress, House of Representatives, 11th Congress, 3rd Session*, pp1093–6.
64 *Annals of Congress, House of Representatives, 12th Congress, 1st Session*, p3.
65 *Annals of Congress, House of Representatives, 12th Congress, 1st Session*, p3.
66 *Annals of Congress, House of Representatives, 12th Congress, 1st Session*, p637.
67 Mark Zuehlke, *For Honour's Sake: The War of 1812 and the Brokering of an Uneasy Peace*,

(Canada: Random House, 2006), p72.

68 The conquest of Canada, Florida, and the Louisiana Purchase provide an interesting context to expansionist goals during the time, although there is some debate as to how much expansionism played a role in declaring war. Certainly men like Clay supported expansion and he is credited with saying while in the Senate in 1810, 'the conquest of Canada is in your power. I trust I shall not be thought to be bold when I state that I truly believe that the militia of Kentucky are alone competent to place Montreal and Upper Canada at your feet.' See *Expansionists of 1812* by Pratt for more on the topic.

69 Murray, p22.

70 Murray, p23.

71 Murray, p63.

72 Murray, p26.

73 Ralph Griffiths and G E Griffiths, 'Conciliation with America: The True Policy of Great Britain', *The Monthly Review*, LXVIII, May to August (1812), p66.

74 Zimmerman, p177.

75 George Dangerfield, *The Era of Good Feelings* (London: Methuen, 1956), p22.

76 Foster to Castlereagh, 21 June 1812, FO 5/86.

77 James Madison, 'War Message to Congress', in *Presidential Document: The Speeches, Proclamations, and Politics That Have Shaped the Nation from Washington to Clinton*, ed Fred Israel (New York: Routledge, 2013), pp28–39.

78 Zimmerman, p175.

79 The Henry affair was a dramatic accusation that Federalists had been selling secrets to the British. The Madison administration paid $50,000 for the evidence that turned out to be nothing more than a useless fabrication. For more about the affair see *The Weight of Vengeance* by Bickham, pp 76–9.

80 Monroe, p409.

81 Monroe, p409.

82 Abijah Bigelow, 'To His Wife 12 January 1814', *Letters of Abijah Bigelow,* American Antiquarian Society (1810–1815), p354.

83 Alexander Dallas and H G Callaway, *An Exposition on the Causes and Character of the War* (Edinburgh: Dunedin Academic Press, 2011), p81.

84 Latimer, p926.

85 Brunsman, p582.

A Boy in Battle

1 Peter Hore, *Nelson's Band of Brothers* (Barnsley: Seaforth, 2015), pp66–70.

2 E J Hounslow, *Nelson's Right Hand Man* (Stroud: The History Press, 2016).

3 Anne Fremantle (ed), *The Wynne Diaries, 1798–1820* (Oxford: Oxford University Press, 1940), p492.

4 Hore, pp15–19.

5 Hore, pp20–3.

6 Fremantle Papers, Centre for Buckinghamshire Studies, Aylesbury (hereafter D/FR) 42/2/12 Charles Fremantle onboard *Ramillies* to his mother, 20 May 1813.

7 D/FR 42/2/41 Claxton onboard *Ramillies* at Halifax to Betsey Fremantle 11 September [1813]. Captain Christopher Claxton (1790?–1868) was later author of the *Naval Monitor*, harbourmaster at Bristol and a friend of Brunel, and a pioneer of steel hulls and the screw propulsion used in SS *Great Britain*.

8 Andrew Lambert, 'War of 1812: Floating Trade', *Trafalgar Chronicle* (2012), p25; Kevin

Phillips, *The Cousins' Wars* (Perseus Books Group, 1999), pp335–7.

9   Stephen Budiansky, 'Anglophile Federalists', *Trafalgar Chronicle* (2011), p83.

10 *The London Gazette,* issue 16750, p1334.

11 The first of six powerful frigates, named by General Washington, armed with twenty-four 42pdrs and thirty-two 4pdrs.

12 D/FR/42/2/13 Charles Fremantle onboard *Ramillies* off New London to his mother, 2 January 1814.

13 Rory Muir, *Wellington the path to victory 1769–1814* (Yale University Press, 2013), pp29–30, description, and numerous entries.

14 Eastport, Hampden, Bangor, Machias, Castin.

15 Gareth Glover and Charles Fremantle, *Wellington's Voice* (Frontline Books, 2012), p43.

16 D/FR/42/2/40 ...CClaxton, onboard *Ramillies* at Eastport Harbour, Moose Island to Betsey Fremantle, 13 July 1814.

17 *The London Gazette*, issue 16941, p1963.

18 D/FR/42/2/17 Charles Fremantle onboard *Ramillies* off the Patuxent River, Chesapeake to his mother, 1 September 1814.

19 Peter Snow, *When Britain Burned the White House* (John Murray, 2013), Chapter 10.

20 D/FR/42/2/35 Claxton, [onboard] Chesapeake Bay to Betsey, 15 September 1814.

21 Edward Lowther-Crofton CB (1783–1821) Commanded *Racoon* 1805/6, Post Captain 1811. Commanded *Leopard* 1814 wrecked on Anticosti Island in fog while carrying 475 Royal Scots Guards to Quebec, all were saved. Acting Captain 1814 *Royal Oak* Gazette 16947, p2078 Cousin of Baron Crofton of the Mote an Irish Peerage,

22 D/FR/42/2/47 T M Hardy onboard *Ramillies* 'on our way to Jamaica' to Thomas Fremantle, October 1814.

23 'The Red Ribband' referred to the award of a knighthood to Thomas Fremantle for his services in services in freeing the Adriatic from the French: the Austrians also gave him a barony.

24 D/FR 211, E L Crofton onboard *Royal Oak* to Charles Fremantle, 16 September 1814.

25 D/FR/42/2/2 Charles Fremantle, *Ramillies* off Baltimore, to his mother, 17 September 1814.

26 Lady Fremantle (Betsey), Journal, 20 April 1815.

27 Later Vice-Admiral Sir Andrew Pellet Green (1777–1858), sailor and spy, who served with Fremantle at Copenhagen and Trafalgar. Our two families still have regular meetings.

28 Ann Parry, *The Admirals Fremantle* (Chatto & Windus, 1971), p137.

The Rocket's Red Glare: Francis Scott Key and the Star-Spangled Banner

1   Built 1812–3 at Topsham, Devon, and abandoned in the Arctic in 1848 during the Franklin expedition. Commanded in the War of 1812 by Commander John Sheridan.

2   Also spelled *Etna*, formerly the *Success*, purchased in 1803 and sold in 1816, she was armed with one 13in and one 10in mortars. Her commander, Irish-born Commander Richard Kenah, was killed on 3 October 1814.

3   Commodore Joshua Barney to Secretary of the Navy William Jones, 4 July 1813, in William S Dudley (ed), *Naval War of 1812: A Documentary History* (Washington DC: Naval Historical Center, 1985–92), 2:373–4.

4   Stephan Budiansky, *Perilous Fight: America's Intrepid War with Britain on the High Seas, 1812–1815* (New York: A A Knopf, 2010), p254; Paul A Gilje, 'The Baltimore Riots of 1812 and the Breakdown of the Anglo-American Mob Tradition', *Journal of Social History* 13:4 (Summer 1980), pp547–64.

5 'Secret Letter from Rear-Admiral George Cockburn to Vice Admiral Alexander Cochrane', 17 July 1814, *Maryland Historical Magazine* 6:1 (March 1911), pp16–19; Charles P Neimeyer, *War in the Chesapeake: The British Campaigns to Control the Bay, 1813–14* (Annapolis, MD: The Naval Institute, 2015), p139.

6 'Official Report of Rear-Admiral George Cockburn', quoted in J Thomas Scharf, *History of Maryland* (Baltimore, MD: J B Piet, 1879), 3:74.

7 John McCavitt and Christopher T George, *The Man Who Captured Washington: Major General Robert Ross and the War of 1812* (Norman, OK: University of Oklahoma Press, 2016), p130.

8 Marc Leepson, *What So Proudly We Hailed: Francis Scott Key, A Life* (New York: Palgrave Macmillan, 2014), pp52–3; McCavitt and George, p171. This was a great cover story for Holden in that he needed to convince Evans that he had been illegally detained by Beanes, or he may have been charged with the far more serious crime of desertion. No one had been killed and Beanes seems to have been responsible for the detention of just five stragglers.

9 Leepson, p53; Courtney C Hobson, 'Patriot or Traitor: John Hodges in 1814', accessed 15 May 2016, http://www.ultimatehistoryproject.com/patriot-or-traitor.html. Hodges was defended by Bladensburg veteran and former US Attorney General William Pinkney. He was easily acquitted of all charges.

10 McCavitt and George, p172.

11 Leepson, pp53–4.

12 Francis Scott Key to John Randolph, 5 October 1814, quoted in Leepson, p57. The 'Star-Spangled Banner' did not become the 'official' national anthem of the United States until 1931.

13 Steve Vogel, *Through the Perilous Fight: Six Weeks that Saved the Nation* (New York: Random House, 2013), pp272–3. The ship's name is also spelled *Surprise* and she was commanded by Vice-Admiral Cochrane's son, Thomas John Cochrane, though some sources give her commander's name as Captain George Henry William Knight.

14 Ibid, pp283–4.

15 Ibid, p319.

16 Ibid, p311.

17 Scott Sheads, *The Rocket's Red Glare: The Maritime Defense of Baltimore in 1814* (Centreville, MD: Tidewater Publishers, 1986), p99. See also https://en.wikipedia.org/wiki/To_Anacreon_in_Heaven, accessed 18 May 2016.

18 Vogel, p345.

19 Walter Lord, *Dawn's Early Light* (Baltimore, MD: The Johns Hopkins University Press, 1972), pp296–7; Vogel, p359; Leepson, p67. For years, many believed that Key watched the bombardment of Baltimore aboard HMS *Minden*, a 74-gun ship of the line. However, it is clear from research that the *Minden* never served in America during the War of 1812. The *Minden* confusion was likely related to a misidentification made by a man named William Curtis Naps who presented a cane to President Abraham Lincoln in 1863, made from the timbers of the ship of this name which had been recently broken up in Canton, China. For more information on the *Minden* misidentification see Ralph E Eshelman and Scott Sheads, *Chesapeake Legends and Lore from the War of 1812* (Charleston, SC: History Press, 2013), pp72–4.

Frédéric Rolette: Un Canadien héros de la guerre de 1812

1 The *Constitutional Act* of 1791 split Canada in two: Lower Canada, which more or less

covered the St Lawrence Valley, and Upper Canada, to the west of the Ottawa River, which covered the area that is now southern Ontario and the Great Lakes region.

2 *Canadien* is the French translation of Canadian. In the beginning of the nineteenth century, *Canadiens* refers to French-speaking inhabitants of the St Lawrence Valley, as the Anglophones were mostly called 'English'. It is only by the second half of the nineteenth century that the term 'Canadians' starts to refer to the Anglophones of Canada, as the Francophones now start to call themselves 'French-Canadians'. Geneviève Joncas, 'Virage à 180 degrés: des Canadiens devenus Québécois', *Revue Cap-Aux-Diamants*, Quebec City, no. 96 (2009), pp25–8.

3 Quebec City, 'Patrimoine urbain', Quebec City. Online: http://www.ville.quebec.qc.ca/culture_patrimoine/patrimoine/patrimoine_urbain/fiche.aspx?fiche=20 (visited 2 June 2016).

4 'Recherches historiques: Le capitaine Frédéric Rolette', *La Minerve*, daily edition, Montreal, morning of Wednesday, 5 February 1868.

5 Benjamin Sulte, *Histoire des Canadiens-français, 1608–1880. Ouvrage orné de portraits et de plans*, vol VIII (1884), p87.

6 Philéas Gagnon, *Bulletin des recherches historiques*, vol I (February 1895).

7 'Major figures of the War of 1812: Charles Frederick Rolette, Canadian Officer of the Royal Navy (1783–1831)', Government of Canada, http://canada.pch.gc.ca/eng/1442597039902/1446050185066.

8 Benjamin Sulte, op cit.

9 'The officers of the Provincial Marine received their commissions from the Commander-in-Chief in British North America, and the whole force was attached to the Department of the Quartermaster-General. On the arrival of the first detachment of the Royal Navy, these gentlemen were informed that their commissions could not be recognized by the rules of a service which subsequent intercourse with Turks and Frenchmen, Sardinians and Russians, had rendered far more cosmopolitan. With a very suggestive show of reticence, the greater part of these officers retired from the Marine and took service in the Militia. Two of the number, Lieutenants George Smith and James Richardson, could not bring themselves to abandon their more natural element, and, to the great satisfaction of the Commodore, accepted rating as "masters," which gave them rank in the gunroom with the commission officers'. William F Coffin, *1812: The War, and its Moral: A Canadian Chronicle* (Montreal: John Lovell, 1864), pp134–5.

10 Collection of the Naval Museum of Québec. Spelling and grammatical errors in the letter have not been altered.

11 *Biography: Lieutenant Frédérick Rolette*, Royal Canadian Navy, http://www.navy-marine.forces.gc.ca/en/navy-life/rolette-bio.page.

12 Philéas Gagnon, op cit.

13 Capture of Detroit: War of 1812, http://www.eighteentwelve.ca/?q=eng/Topic/14.

14 Philéas Gagnon, op cit.

15 Letter from Felix Throughton to Frédéric Rolette, 1813, Chatillon family collection.

16 Letter from Major-General Henry Procter to Frédéric Rolette, 1816, Chatillon family collection.

17 Philéas Gagnon, op cit.

18 Letter from L'loyd, Surgeon, Royal Artillery, December 1815. Chatillon family collection.

19 Battle of Lake Erie (Put-In-Bay): War of 1812, http://www.eighteentwelve.ca/?q=eng/Topic/35.

20 Robert B Townsend, 'Battle of Put-In-Bay', Excerpt from *Freshwater Navies of Canada*.

21 Excerpt from *The Quebec Gazette*, 21 March 1831.

22 The sword has a funny spelling mistake. It is indeed written 'patrotic' when it should be written 'patriotic'.

23 Jeune Bibaud, *Dictionnaire historique des hommes illustres du Canada et de l'Amérique*, Montreal, 1857, p280.

24 LS Fabrice Mosseray, 'HMCS Carleton, Arctic Offshore Patrol Ship Named after a Quebec Hero, Royal Canadian Navy', http://www.navy-marine.forces.gc.ca/en/news-link/link-view.page?doc=arctic-offshore-patrol-ship-named-after-a-quebec-hero/ilnc7p0d. We must know that Rolette has different spellings in the archives: Rolette, Rollet, Roulette, and Frédéric has also been spelled Frédérick.

Pathfinders: Front-line Hydrographic Data-gathering in the Wars of American Independence and 1812

1 Roger Knight, *Britain Against Napoleon: The Organisation of Victory 1793–1815* (London: Allen Lane, 2013), xxii–xxiii, p103.

2 Michael Barritt, 'Agincourt Sound Revisited', in *Mariner's Mirror* (hereafter MM), 101:2 (May 2015), pp184–99. The argument will be elaborated in a book in course of preparation.

3 Alexander Dalrymple, Introduction to a *Collection of nautical memoirs and journals ... reprinted for the use of the Royal Navy* (London, 1806).

4 The National Archives (hereafter TNA) ADM 1/3461, Memorial of Thomas Hurd to the Board of Admiralty, dated 16 November 1818.

5 Canadian Dictionary of National Biography online, http://www.biographi.ca/en/index.php, accessed 1 April 2016.

6 United Kingdom Hydrographic Office Miscellaneous Papers (hereafter UKHO MP) 36 (Ab4ii), pp71, 108.

7 TNA ADM 1/487, f174.

8 TNA Colonial Office (hereafter CO) 37/44/15, p265; TNA ADM 1/493, letter dated 27 May 1795.

9 The survey of Bermuda is described and analysed in detail in Adrian Webb, *Thomas Hurd, RN and His Hydrographic Survey of Bermuda 1789–97* (Bermuda: National Museum of Bermuda Press, 2016).

10 TNA ADM 36/8433.

11 J Ralfe, *The Naval Biography of Great Britain* (London: Whitmore and Fenn, 1828), vol II, pp352–6; J Marshall, *Royal Navy Biography*, vol I (London: Longman, Hurst, Rees, Orme and Brown, 1823), p157; Stephen J Hornsby, *Surveyors of Empire: Samuel Holland, J F W Des Barres and the Making of the Atlantic Neptune* (Montreal and Kingston: McGill Queens University Press, 2011), pp200–1.

12 TNA ADM 52/1789, Part 9 *Haerlem*; ADM 51/293, Part 4 *Eagle;* Knight's work at Sandy Hook is shown on Plate 13 in BL Maps 184.m.3.

13 J K Laughton (ed), *The Naval Miscellany*, volume I (London: Navy Records Society, 1901), p163.

14 S Fisher, 'Captain Thomas Hurd's Survey of the Bay of Brest during the Blockade in the Napoleonic Wars', in MM 79:3 (August 1993), pp293–304; M K Barritt, *Eyes of the Admiralty* (London: National Maritime Museum, 2008), pp45–51, 116–17.

15 J D Ware and R R Rea, *George Gauld, Surveyor and Cartographer of the Gulf Coast* (Gainsville Tampa: University of Florida, 1962), pp59–79.

16 Clements R Markham, *A Naval Career during the Old War* (London: Sampson Low,

Marston, 1883), p46.

17 Melville Papers, Clements Library, quoted in Andrew Lambert, *The Challenge: Britain Against America in the Naval War of 1812* (London: Faber and Faber, 2012), Chapter 3 (Kindle edition).

18 W A Spray, 'British Surveys in the Chagos Archipelago and Attempts to form a Settlement at Diego Garcia in the Late Eighteenth Century', in MM 56:1 (February 1970), pp74–5; G Cornwallis-West, *The Life and Letters of Admiral Cornwallis* (London: Robert Holden, 1927), pp151–2.

19 G S Graham and R A Humphreys (eds), *The Navy and South America 1807–1823* (London: Navy Records Society, 1962), pp72–4, 77, 79–80.

20 Ibid, pp86, 90–2; TNA ADM 1/1947 Cap H210; E Tagart, *A Memoir of Captain Peter Heywood RN, with Extracts from his Diaries and Correspondence* (London: E Wilson, 1832), pp 255–71.

21 Graham and Humphreys, pp90, 98–100, 105–6, 128–9, 132–3, 135–7.

22 UKHO Letter Book (hereafter LB) 1, letter dated 2 September 1815.

23 UKHO MP. 54(Ad1), pp501–4.

24 TNA ADM 12/188, Cut 57.

25 Clements R Markham, *A Memoir of the Indian Surveys* (London: W H Allen, 1878), pp14–16, 23.

26 TNA ADM 3/260 contains the Admiralty's orders to Hillyar in May 1812. Remarks from the *Racoon*, which Hillyar detached to the River Columbia, have been transcribed and published by M Rees as *The Remarkable Voyage of HMS Racoon 1813–14* (Seattle: University Book Store Press, 2011).

27 Hillyar's journal is at NMM MS87/026. Gardiner's journal, edited by John S Rieske with an introduction by Andrew Lambert, was published as *Hunting the Essex* (Barnsley: Seaforth, 2013).

28 Brady's surveys are preserved in the UKHO archive and his views in the TNA ADM 344 series.

29 TNA ADM 1/1950, No. 300B, letter from Hillyar dated 26 June 1812

30 UKHO 132 on Pb.

31 TNA ADM 1/1950, No. 265, letter dated 13 April 1812; G Vancouver, *A Voyage of Discovery to the North Pacific Ocean and round the World 1791–1795* (London: Hakluyt Society Edition, 1984), vol II, pp781–4, in which the description is from a sketch survey by Lieutenant Richard Hergest, a veteran of Cook's second and third Pacific voyages and the embarked astronomer, William Gooch, during the voyage of the storeship *Daedalus* to join Vancouver.

32 UKHO 135 on Pv* is Pipon's, and 584 on Pv is Staines'.

33 TNA ADM 37/3532, Muster Book Nos. 208 and 209.

34 Captain Basil Hall, *Extracts from a Journal, written on the coasts of Chili, Peru, and Mexico in the years 1820, 1821, 1822* (Edinburgh: Constable, 1825), vol II, Appendix No. 1, pp 4–5.

35 Lieutenant Poyntz's surveys of Penetanguishene and the approaches are at UKHO 190 and 191 on Aa2 and his remarks are in MP 31(Aa1ii).

36 TNA ADM 1/2264 Cap. O 299, dated 7 October 1815.

37 TNA ADM 1/2264 Cap. O 271, dated 3 August 1815.

38 TNA ADM 1/2264 Cap. O 41, dated 28 Oct 1815

39 Captain James Scott RN, *Recollections of a Naval Life* (London: Richard Bentley, 1834), vol III, Chapter V.

40 The correspondence relating to the appointments is at TNA ADM 1/506, O22, ff151–5.

41 William James, *Naval History*, vol VI, p187; United Services Journal (1836), Part III, pp25–6.

42 UKHO MB1, f231, 25 March 1829.

43 Cochrane's report of the operation is at TNA ADM 1/506, ff1191–5.

44 UKHO LB1, Nos. 343 and 443.

45 TNA ADM 1/503, O 100, 557, report from Warren, dated 28 May 1813.

46 His survey of the Patuxent is at UKHO 303 on Ra. His other surveys from the Chesapeake have not survived. De Mayne's contribution and the coverage of BA Chart 305 are discussed in R Morrison and R Hansen, *Charting the Chesapeake* (Hagerstown: Maryland State Archives, 1990), p55.

47 For his influence on Admiralty Board oversight of hydrographic administration see Adrian Webb, 'The Expansion of British Naval Hydrographic Administration, 1808–1829' (unpublished doctoral thesis, University of Exeter, 2010), pp44–5.

Charting the Waters: The Emergence of Modern Marine Charting and Surveying during the Career of James Cook in North American Waters, 1758–1767

1 J C Beaglehole, *The Life of Captain James Cook* (Stanford: Stanford University Press, 1974), p32.

2 L A Brown, 'The Atlantic Neptune', *Pennsylvania Magazine of History and Biography* (Philadelphia: Historical Society of Pennsylvania, 1943), vol 67, no. 4.

3 R Skelton and R Tooley, *The Marine Surveys of James Cook in Newfoundland* (London: Map Collectors' Circle, 1967), p13.

4 Skelton and Tooley, op cit, p17.

5 John Robson, *Captain Cook's War and Peace* (Barnsley: Seaforth Publishing, 2009), p98.

6 Victor Suthren, *To Go Upon Discovery: James Cook and Canada 1758–1779* (Toronto: Dundurn Press, 2000), p7.

7 Brown, op cit, vol 67, no. 4.

8 Beaglehole, op cit, p58.

9 Robson, op cit, p182.

10 Ibid, p137.

11 Beaglehole, op cit, p89.

Captain Archibald Kennedy, an American in the Royal Navy

1 George Washington used No. 1 Broadway as his headquarters for a period when the Revolutionary war broke out in 1775. When the British reoccupied the city in 1776 the property became the headquarters of the British commander-in-chief, Sir Henry Clinton.

2 The National Archive, ADM 1/2009 Captains' Letters K Kennedy, 29 April 1753.

3 *Halifax*: this brigantine was built on Lake Oswego 1756. She was later taken and burnt by the French. David Lyon, *The Sailing Navy List All the Ships of the Royal Navy Built, Purchased and Captured 1688–1860* (Conway, 1993), p302.

4 TNA ADM 1/ 2009 Captains' Letters K 1751–6 Kennedy, 30 November 1756.

5 TNA ADM 1/2010 Captains' Letters K 1757–9 Kennedy, 18 August 1757.

6 John Charnock, *Biographia Navalis* (London 1798), vol VI, p263. *Vestal* 32-gun 5th rate O 1756 K 1756 L 1757, Lyon, p82.

7 *Flamborough* 20-gun 6th rate O 1755 K 1755 L 1756, Lyon, p89.

8 TNA ADM 1/2011 Captains' Letters K 1760–62, 14 April 1760

9 This image has been made available by Rob Gardiner of Seaforth Publishing. The original

is held by the Beverley R Robinson Collection, Annapolis.

10 Marquis of Ailsa, 19th Earl of Cassillis, 22nd Lord Kennedy. Both painting and salver remain at Culzean Castle.

11 Reproduced by kind permission of the National Trust of Scotland photo library.

12 Mather Brown (1761–1831) was American-born, and arrived in London in 1781 and quickly began painting American citizens such as John Adams and Thomas Jefferson. He painted a companion piece to the portrait of Archibald Kennedy, that of his wife Ann Watts. His success led to his appointment as official portrait painter of the Duke of York.

13 A B McLeod, *British Naval Captains of the Seven Years' War* (Boydell and Brewer, 2012), p144.

14 McLeod, *British Naval Captains*, p56.

15 *Coventry* 28-gun 6th rate O 1756 K 1756 L 1757, Lyon p85.

16 TNA ADM 1/2012 Captains' Letters K 1763–70 Kennedy, 29 October 1763.

17 Interested readers can find several views of this mansion in the collection of the New York Picture Library http://digital.nypl.org/mmpco/searchresultsK.cfm?keyword=kennedy+mansion+1+broadway.

18 TNA ADM 1/2014 Captains' Letters K 1771–81 Kennedy, 16 November 1781.

19 TNA ADM 1/2014 Captains' Letters K 1771–81 Kennedy, 16 November 1781.

20 In 1509 Sir David Kennedy, the 3rd Lord Kennedy, was created Earl of Cassillis, which is why the titles are not in step. Clan Kennedy, Wikipedia [accessed 2 February 2016].

Admiral Sir Isaac Coffin: Nelson's American Pallbearer

1 Most of the information in this article about Sir Isaac Coffin is readily available in the public domain, not least in the *Oxford Dictionary of National Biography*, in the *Naval Chronicle* (especially volume 12), in *Royal Naval Biography*, Marshall, vol 1, and in Wikipedia, and it will consequently not be overburdened with unnecessary references for all the basic details. It may, however, be of interest to check out the following: http://www.oxforddnb.com/view/article/5807?docPos=1; https://archive.org/stream/lifeofadmiralsir00inamor/lifeofadmiralsir00inamor_djvu.txt; http://www.biographi.ca/en/bio/coffin_isaac_7E.html; http://www.historyofparliamentonline.org/volume/1820-1832/member/coffin-sir-isaac-1759-1839; https://en.m.wikipedia.org/wiki/Sir_Isaac_Coffin,_1st_Baronet.

2 Established on 23 April 1635, it is generally accepted to be both the first and oldest public school in the United States.

3 In 1827 Coffin gave £2,500 for the creation of the Sir Isaac Coffin's Lancasterian School on the brig *Clio*, which he had purchased for the purpose on his last visit to Nantucket. After a large fire in 1854 the school had to be rebuilt and eventually became today's Egan Maritime Institute.

4 Coffin, Nathaniel, *Dictionary of Canadian Biography*, volume VII (1836–1850).

5 Refer to Peter Hore's comments in *Nelson's Band of Brothers*.

6 *Europe* was renamed from *Europa* early in 1778, causing some confusion to historians.

7 *The Life of Admiral Sir Isaac Coffin, baronet, his English and American ancestors*, by Thomas C Amory (Thomas Coffin) (1812–1889).

8 The English fleet comprised twenty-two sail of the line and the French fleet comprised one ship of 110 guns, twenty-eight two-decked ships, and two frigates.

9 See note 5.

10 31st Article of War: 'Every officer or other person in the fleet, who shall knowingly make or sign a false muster or muster book, or who shall command, counsel, or procure the

making or signing thereof, or who shall aid or abet any other person in the making or signing thereof, shall, upon proof of any such offence being made before a court martial, be cashiered, and rendered incapable of further employment in His Majesty's naval service.'

11 Seamen did not readily learn to swim. Swimming was generally seen by the lower decks as a method of prolonging the adverse experience of drowning, which was much more acceptable if completed quickly, preferably without the early involvement of sharks.

12 Or recruiting officer, responsible for the press.

13 In 1796 the Navy Board was reconstituted: the post of Clerk of the Acts was abolished, as were the three Controllers of Accounts. Henceforward, the board would consist of the Controller and a Deputy Controller (both of whom were normally commissioned Officers), the Surveyor (usually a Master Shipwright from one of the Dockyards) and around seven other Commissioners (a mixture of officers and civilians) to whom no specific duties were attached.

14 Letter to J E Blackett, Esq, *Excellent* – Ajaccio, Corsica, 14 March 1796. 'This part of Corsica is still more barbarous than San Fiorenzo: the least offence offered to one of the inhabitants is resented by a stab, or a shot from behind a wall. [...] Some bad carpenters were discharged from the yard on Saturday, because they were not wanted, and on Sunday morning they took a shot at Commissioner Coffin, as he walked in his garden, but missed him.', in G L Newnham Collingwood, *A Selection from the Public and Private Correspondence of Vice-Admiral Lord Collingwood* by (New York, 1829).

15 Captain W V Anson, *Life of John Jervis, Admiral Lord St Vincent* (1913).

16 Coffin to Admiralty, 13 April 1801, TNA: PRO, ADM 106/1844.

17 After Nelson's coffin was carried to the western entrance of St Paul's by sixteen sailors, it was accepted by ten admirals acting as pallbearers at the funeral. The four next to the coffin were Orde (a last-minute replacement for Savage who was indisposed), Whitshed, Harvey and Taylor, and then there were six more supporting the canopy: Coffin, Domett, Wells, Drury, Aylmer and Douglas, all in mourning cloaks, over their respective full uniform coats, black waistcoats, breeches, and stockings, crepe round their arms, and crepe hatbands. See Ludovic Kennedy, *Nelson and his Captains*.

18 *The Life of Admiral Sir Isaac Coffin, baronet, his English and American ancestors*, by Thomas C Amory (Thomas Coffin) (1812–1889).

19 Ibid.

20 http://www.historyofparliamentonline.org/volume/1820-1832/member/coffin-sir-isaac-1759-1839.

21 He claimed to have crossed the Atlantic on thirty occasions (his last visit coming in 1829) and was responsible for importing English racehorses, plants, and stocks of European turbot for commercial fishing.

22 *The Times*, 11 June 1839.

What Did HMS Victory Actually Look Like at the Battle of Trafalgar?

1 Goodwin, *Nelson's Ships*, p262.

2 John McKay, *The 100-Gun Ship Victory* (London: Conway Maritime Press, 2000), p9; Goodwin, *Nelson's Ships*, p263.

3 Finberg LXXXVII.

4 The visitor at Dover was a reporter identified as 'RJ' in Adkins, pp308–9.

5 Bugler, *HMS Victory*, p 26.

6 Finberg LXXXIX. This sketchbook also includes sketches of the bow of a ship identified

as *Temeraire*, which was undergoing repairs at Portsmouth during the Christmas period of 1805, and a sketch of the Spanish *Santísima Trinidad* in her four-decker configuration. She was sunk at Trafalgar, and was never anywhere near England for Turner to draw.

7 Finberg LXXXIX D05467_E, 'The "*Victory*": Starboard Side 1805'.
8 Finberg LXXXIX D05483_E, 'The "*Victory*": Three-Quarter Stern View 1805'.
9 Bugler, *HMS Victory*, p29.
10 Roy Adkins, *Nelson's Trafalgar: The Battle That Changed the World* (New York: Penguin Group, 2004), p98.
11 Finberg LXXXIX D05486_E, 'The "*Victory*": Fore Part of Starboard Side 1805'.
12 Bugler 1966, p28.
13 Goodwin, *Nelson's Ships*, p261.
14 Finberg LXXXIX D05487_E, 'The "*Victory*": Port Side, Smaller Vessels Alongside [*sic*] 1805'.
15 Finberg CXXI S D08275_9, 'The "*Victory*": From Quarterdeck to Poop 1805'.
16 J R Piggott, '"The High Raised Nelson Star": Turner, Nelson and the Royal Navy', *Trafalgar Chronicle*, No. 18 (2008), p143.
17 Roy Adkins, *Nelson's Trafalgar* (London: Penguin Books, 2004), p124.
18 Goodwin, *Nelson's Ships*, p249.
19 Tate Britain D08243, 'HMSV Forward from Mizzen Shrouds'.
20 Bugler, *HMS Victory*, pp28–9.
21 Brian Lavery, *The Arming and Fitting of English Ships of War, 1600–1815* (London: Conway Maritime Press, 1987), p253.
22 James Lees, *The Masting and Rigging of English Ships of War, 1625–1860* (London: Conway Maritime Press, 1979), p45.

Thomas Buttersworth: A Biographical Note of a Sailor Turned Artist
1 The National Archives (hereafter TNA) ADM 73/40 General Entry Book of Officers and Pensioners. Other contemporary naval officer-artists included Thomas Yates, Robert Strickland Thomas, and Robert Cleveley.
2 TNA, ADM 29/14/122 Thomas Buttersworth; rating; born: Isle of Wight; age on entry not given; dates served 25 August 1790 to 15 August 1802.
3 Rif Winfield, *British Warships in the Age of Sail, 1793–1817* (Seaforth, 2005), p143.
4 TNA, ADM 7/361 Return of men raised at the Port of London 1795.
5 TNA, ADM 51/1261, log book of *Caroline.*
6 TNA, ADM 51/1261, log book of *Goliath*; National Maritime Museum (hereafter NMM), ADM/L/B/182 Lieutenant's log book of *Britannia*. In many ways, George Buttersworth had a somewhat more common experience in the navy than his brother. He volunteered in 1793, served on three ships before 1800, when he deserted while on leave. He was pressed onboard *Latona* a month later and served for another twelve years.
7 NMM, ADM/L/B/182, Lieutenant's log book from *Britannia*.
8 NMM PAH9508 The *Arrogant, Intrepid* and *Virginie* chasing French and Spanish Squadron off coast of China, 27 January 1799.
9 See, for example, Nicholas Tracy, *The Miracle of the Kent* (2008), p202.
10 TNA, ADM 51/1381 Captain's log. HMS *Caroline*, 20 September 1798 to 7 April 1802.
11 TNA, ADM 102/707 Admiralty: Naval Hospitals' and Hospital Ships' Musters, and Miscellaneous Journals, Port Mahon.
12 TNA, ADM 35/1536 Navy Board: Navy Pay Office: Ships' Pay Books, HMS *Resource,* 2 September 1793 to 2 March 1802

13 Isle of Wight Record centre, Will of James Buttersworth, proved 16 November 1790.
14 TNA, CP 40/386 Chief Justice's roll, 49 Geo III, Hilary term, 1809.
15 Ben Weinreb and Christopher Hibbert (eds), *The London Encyclopedia* (Macmillan, 1983), p561.
16 Parish registers of St George the Martyr, Southwark, 1 May 1804 'Church of England Baptisms, Marriages and Burials, 1538-1812'.<www.ancestry.co.uk> [accessed 3 May 2016].
17 London Metropolitan Archives, LABG/140/006.
18 NMM, PAG 8678 Plate depicting ships captured by Nelson 1793–1801 and also the Battle of Genoa, Battle off Cape St Vincent, Battle of the Nile and Battle of Copenhagen.
19 British Library, Egerton Ms 1614, fol. 51.
20 NMM, PAG 7151 Representation of the advanced Squadron under the command of Rear Admiral Lord Nelson during the blockade of Cadiz exhibiting a View of the Harbour and fortifications, 1797.
21 NMM, PAH 7919 Plate representing the *Captain* ... boarding the *San Joseph* ... and the *San Nicholas*.
22 NMM, PAI 5757 To the Right Honble Viscount Nelson ...The *Magnanimous* Attack on El Muros Fort and Town, by ... Frigate *La Loire* ...4th of June 1805.
23 NMM, Phillips Croker papers, CRK/15/20.
24 James Hamilton, *A Strange Business: Making Art and Money in Nineteenth-Century Britain* (London: Atlantic Books, 2014), p203.
25 *Manchester Courier and Lancashire General Advertiser*, 5 February 1825, p3.
26 Peter Hore (ed), *Nelson's Band of Brothers: Their Lives and Memorials* (Seaforth, 2015), p45.
27 See, for example, Christies Sale 3562, 24 March 1987, Lot 16; Christies Sale 7660, 29 October 2008, Lot 56.
28 See, for example, Rudolph Schaefer, *J E Buttersworth: 19th Century Marine Painter* (Mystic, Connecticut: Mystic Seaport, 1975)
29 Parish records of St Mary's Lambeth, 1 May 1816 'Church of England Births and Baptisms, 1813–1906', www.ancestry.co.uk [accessed 27 May 2016]
30 General Register Office of England, Death Certificate for Thomas Buttersworth, #DXZ 636643, copy obtained 8 September 1999, application # B005995.
31 General Register Office of England, Death Certificate for Thomas Buttersworth, # DYB 114689, copy obtained 26 July 2006, application # COL472674. The attribution to Thomas Buttersworth senior of a painting of Queen Victoria's visit to Edinburgh in 1842 is wrong.

Port Mahon under Admiral Fremantle 1810–11
1 Max Adams, *Admiral Collingwood; Nelson's own hero* (Phoenix, 2006), p221.
2 Ibid, p250.
3 Ann Parry, *The Admirals Fremantle* (Chatto & Windus, 1971), p80.
4 D/FR/35.2/1.
5 Ann Fremantle (ed), *The Wynne Diaries* (OUP, 1935), vol 3, p326. On 25 September Betsey wrote 'he says Charles was delighted, had not been on board five minutes ere he was at the masthead, and that he climbs the rigging as if he had been at sea for years.'
6 Ibid, vol 3, p328.
7 D/FR/35/2/25.
8 Ann Fremantle (ed), *The Wynne Diaries* (OUP, 1935), vol 3, pp328–30.

9 Ibid, p330.
10 C F Fremantle from Fremantle Archives.
11 Mahon Dockyard Regulations 1811.
12 D/FR/235/2.
13 *The Admirals Fremantle*, p83.
14 John Sugden, *Nelson: A Dream of Glory* (Jonathan Cape, 2004), p196.
15 Wikipedia, Capture of Menorca.
16 Charles Fremantle from Fremantle Archives.
17 D/FR/35/2/42.
18 D/FR/35/4.
19 *The Admirals Fremantle*, p83; letter to William Fremantle, dated 5 January 1811.
20 D/FR/35/3/3.
21 *The Admirals Fremantle*, p86; letter to Sir Charles Cotton, dated 3 June 1811.
22 Ibid; letter to William Fremantle, dated 29 June 1811.
23 Ibid, p88.
24 *The Wynne Diaries*, vol 3, p85.
25 D/FR/35/4.
26 D/FR/35/3/13.
27 D/FR/35/3/41.
28 D/FR/35/3/55.
29 D/FR/35/3/19.
30 D/FR/35/3/31.
31 D/FR/35/3/19.
32 D/FR/35/2/1.
33 D/FR/35/3/46.
34 D/FR/35/1.
35 *The Wynne Diaries*, vol 3, p345 et seq.
36 D/FR/35/4.
37 *The Admirals Fremantle*, pp87–8.

Sir Richard Strachan

1 HMS *Naiad* (38) had survived after 1846 as a coal depot ship, first in Valparaiso, Chile, and then from 1851 in Callao, Peru, until she was broken up in 1898.
2 Strachan's original dispatches for the battle are in the *London Gazette*, 11 November 1805, 15860, pp1389–92 (pp3–4 are missing) and 12 November 1805, 15861, pp1399–1400. Accounts of the battle also appear in William James, *Naval History of Great Britain, 1793–1827* (London: Richard Bentley, 1837), iv, pp107–15 and Bartlett Library Researchers, *Trafalgar: Gilding The Gingerbread,* National Maritime Museum, Cornwall, 2005. http://www.ranops.net/news-and-interest/trafalgar—-gilding-the/gilding-the-gingerbread.pdf [accessed 1 June 2016].
3 The parlous state of the ship can be judged by the 1925 British Pathé newsreel *She Braved Battle And The Breeze*, http://www.britishpathe.com/video/she-braved-battle-and-the-breeze [accessed 1 June 2016].
4 The scuttling is the subject of the 1949 British Pathé newsreel *Implacable To The End* http://www.britishpathe.com/video/Implacable-to-the-end [accessed 1 June 2016].
5 Maritime Diary, *Marine Times*, December 2011, p24.
6 *Oxford Dictionary of National Biography*, vol 52, pp993–4 (J K Laughton, rev Michael Duffy). His life and career also appear at https://en.wikipedia.org/wiki/

Sir_Richard_Strachan,_6th_Baronet [accessed 1 June 2016] and in Thomas A Wise, 'Life and Career of Admiral Sir Richard J Strachan, Baronet, GCB', *Transactions of the Royal Historical Society* (1873), ii, pp32–53.

7   http://www.genealogics.org/getperson.php?personID=I00114557&tree=LEO [accessed 1 June 2016].

8   *Oxford Dictionary of National Biography*, vol 52, p991 (J K Laughton, rev Philip Carter).

9   William James, op cit, i, pp118–19.

10 *London Gazette*, 28 April 1794, 13646, p379.

11 *London Gazette*, 21 April 1804, 15695, p496.

12 The *Hero* (74), *Courageux* (74), *Namur* (74) and *Bellona* (74) under Captains the Honourable Alan Hyde Gardner, Richard Lee, Lawrence Halstead and Charles Dudley Pater respectively. During the chase of Dumanoir, the *Bellona* could not keep up with the other ships and was not present at Cape Ortegal.

13 The *Santa Margarita* (36) and *Aeolus* (32) under Captains Wilson Rathbone and Lord William Fitzroy respectively. The *Revolutionaire* (38) and the *Phoenix* (36) under Captains the Honourable Henry Hotham and Thomas Baker were technically not part of the squadron, but were present at Cape Ortegal.

14 *London Gazette*, 5 November 1805, 15859, pp1373–5.

15 *London Gazette*, 25 February 1806, 15894, p264.

16 *London Gazette*, 28 January 1806, 15885, p128. He was advanced to GCB in 1815.

17 Strachan's original dispatches for the Walcheren expedition appear in the *London Gazette*, 7 August 1809, 16282, pp1232–3; 15 August 1809, 16287, pp1297–9; 20 August 1809, 16289, pp1325–8; 16 December 1809, 16325, pp2006–7 and 26 December 1809, 16328, pp2056–7.

18 Cited in https://en.wikipedia.org/wiki/Sir_Richard_Strachan,_6th_Baronet and citing as its source the now defunct version of the Clan Strachan website [accessed 1 June 2016].

19 *London Gazette*, 24 October 1809, 163039, pp1685–6.

20 *London Gazette*, 28 July 1810, 16391, pp1117–8.

21 *London Gazette*, 11 August 1812, 16632, p1584.

22 *London Gazette*, 7 June 1814, 16906, p1187.

23 *London Gazette*, 20 July 1821, 17727, p1511.

24 *The Creevey Papers*, ed Sir Herbert Maxwell, 2nd edn (John Murray, London, 1904), i, p95.

25 *The Creevey Papers*, ibid.

26 NLI MS 10, 166/828, cited in Maria Edgeworth, *The Absentee*, ed W J McCormack and Kim Walker (OUP, 1988), p293.

27 https://www.geni.com/people/Lt-Gen-Hon-Arthur-Dillon/6000000002188517376 [accessed 1 June 2016]; http://geneall.net/en/name/100463/marie-francoise-laure-de-girardin-de-montgerald/ [accessed 1 June 2016]

28 *Oxford Dictionary of National Biography*, vol 16, pp200–1.

29 North pillar, fourth column, below Grouchy and Villaret-Joyeuse.

30 Her grandmother, Marie Françoise des Vergers de Sannois, was the sister of Joseph François des Vergers de Sannois, the grandfather of the Empress. His daughter, Rose Claire des Vergers de Sannois (1736–1807), married Joseph Gaspard Tascher de la Pagerie (1735–1790): http://gw.geneanet.org/favrejhas?lang=fr&p=rose+claire&n=des+vergers+de+sannois [accessed 1 June 2016].

31 Andrea Stuart, *Josephine: the Rose of Martinique* (PanMacmillan, London, 2004), p59.

32 https://georgianera.wordpress.com/2014/12/07/countess-francoise-elisabeth-bertrand-

fanny-dillon-25th-july-1785-to-6th-march-1836/ [accessed 1 June 2016].

33 His illegitimate grandson, Sir Richard Wallace, was the creator of the Wallace Collection. Hertford had in 1798 married Maria Emilia ('Mie-Mie') Fagnani, probably the illegitimate daughter of the 4th Duke of Queensberry ('Old Q'), but they were estranged by 1802. She remained in Paris, while the 3rd Marquess established splendid residences in London at Dorchester House (on the site of the present Dorchester Hotel) and at St Dunstan's Villa in Regent's Park (demolished in 1937).

34 Lady Charlotte Schreiber, *Journals: confidences of a collector of ceramics and antiques throughout Britain, France, Holland, Belgium, Spain, Portugal, Turkey, Austria and Germany from the year 1869–1885*, ed Montague J Guest (London: John Lane, The Bodley Head 1911), i, p15. See also Peter James Bowman, *The Fortune Hunter: A German Prince in Regency England* (Oxford: Signal Books, 2010), pp5–6.

35 British Museum No. 1868,0808.12919 http://www.britishmuseum.org/research/ collection_online/collection_object_details/collection_image_gallery.aspx?assetId=687256 001&objectId=1664207&partId=1 [accessed 1 June 2016].

36 British Museum No. 1868,0808.8501 http://www.britishmuseum.org/research/ collection_online/collection_object_details/collection_image_gallery.aspx?assetId=752260 01&objectId=1488112&partId=1 [accessed 1 June 2016].

37 British Museum No. 1868,0808.8687 http://www.britishmuseum.org/research/ collection_online/collection_object_details/collection_image_gallery.aspx?assetId=684185 001&objectId=1660695&partId=1 [accessed 1 June 2016].

38 Bernard Falk, *'Old Q's' Daughter* (London: Hutchinson & Co, 1937), pp134–5.

39 Bernard Falk, op cit, pp135–6.

40 In 1833 she married Graf Anton Maria Berchtold, Freiherr von und zu Ungarschitz, Fratting und Pullitz (1796–1875). By him she had three sons and two daughters. Hertford offered the barbed comment in a letter to Lady Jersey in 1834: 'I hope to present to you Matilda under her new name of Css [Countess] Berthold. Her husband is a handsome likeness of Leopold [King of the Belgians] in his best days, supposing him to have swallowed a poker', Bernard Falk, op cit, p177. On the first anniversary of her coming out, the marquess threw an extravagant party for her, the guest of honour being none other than Prince Talleyrand: *The Southern Review* (November 1831), p179.

41 Bernard Falk, op cit, p136.

42 In 1838 she married Don Vincenzo Ruffo, Principe di Antimo and Duca di Bagnara (1801–1880). By him she had two sons and two daughters: http://www.angelfire.com/ realm/gotha/gotha/ruffo.html [accessed 1 June 2016].

43 Graf Emanuel Zichy-Ferraris de Zich et Vasonkeo (1808–1877). The marriage was childless.

44 Bernard Falk, op cit, p187.

45 The whole extraordinary saga can be found in the law reports under the following titles: *The Countess de Zichy Ferraris and J W Croker* v *The Marquis of Hertford* (KB, 17 March 1843) 163 ER 794; *Marquis of Hertford* v *Lord Lowther* (Ch, 12 December 1843) 49 ER 1003; *The Marquis of Hertford* v *Lord Lowther* (Ch, 14 December 1843) 49 ER 962; *Countess Berchtoldt* v *Marquis of Hertford* (Ch, 19 January 1844) 49 ER 1029; *The Right Hon John Wilson Croker* v *The Marquis of Hertford and Others* (PC, 21 February 1844) 13 ER 334; *Zichy* v *The Earl of Lonsdale* (KB, 09 June 1845) 71 ER 839; *The Marquis of Hertford* v *The Count and Countess de Zichi* (Ch, 05 November 1845) 50 ER 246; *The Marquis of Hertford* v *Lord Lowther* (Ch, 20 January 1846) 50 ER 345; *The Earl of Lonsdale* v *The Countess Berchtoldt* (Ch, 30 June 1854) 69 ER 274; *The Earl of Lonsdale*

v *The Countess of Berchtoldt* (Ch, 16 January 1857) 69 ER 1074; *Chatfield* v *Berchtoldt* (1871) LR 12 Eq 464; *Chatfield* v *Berchtoldt* (1871–72) LR 7 Ch App 192.

46   Bernard Falk, op cit, p292.

47   Charles C F Greville, *A Journal of the Reign of Queen Victoria from 1837 to 1852* (Longman & Green, London, 1885), pp91–2. http://www.gutenberg.org/ebooks/46310 [accessed 1 June 2016].

48   http://www.naplesldm.com/maraval.htm [accessed 1 June 2016]. It is now a prime Neapolitan wedding venue: http://www.classvenues.com/wedding-venue/1016/wedding-venues-in-italy/villa-rocca-matilde [accessed 1 June 2016], having in the interim passed through the hands of the Khedive of Egypt and the shipping magnate Achille Lauro.

Samuel Brokensha, Master RN

1   Note: names and extracts from records and other documentation held in various public record offices quote original spellings, grammar and punctuation.

2   *Trafalgar Chronicle*, no. 21 (2011), p49; *Trafalgar Chronicle*, no 23 (2013), p192. The brothers spelled their names differently. Luke Brokenshaw (1779–1840) joined the navy in 1801, gaining rapid promotion to master's mate under his brother Samuel; was lavishly praised by Captain Phillippe d'Auvergne, Royal Navy when, as master of *Severn*, his ship was wrecked on Jersey; wounded at Trafalgar in *Revenge*, present at the Second Battle of Copenhagen in *Ganges,* at the end of the Great War he sailed the brand-new *Nelson* (120) from Woolwich to be laid up at Portsmouth. After the war, Luke set up a naval academy in Cornwall. He is buried in St Michael Caerhays, Cornwall, where his headstone has been conserved by the 1805 Club.

3   Cornwall Record Office (CRO) P147/1/2 Mevagissey Parish Church Register of Baptism, Marriage and Burials 1721–1776.

4   CRO P147/1/5 Mevagissey Parish Church Register of Marriages and Banns of Marriage 1774–1809, p107.

5   CRO MSR1 Fowey Ship Registers 1786–1823.

6   *Gentleman's Magazine*, 1xv, Pt 1, 75–6, 1795.

7   Wikipedia – Henry Wellesley, 1st Baron Cowley.

8   [8] ADM 6/138 Masters' Certificates of Service.

9   ADM 51/1117 No. 9 Captain's Log HMS *Dryad* 28 June 1795 – 7 October 1795; ADM 35/519 Pay Book HMS *Dryad* 25 June 1795 – 31 December 1796.

10   ADM 52/2957/1 Master's Log HMS *Dryad* 29 July 1795 – 28 August 1796.

11   ADM 36/12705 Muster Book HMS *Dryad* 28 June 1795 – 31 August 1795.

12   ADM 51/1112 No. 5 Captain's Log HMS *Dryad* 6 October 1795 – 19 November 1795.

13   Wikipedia – Ernest Augustus 1 of Hanover 'Early life 1771–1779'. The background to this voyage is beyond the scope of this essay but the Wikipedia entry for Prince Ernest Augustus makes intriguing reading.

14   ADM 51/1137 No. 8 Captain's Log HMS *Dryad* 20 November 1795 – 20 November 1796; ADM 35/519 Pay Book HMS *Dryad* 25 June 1795 – 31 December 1796.

15   ADM 51/1192 No. 1 Captain's Log HMS *Dryad* 20 November 1796 – 20 November 1797.

16   ADM 52/2957/5 Master's Log HMS *Dryad* 29 July 1797 – 28 July 1798. The fair copy of this log, ADM 52/2957/6, is erroneously annotated as running between 29 July 1798 and 28 July 1799.

17   ADM 51/1237 No. 2 Captain's Log HMS *Dryad* 21 November 1797 – 20 February 1799.

18   ADM 52/2958/2 Master's Log HMS *Dryad* 29 July 1799 – 28 July 1800.

19   ADM 52/2958/3 Master's Log HMS *Dryad* 29 July 1800 – 30 December 1800.

20 ADM 36/14482 Muster Book HMS *Fortunee* 1 December 1800 – 31 October 1801; ADM 52/3030 Master's Log HMS *Fortunee* 31 December 1800 – 30 December 1801 (Piece 12), 31 December 1801 – 10 October 1802 (Piece 11).

21 ADM 36/14483 Muster Book HMS *Fortunee* 1 October 1801 – 31 October 1802.

22 ADM 51/1431 No. 3 Captain's Log HMS *Fortunee* 20 April 1802 – 21 July 1802.

23 ADM 51/1397 No. 14 Captain's Log HMS *Fortunee* 22 July 1802 – 10 October 1802.

24 Various authors, *Encyclopaedia of Ships* (Silverdale Books). Skuta: A Scandinavian shallow-draught clinker-built cargo vessel of one, two or three masts depending on size, square-rigged with a square topsail on the mainmast. Typically carried cargo on an open deck.

25 ADM 37/1321 Muster Book HMS *Shannon* 20 June 1806 – 30 April 1807.

26 ADM 52/4609 Master's Log HMS *Shannon*. Surviving pages between about 25 November 1806 and 14 April 1807 only.

27 ADM 51/1653 No. 3 Captain's Log HMS *Shannon* 1 September 1806 – 31 August 1807.

28 ADM 102/831 Muster Book Yarmouth 1806 – 1807.

29 ADM 37/1227 Muster Book HMS *Emerald* 1 February 1807 – 30 November 1807.

30 ADM 51/1656 No. 2 Captain's Log HMS *Emerald* 30 November 1806 – 30 November 1807.

31 ADM 53/466 Ship's Log HMS *Emerald* 29 January 1807 – 20 May 1808.

32 ADM 51/1820 No. 2 Captain's Log HMS *Emerald* 1 December 1807 – 30 November 1808.

33 *London Gazette*, no. 16130, pp416, 417, 22 March 1808.

34 ADM 171/8 Nominal Roll of Surviving Officers and Men Entitled to Clasps of the Naval General Service Medal. Page 184 *Emerald* 13 March 1808 Destruction of batteries and vessels of war at Vivero.

35 ADM 37/1228 Muster Book HMS *Emerald* 1 December 1807 – 30 November 1808.

36 ADM 6/200 Leave Books 1804.

37 ADM 37/1191 Muster Book HMS *Ruby* 1 May 1808 – 28 February 1809.

38 ADM 52/3858 No. 10 Master's Log HMS *Ruby* 3 September 1808 – 15 December 1808.

39 ADM 51/1984 No. 3 Captain's Log HMS *Ruby* 9 July 1808 – 30 June 1809.

40 ADM 37/2151 Muster Book HMS *Norge* 10 November 1808 – 21 July 1809.

41 ADM 52/4203 Master's Log HMS *Norge* 18 December 1808 – 30 June 1809.

42 ADM 51/2591 Captain's Log HMS *Norge* 4 November 1808 – 31 August 1815.

43 ADM 35/2959 Pay Book HMS *Norge* 27 October 1808 – 30 September 1813.

44 ADM 37/2017 Muster Book HMS *Bedford* 1 July 1810 – 31 December 1810.

45 ADM 37/2722 Muster Book HMS *Bedford* 1 January 1811 – 30 October 1811; ADM 37/3311 Muster Book HMS *Bedford* 1 November 1811 – 30 June 1812.

46 ADM 107/45 Lieutenant's Passing Certificates.

47 ADM 37/4112 Muster Book HMS *Raisonnable* 1 February 1813 – 10 September 1813.

48 ADM 51/2751 Captain's Log HMS *Raisonnable* 1 January 1808 – 1 July 1814. Further reading: K R Gulvin, *The Medway Prison Hulks* (Light Industrial Workshop, 2010).

49 ADM 37/4113 Muster Book HMS *Raisonnable* 1 October 1813 – 1 June 1814

50 PROB 11/1922/203 Will of Samuel Brokensha.

51 Plymouth and West Devon Record Office (PWDRO) 1421/16 Newton Ferrers Churchwardens and Overseers Parish Register for 1829.

52 PWDRO 1421/10 Newton Ferrers Parish Register Burials 1813–1877.

53 ADM 45/35/532 Navy Board, and Admiralty, Accountant General's Department: Officers' and Civilians' Effects Papers.

54 CRO P147/1/4 Mevagissey Parish Church Register of Baptisms 1777–1813.